INDIA'S

Tavleen Singh's last book, *Durbar*, dealt with the betrayal of India by an inexperienced ruling class. She has written three other books, *Kashmir: A Tragedy of Errors*; *Lollipop Street: Why India Will Survive Its Politicians* and *Political and Incorrect*. She currently writes three weekly political columns in English and Hindi.

Praise for *India's Broken Tryst*

'[A] good book, fun to read, and evocatively written. You should read it.' – Vir Sanghvi, *Business Standard*

'Typically pointy and punchy, Tavleen Singh gets to the heart of what has been ailing India over the last four decades ... Singh brings a journalist's best quality – her empathy – to understanding why in the battle between the Indian state and Indian democracy, the state has usually triumphed to the detriment of the people. ' – Kaveree Bamzai, *India Today*

'[Singh] not only writes with feeling about the drug addicts and alcoholics, the vendors who fight municipal authorities to make a living, and the runaway children who are trafficked and abused, she even uses her privileges to make a difference by helping to feed kids, getting them out of remand homes or helping set up small businesses. It's more than what most of us do and you feel a grudging admiration for her ... It has made her an always-readable chronicler of our times.' – Manjula Narayan, *Hindustan Times*

'The narrative has a feel of reportage which makes it an easy read ... The anecdotes mentioned in the book should be of particular interest.' – Aniruddha Chakraborty, *Telegraph*

'[The book] is certainly written well and isn't a collection of columns masquerading as a book.' – Bibek Debroy, *Sunday Standard*

'*India's Broken Tryst* takes an unflinching look at India as it is – politics, poverty, cronyism, administration, justice and injustice. It is one of the few books to cover India from the very poor to the very rich.' – *Millennium Post*

INDIA'S BROKEN TRYST

Tavleen Singh

HarperCollins *Publishers* India

First published in hardback in India in 2016 by
HarperCollins *Publishers* India

First published in paperback in India in 2017 by
HarperCollins *Publishers* India

P-ISBN: 978-93-5264-391-2
E-ISBN: 978-93-5177-758-8

2 4 6 8 10 9 7 5 3 1

Tavleen Singh asserts the moral right
to be identified as the author of this work.

The views and opinions expressed in this book
are the author's own and the facts are as reported by her,
and the publishers are not in any way liable for the same.

HarperCollins *Publishers*
A-75, Sector 57, Noida, Uttar Pradesh 201301, India
1 London Bridge Street, London, SE1 9GF, United Kingdom
Hazelton Lanes, 55 Avenue Road, Suite 2900, Toronto, Ontario M5R 3L2
and 1995 Markham Road, Scarborough, Ontario M1B 5M8, Canada
25 Ryde Road, Pymble, Sydney, NSW 2073, Australia
195 Broadway, New York, NY 10007, USA

Typeset in 11/14.5 Sabon LT Std
by Jojy Philip, New Delhi

Printed and bound at
Thomson Press (India) Ltd

CONTENTS

1

A TELEPHONE CALL AND A TAX RAID

On a Sunday morning some months after Sonia Gandhi's government lost the general election, I was in my garden by the sea in a contemplative mood. Birds sang, butterflies danced in beams of soft sunlight and waves washed gently up against the garden wall. A blissful moment. So when my phone rang and I saw that it was one of Sonia's devotees I let it ring. The caller was a former minister whom I had not spoken to in a long while. When it rang again I responded out of curiosity. The voice I had not heard in years began our conversation this way. 'I got the invitation for Aatish's book launch. Please congratulate him for me. I won't be able to come, alas, since I won't be in Delhi.'

'Oh, I'm sorry,' I said.

'I will buy the book.'

'You should. I think it's his best one yet.'

'By the way if you are wondering why we haven't spoken in such a long while...You were absolutely right about her.'

'Oh?'

'More than you can imagine...much more than you can imagine.'

'Tell me.'

'Would you believe me if I told you that my problems with her began because after she made me a minister she and her children wanted me to do things that were in the interests of their friends and family but against the national interest?'

'Yes.'

'There were rules that I made towards achieving the stated goals of our party but I was forced to change them because some friend of Priyanka and Rahul would have been directly affected by the changes.'

'I am not surprised,' I said, 'and now Sanjaya Baru and Natwar Singh have confirmed in their books that Sonia was India's real prime minister.'

'True. Do you know that she called me in one day and yelled at me for several minutes because she objected to my friendship with you...I was reduced to tears.' The minister and I had been friends for more than thirty years.

We talked for almost an hour, at the end of which the ex-minister said, 'I've told you these things in confidence. I hope you will respect my confidence because you know what she is capable of.' So I will not reveal the minister's name. Our conversation on that perfect Sunday morning in my garden by the sea put into perspective things I had only suspected. Bad things had happened in my life and to people in my life under Sonia Gandhi's reign.

Among these was a tax raid. It was aimed at Ajit and not me, but I sensed it had less to do with anything he had done and more to do with other factors. Months before my conversation with the ex-minister, when it was not completely clear that Narendra Modi would become India's next prime minister, I was in this same house by the sea when it was raided. The raid was ordered by the Government of India and not the Government of Maharashtra. By then Prime Minister Manmohan Singh had retired behind his veil of silence and everyone with the smallest interest in politics knew that India's real prime minister was Sonia Gandhi.

The raiders came on a Saturday. I had returned after a frenzied week of travel between Delhi and Jaipur. My friend Vasundhara Raje had been sworn in as chief minister of Rajasthan two days earlier, and I spent hours on the Jaipur road juggling column deadlines and the inaugural ceremony. So I came back with the hope of enjoying a restful weekend in our home in the seaside village of Kihim. Curled up in the study on a lounger I was watching something forgettable on television in a sleepy sort of way when I heard loud shouting from the courtyard below. Assuming that it must be some problem with the dogs, I continued to lie half asleep on my reclining chair. Suddenly a group of people that included one short woman burst into my tiny study and ordered me to 'go down at once'. 'We are from the Government of India,' they yelled menacingly, 'and you have to come down at once.'

'Who are you?' I asked with some alarm, thinking for a moment that they could be local thugs.

'Enforcement Directorate,' they shouted, even more menacingly. 'Come down at once.'

'You go down and I will follow,' I said, not sure if my clothes were in suitable array beneath the blanket under which I lay.

'No, no. You will come down with us now,' said the woman in a shrill, grating voice.

'Okay,' I said, standing up after adjusting my clothes. And because she was just ahead of me, I happened to touch her back as we were going down the stairs.

'Don't touch me,' she screeched. 'I am an officer of the Government of India.'

'I didn't touch you,' I said firmly, by now sure that this was indeed a tax raid and that the inspectors would be hostile and ugly. I had been in a tax raid once before when another of Ajit's homes in Mumbai was raided. Ajit and I have been life partners for thirty years, but since we are not married the raiders technically had no right to treat me as a suspect in the raid. But these are niceties they pay no attention to.

When we got to the veranda downstairs, I saw that the raiding party consisted of more than thirty people. They were nearly all men, but other than the short woman there were a couple of policewomen in plain clothes. When the raiders handed me a form listing my rights and obligations, I could have said that the house was not mine and that since Ajit was abroad they had no right to conduct their raid, but it would have been pointless. So I read the badly printed, government-issue form they set before me and drew attention to the rule that said I needed to be shown their identity cards before they proceeded further. They produced small, laminated cards in a flurry with a lot of noise and bluster, after which I said, 'All right then, go ahead and conduct your raid.'

At this point the short woman started jumping around. 'Please use parliamentary language only.'

'What did I say wrong?' I asked, genuinely puzzled.

'You said bloody,' she screamed.

'I did not,' I said indignantly. 'It is not a word I ever use.' I was tempted to add that if I had used an abusive word, it would have been the 'F' one but knew that there would be more hysterical screeching from the woman.

So the raiders set forth in small groups to look into every nook, cranny, floorboard, drawer and cupboard in a house that is built in such a way that it is impossible to conceal anything. They soon discovered this and became mellower in their manner, even allowing me to go into my gym and work out. Mid-workout I got a call from my son, and although there was a woman inspector parked by my treadmill to watch my every move, I managed to tell Aatish that there was a government inspection on and that I could not talk.

Clever creature that he is, he sensed what was happening and called my friend and neighbour in Kihim village, Uma Dubash, to tell her what he suspected. She and I were meant to have dinner in my house that evening, and I had been permitted by the raiders to call her and tell her that she could not come. 'But you mustn't tell her that you are being raided,' they warned. Uma had personal experience of tax raids and knew that they could be a lonely, frightening business, so after her conversation with Aatish she drove straight over, clad in a Moroccan kaftan, with a toothbrush in her evening bag.

When they asked her who she was, she announced grandly that she was 'Uma, Princess of Morvi'. And then sailed into the dining room, where we were in the process of having my jewellery valued by a government jeweller. When I saw this bejewelled, perfectly groomed and scented vision manifest itself so unexpectedly, I could hardly believe my eyes. I told her that I had never in our long friendship been more delighted to see her. Not only is Uma hard to scare, she has the unusual ability to retain a sense of humour in difficult situations.

'A free jewellery evaluation,' she said when she saw what was happening, then turning to the jeweller said sweetly, 'Could you please do mine when you have finished doing hers?'

One diamond ring on her finger was worth twice as much as my meagre collection of beach house jewellery, so even the jeweller seemed to realize there was something odd about the situation. He became more chatty. We got into a conversation about the value of corals and rubies till a glum tax inspector came in and told us we were not allowed to talk. When I saw his face I realized that they were very disappointed to find nothing more than a closed safe that nobody had ever used because it was too cumbersome. I told him he would be doing me a favour if he ordered it broken open and taken away.

By now it was late evening. The gaggle of inspectors on the veranda had ordered takeaway food from the village that they ate out of plastic boxes, looking thoroughly put out at having found nothing more than Rs 40,000 in my cupboard and jewellery worth barely anything. I asked if Uma and I could eat dinner and they gloomily granted permission. One of the rules of tax raids is that both raider and victim are permitted nourishment.

Uma and I repaired to the drawing room and ate the grilled fish and salad I had ordered for us, and to really annoy the raiders I asked Deepak, my butler, to go ahead and serve the red wine that we would have had if we had been eating alone. So while the raiders dined out of plastic boxes and bottles on the veranda, we dined in considerable style in the drawing room, through the glass doors of which they could see exactly what was happening. 'It's like a Fellini film,' Uma said, grinning at the people who stared at us through the glass.

Around midnight the woman appeared in the drawing room with a laptop and asked sulkily if she could record my statement. Then with a sneering glance at my glass of wine said, 'Of course, if you prefer to do this tomorrow we can postpone.'

'No, I would like to do it right now,' I said, horrified at the thought that they would come back the next day. When I noticed one of the inspectors video-taping our conversation with his cellphone, I requested him to be careful to record everything I had to say. And at the end of giving my name, address, date of birth and other such details, when they asked me if I had anything more to say, I added, looking straight at his camera phone, 'You people came into my house like terrorists and behaved in a needlessly hostile manner.'

'You cannot say that,' said a man who was playing the good cop to the woman's bad cop.

'Yes, I can,' I said, 'because that is exactly what happened.'

'But we allowed you to drink wine.'

'So? You allowed me to have dinner and I drink wine with dinner.'

'You cannot say that we came like terrorists. We work for the Government of India.'

'Exactly.'

India is proud of being a democracy, but the Indian state has perfected the art of using totalitarian methods of control under the veneer of democracy. Repression is easier to fight when it comes in the form of totalitarianism, but this is much harder to do when it comes disguised as democracy. The raid was not Sonia Gandhi's only act that seemed vindictive. After the general election that reduced her party to forty-four seats in the Lok Sabha, I discovered that she had personally ordered the closure of Lavasa. Lavasa was India's first new city since Chandigarh was built in the 1950s. Its closure caused a loss of more than Rs 2,000 crore to Ajit's company and nearly destroyed his attempt to build it. Ajit is a passionate nationalist and it was this rather than reasons of profit that made him take the risk of trying to build a city in the Western Ghats despite knowing that at every step there would be small armies of petty officials trying to stymie the project. It is the Indian way. What he had not bargained for was the possibility that Sonia Gandhi would close Lavasa down. We originally thought she had done what she did to get back at Sharad Pawar. Pawar, a Maharashtrian leader, was part of Sonia's United Progressive Alliance and a senior minister in both her governments, but she appears never to have forgiven him for raising the issue of her Italian birth when she first entered politics. But gradually from the newsrooms of Delhi I gleaned that part of the reason why construction was shut down had to do with me.

Sonia and I had been friends in the days before Rajiv became prime minister. Tensions built up when I criticized his policies, and our friendship ended completely when she entered politics and showed that she wanted very much to become prime minister herself. There was nothing personal about my objections to her political role. They were based on my conviction that an Italian prime minister of India would seriously damage the already fragile sense of self-worth that most Indians have. Centuries of being ruled by foreigners have caused a congenital kink in the Indian psyche.

Even self-respecting Indians kowtow naturally before whites. They are served first in restaurants and shops, and at least two generations of Indians have grown up since Independence with a reverence for whites that makes me cringe. But if there is reverence there is also shame at this reverence, and in retrospect I believe that if Sonia Gandhi had agreed to become prime minister in 2004, she would have certainly not won a second term for her government.

At every turn she would have been accused of being the 'foreign woman', and every calamity would have been blamed on her personally. So she was well advised by her 'inner voice' to reject the job when she was offered it in 2004. This transformed her into the Mother Teresa of politics in the eyes of not just ordinary Indians but even senior political commentators. In an exchange I had on CNN-IBN with the venerable editor Vinod Mehta on Karan Thapar's show once, he said, 'Indians love people who sacrifice high office and this is why Sonia Gandhi is so loved.' She had only sacrificed accountability, not power, I reminded him, and he had no response, but he was not the only one who sang Sonia's praises after her 'sacrifice'.

Since that day of 'sacrifice', sycophants had in the name of protecting secularism crawled out of everywhere. Journalists, bureaucrats, businessmen, movie stars and political leaders united to praise Sonia's 'sacrifice'. Why she listened to her 'inner voice' instead of to the devotees who begged her to become India's prime minister remains a mystery. Natwar Singh, an ex-devotee, wrote in his memoir *One Life Is Not Enough* that she wanted to take the job but was prevented from doing so by her son. This does not fully explain what happened on that hot May day in 2004 when Atal Behari Vajpayee's government was voted out of power and Sonia Gandhi's Congress unexpectedly won.

She, who till then had almost never spoken to journalists in all her years in public life, called a press conference after the results. Under a hastily erected shamiana that barely kept out the sun, she smiled happily when a reporter asked her if she planned to become prime minister, before saying in Hindi, 'Is that not what usually happens?' I remember thinking as I watched the press conference that in the twenty years I had known her, I had never seen her look so utterly happy.

The next day she set off for Rashtrapati Bhavan, still looking very pleased with herself. But emerged from her meeting with the president in a different mood. The jauntiness had gone out of her step and the smile had disappeared from her face. She spoke to nobody until she appeared in Parliament's Central Hall to announce to her newly elected MPs that her 'inner voice' had advised her against becoming prime minister and she intended to obey it. Her announcement caused hysterical shrieks and wails to rise in that high-ceilinged hall as men and women elected by the people of India to represent them in Parliament behaved like children suddenly bereaved of a parent.

Outside Parliament wild and wondrous rumours in hectic whispers immediately began to swirl through the political circles and they soon found their way into newsrooms. The president had warned her, some said, that there could be problems with the armed forces on account of her Italian birth. Officers marrying foreigners have to choose between marriage and their jobs. So why should they listen to a foreigner who had become prime minister only because she married into the right family? More spellbinding was the story of the Russian spymaster. In a city that thrives on conspiracy theories, people easily believed that a Russian spy plane had landed at Delhi airport in the middle of the night to warn Sonia that the Americans had information that they would use against her. This story was as bizarre as the story that the KGB had trained young women to ensnare the sons of powerful leaders during the Cold War and that Sonia was one of them. But the story I was told was embellished with vivid details. My informant was a low-level political worker who could hardly contain his excitement as he said, 'A black car with darkened windows met the plane on the tarmac and took the spymaster straight to 10 Janpath, where he talked alone to Sonia and her children, and it was this that convinced her to not become prime minister.'

While rumours of this kind circulated and the weeping and

wailing from Parliament's Central Hall got more hysterical, I got a call from one of Sonia's oldest friends.

She sounded worried and dazed.

'I cannot believe what is happening,' she said. 'I cannot believe that she has come so close to becoming prime minister. Do you think she will change her mind and take the job?'

'No. Because in any case she will be de facto prime minister.'

'But she hates politics and politicians,' the friend said.

'But she likes power,' I pointed out. There was a moment of silence before this friend said, 'That is true. But why shouldn't she? Ever since she came to India, she has lived in the house of the prime minister.'

Sonia had never lived outside the prime minister's house. She moved into it as a bride when her mother-in-law was prime minister and except for brief intervals never lived anywhere else. Power without accountability had always been the leitmotif of her life in India. Could this have been why she was forced into a career she had always disdained? When Rajiv was killed so tragically at that political rally in the last days of the general election in 1991, she was offered a choice. She could have retired to a life of peace and seclusion. She chose not to. She turned down the offer of becoming president of the Congress when the party's highest officials offered it to her on the night that Rajiv was killed. That the rejection of a career in politics was temporary soon became clear.

By the time another general election came around in the winter of 1997, she launched her career in electoral politics with a rally in Sriperumbudur, the Tamil Nadu town where her husband was killed. Even before this she never quite broke her ties with politics. During the year she withdrew behind the high walls of 10 Janpath to mourn for her husband and to assuage her grief by writing a book about his life, she saw almost nobody other than politicians and visiting foreign leaders. When I commented on this in my columns and started pointing towards what for me was the ominous possibility that she would become prime minister, her friends attacked me whenever I saw them.

'Why do you write about her when she is not even in politics?'

'If she isn't in politics why does she meet so many politicians every day?'

'If people from the Congress come to see her, she can hardly turn them away.'

'But when she meets people who openly defy the prime minister she has personally chosen, doesn't she send a clear message?'

'That is her business.'

'No. It isn't. If she interferes in political matters it stops being her personal business.'

'You've got it all wrong.'

'Are you sure she has no interest in politics?'

'Absolutely.'

'She has no interest in becoming president of the Congress party?'

'None.'

It should have been clear to even her most ardent devotees that she was always going to take over the Congress party that had been reduced by then to being little more than a family firm, but for some reason it was not. She even managed to fool experienced editors whom she granted privileged access while keeping other journalists at a safe distance. Shekhar Gupta was one of the privileged few who was granted regular audiences, and he came back convinced that it was Sonia's overwhelming love for her late husband that motivated her. Vir Sanghvi was convinced that she came into politics only to save secularism in India. She told him that she had not been able to walk past portraits of Jawaharlal Nehru and Indira Gandhi without feeling guilty about not taking their legacy forward.

On that day of Sonia's 'sacrifice', my mind filled with images from that time long ago when I first met her. Images of dinner parties and her always in Western clothes and always clinging to Rajiv's hand if there were none of her foreign friends around. Beautifully dressed and groomed always, but reserved to the point of being uneasy with conversation of any kind. Ladies would encircle her and titters would rise from the circle along with chitchat about clothes and jewellery, children and holidays. Never politics. It was not a good idea anyway. There was an Emergency and there was press censorship. And it was a time when monkey-wallahs could be arrested for making political jokes.

There were ladies in her circle who salved their privileged consciences by 'helping' Mother Teresa and they liked to talk of this at dinner parties. Sonia sometimes went to help as well but seemed to do this without real interest or consistency. India in the 1970s was a land of horrible poverty. The death rate for newborn babies was more than 100 per thousand. In Gandhiji's 'real India', it was hard to find a village of 'pucca' houses or people in those villages who could write their names. These were things never discussed in the drawing rooms in which Rajiv and Sonia spent their evenings, so the India of poverty, disease, deprivation and dirt never intruded into the life of the woman who would one day become de facto Empress of India. Later she loved saying in the handful of interviews she gave that she had never understood why anyone saw her as a foreigner because that is not how she saw herself. And the carefully vetted interviewers never asked why then she had become an Indian citizen only after her husband became a politician.

Was it her fault, though, that Indian politics had thrown up such pathetic leaders that she could become the most powerful of them? No. And for me personally that is the most shaming thing of all. Why was a country of more than a billion people incapable of producing a real leader? Why was even a man like Atal Behari Vajpayee incapable of stopping her when he could have?

Other memories came back on that day of 'sacrifice'. Memories of an evening in the house of Jaswant Singh, who would go on to become minister of external affairs in the Vajpayee government. It was summer and the dark garden of his house in Teen Murti Lane was filled with the scent of flowering trees. As I walked in for what I imagined was just an evening of cocktails and chitchat, the scents of jasmine and raat-ki-rani followed me into the drawing room through open windows. But the cocktail party I thought I was attending was in fact a political conclave.

I do not know how or why I was invited to this very private gathering, at which the only other guests were L.K. Advani, Arun Jaitley and Arun Shourie. We sat around a table and I listened silently as the most important leaders of the Bharatiya Janata Party discussed strategies for the coming general election. When the question of Sonia Gandhi as a potential opponent came up, I said something to the effect that she did not even speak Hindi so she could hardly be treated as a serious opponent. Vajpayee looked at me quizzically for a moment and then said, 'She doesn't need to speak Hindi. All she needs to do is hold her hands together in a namaste and stand on stage with her head covered and she could win.'

In Sriperumbudur at her first political rally I saw what he meant. The streets of the small rustic town were decorated that day with large garish cutouts of Sonia Gandhi with her head covered and her hands in a namaste. The colours used to paint her sari and the backdrop against which she stood were bright green, shades of luminous pink and electric blue, but the most striking thing was how white her skin was made to look. Her skin was given a pearly sheen that made it look surreal in its whiteness. At the grounds where the rally was being held there were more posters and more cutouts, shining in the harsh light of the day. I arrived early in the hope of talking to ordinary people. It was January but it was as hot as a summer day in Delhi. The white sky and the humid air, though, did not bother those who had come to listen to Sonia Gandhi. A small crowd gathered round as I started to ask questions with the help of a Tamil interpreter. When I asked if they thought it would be wrong for India to get a prime minister who was born Italian, they said this did not bother them at all. They translated proudly for me a song playing in the background that said, 'You have white skin so you are God.'

When 'God' arrived in a dark green sari with a maroon border, a wave of hysteria washed through the crowd. Sonia's hair was carefully groomed and the dark green made her skin look whiter still in the sunlight that made an interesting contrast with the sea of dark faces in her audience. She seemed nervous and seemed to be trying hard to conceal this. She waved in short, jerky movements to the vast, cheering crowd. Her daughter in a red sari was much more at ease as she stood by her mother, waving and smiling.

When the ladies walked on to the stage I noticed that Sonia had changed her style of walking and had cultivated the hurried, jerky manner in which Indira Gandhi used to walk. Cruel people in Delhi had long whispered about how in her year of isolation and mourning she had watched old videos of her mother-in-law's speeches. If this was not true then what was certainly true was that she had obviously modelled herself on her. From the front row at this rally I noticed that she had even developed Indira Gandhi's manner of twitching one side of her face, and that when she began her speech her voice had the shrill edge that I remembered from the other Mrs Gandhi.

When she saw me sitting in the front row, she scowled. And when our eyes met for a moment, she gave me what can only be described as a dirty look. She made a bad speech in stilted English in which the only point she made forcefully was that the reason she had decided to campaign for the general election due was that she did not want to allow parties who mixed religion with politics to win. She did not want political power, she said, in an early hint of the 'sacrifice' she would make five years later. The Congress workers in their shiny white clothes and the people who had come to listen to her seemed more interested in just seeing her. Not in listening to what she had to say. It was easy for me to see why.

The Gandhi ladies exuded an aura that royalty usually manages effortlessly to exude. They looked very much as if they knew they had a right to rule India and that this was a right lesser political leaders did not have. I remember thinking as I watched them on the stage at this first rally Sonia Gandhi addressed, they looked so good compared to the shabby dreariness that defines most Indian political leaders. Even someone like Vajpayee, with his ability to mesmerize audiences with his words, looked more like a small-town schoolteacher than a charismatic leader. The ladies on that stage in Sriperumbudur looked like movie stars, and the people were so dazzled by their appearance and by Priyanka's smiles and waves that serious political and economic issues became inconsequential.

Vajpayee was right about her being a formidable opponent. But he could perhaps have reduced her powers in the election that came later that year had he once indicated that having a foreign woman as his main opponent was unacceptable. This he did not do. I used to do a weekly programme called 'Ek Din, Ek Jeevan' at the time for Star Plus and during the election campaign took to spending a day with the main contestants. So it was that I caught up with Atalji in a remote, rural part of Madhya Pradesh. He was staying in a dak bungalow that had fallen to rack and ruin. Because things were worse indoors than in the wildly overgrown, weed-infested garden, it was here in the shade of a tree that I interviewed him.

Very deliberately I asked what I believed to be the most important question of this interview. 'Your main opponent,' I said, 'is an Italian woman. Do you have any problems with this?'

'No problems at all,' he replied with an enigmatic smile. Afterwards, when the camera was turned off I asked why he had not expressed some small measure of concern if nothing else. He could have said, I pointed out, that it was shameful for the political party of India's freedom movement to be led by someone who had not bothered to get an Indian passport till her husband became a candidate for prime minister. He said that he believed that if he said something like this it would help Sonia Gandhi rather than harm her.

It is hard to say if this was true or not. What is true is that Sonia Gandhi's very successful political career was built with the help of many, many powerful Indians. High officials kowtowed before her as before no other political leader, even after her 'inner voice' persuaded her not to become prime minister. Fearless investigative journalists never bothered to investigate her role in the Bofors bribery scandal even after bribe money was found in the Swiss bank accounts of her two best friends, Ottavio and Maria Quattrocchi, and major politicians accepted her suzerainty. And Delhi's drawing rooms reverberated with praise of the new Empress of India. This is truly what she was, because except in matters of daily governance she remained in total charge of the government.

2

BOMBAY/MUMBAI

In 1994 I moved to Bombay to live with Ajit Gulabchand. My first home in the city that was still called Bombay was a tiny apartment in a bleak building called Beach Towers in Prabhadevi. The building's name was a misnomer. There was not a beach to be seen from its high windows, and the small glimpse of the sea that I got if I craned my neck out of the windows of my flat on the seventh floor was of a black sewer emptying its contents into the water. The flat was so tiny that all of it could have fitted easily into a large bedroom in an old-fashioned Delhi house. The matchbox rooms had low ceilings that enhanced the feeling of claustrophobia. I knew it was a temporary arrangement but tried in the two years that we lived there to cheer things up with some nice furniture. But every time I bought something too nice, Ajit would remind me that we would be moving soon.

By the time we moved to the NCPA Apartments at the end of Marine Drive, Maharashtra's Shiv Sena government had changed Bombay's name to Mumbai. It was a pointless thing to do since everyone still calls it Bombay, and I got into endless futile arguments with Maharashtrians about how needless the change was. As a new resident of this city by the sea, I tried pointing out how wrong it was to change a name that resonated with so much romance and history. I reminded people that Paris was called Paris in English and Paree in French as London became Londres in French, Roma in Italian became Rome in English, but it was useless. There was an ugly kind of Marathi nationalism in the air that seemed to affect even socialites without a political thought in their heads. I remember in particular a long conversation with a Marathi lady at a Godrej dinner party.

The party was on the fairy-lighted terrace of a Godrej office building in the business district. All around us was the squalor that defines Bombay because the men who ruled over it have chosen to bleed it dry to invest in rural Maharashtra. When I pointed this out to the lady, she bristled. 'Bombay is a Marathi city,' she said coldly, 'and in Marathi its name is Mumbai after the Mumba Devi temple.'

'I thought it was called Bombay from the Portuguese word for good bay...'

'Rubbish. It is a much older city than that and has always been called Mumbai.'

'But wouldn't it be better to do something to improve the city rather than waste money on changing its name?'

'Only someone from Delhi would say a thing like that.' End of conversation. It is how nearly every conversation on the subject ended.

The Shiv Sena had come to power in Maharashtra for the first time ever in alliance with the Bharatiya Janata Party, and the consensus that Bombay needed to alter its cosmopolitan image and become more Marathi was widespread.

There was a dangerous mix of communalism and chauvinism in the air because the year before Muslim gangsters led by Dawood Ibrahim had set off a series of bombs across the city that had killed more than 200 people. This was Dawood's way of avenging the killing of Muslims during communal riots provoked by the demolition of the Babri Masjid the year before. So my first impressions of Bombay/Mumbai were bad. I seemed everywhere to run into people filled with ill-feeling towards Muslims and 'outsiders'. As one of the hated outsiders, I tried to atone for this unintentional sin by making a real effort to understand why Ajit's Maharashtrian friends and family were so filled with provincial chauvinism. I failed. Ajit explained that it came from a complex Maharashtrians living in Mumbai had about being a minority in a city that was part of their home state. 'Bombay was built by Gujaratis, Parsis and Arabs,' he said, 'and this makes Marathi people feel insecure.'

It did not help that in those first two years of living in Bombay the only interesting people I met were from Bollywood, and I lived a long way from Juhu and Bandra where Bollywood had its studios and its stars. What did help was that I had a job with Plus Channel, whose offices were in Juhu. I had been in charge of the Delhi bureau ever since it was started by Amit Khanna three years before I moved to Mumbai, so it was an easy transition to working full time in the Juhu office. Private television channels had not taken off then. We made programmes for Doordarshan, and although my own role was restricted to the business channel I admit to being dazzled by every Bollywood celebrity who wandered by. Aamir Khan appeared from time to time, Mahesh Bhatt was a regular fixture and Amitabh Bachchan had his offices in the same building on Juhu Tara Road.

When I left Delhi I realized that I would have to make a definitive change in my career. No longer could I be the political reporter I had always been. I would have to start doing something that I could do from Mumbai. In any case I had by then lost my taste for wars and riots. By the 1990s I had already seen too many, and what convinced me that it was time to move on was a visit to Sri Lanka. There was trouble in the eastern province of Batticaloa, where I had been often before to report for the *Sunday Times*, London, but this time something happened on the way there that made me realize that I no longer wanted to risk my life covering a story. I lost my nerve on the road to Batticaloa and concluded that I was too old to be covering wars and violent conflicts.

What happened that day was so bizarre that I saw it as a sign from the gods. I was staying at the Taj Samudra Hotel in Colombo and my plan was to drive up to Batticaloa, get a sense of what was happening in the renewed fighting between Tamil militants and the Sinhalese army, and drive back the next day or the next. I had a lovely room with a view of the sea and remember thinking that it was such a shame that I had to leave its comforts for a long drive and a war. While I was packing the bag that I was leaving in the hotel I found myself putting things away more neatly than usual and thinking as I did this that when they open it they should not find a mess. The thought jolted me: why was I thinking of someone else opening my bag? I quickly put the thought out of my head but realized that I was not very comfortable about leaving Colombo that morning.

This anxiety became worse when I got into the car and discovered that my driver was Sinhalese. 'But we are going into an area where the Tamils seem to be winning the war,' I remember saying. He smiled cheerfully and said that he was not worried at all. We set off. It was a beautiful, luminous morning and this made me feel better. We stopped in Anuradhapura to eat a delicious breakfast of hoppers and beef stew, and I ate as if it were my last breakfast. When I thought about this the anxiety attack came back. I could not understand why I was so anxious. I calmed myself down with the thought that I had the numbers of important LTTE leaders in case I ran into trouble.

We were less than fifteen minutes away from Batticaloa when we did. At a Sri Lankan military barricade the men who checked us through told us in so many words that we were now going on at our own risk. 'We cannot be responsible for your safety beyond this point,' the military officer said. I asked my driver if he was worried about this and he said that he was not, so we went on, but I felt the knot of anxiety in my stomach grow tighter as we got back into the car and drove on. We had not gone far when a group of men in civilian clothes stopped us. Assuming that they must be Tamil militants I told them that I was from India and showed them the name of the Tamil leader I was supposed to meet in Batticaloa. 'We are Sri Lankan army,' they said, 'and it isn't safe for you to go to Batticaloa. People are fleeing because the fighting has got so bad.'

Barely were these words said than two trailer trucks came hurtling towards us from Batticaloa. In the trailers were Sri Lankan Muslims who told my driver in frightened tones that they had been forced to leave because of the shooting and the bombs. My driver listened carefully to what they said and after translating for me said he did not want to go any further. When he said this a feeling of such relief came over me that I could have hugged him. We turned around and headed towards Trincomalee, and instead of being sad that I was missing a really good story I was relieved. That told me that some kind of fundamental change had occurred in the way I viewed my career.

There was no story to cover in Trincomalee, but on the way there we were stopped at barricades and made to pay taxes imposed by an LTTE provisional government. This indicated to me that Vellupillai Prabhakaran was winning larger and larger swathes of territory. He was no hero of mine, and although I had some sympathy for the Tamil struggle for equal rights, I did not believe that the demand for a separate Eelam was right. Sri Lanka was too small a country to be divided.

When we got to Trincomalee late that evening I met Sri Lankan army officers who echoed these feelings. We talked in a fine army mess and when I told them I had nowhere to spend the night, hoping they would offer me a room, they said it would not be possible for me as a foreigner to stay in a military establishment but they would find me a place. They dragooned an elderly Sinhalese couple into letting me spend the night on a couch in their living room. I slept badly because of the noises of severe geriatric flatulence that emanated from the bedroom and because the single toilet was so filthy I could not use it. The next morning, before my hosts rose, I evacuated my bursting bladder in a corner of the garden and drove back to Colombo filled for the first time with relief at having been unable to enter a war zone.

I tell this story to emphasize that moving to Bombay was a welcome turning point in my career. I decided that instead of reporting I would try and take my career in a new direction by doing more television work, writing columns and the book on Kashmir that I had been wanting to write for long. The book came out the following year and soon I was doing 'Ek Din, Ek Jeevan', so work-wise my life was full. But it was not till I moved from the Beach Towers apartment to one with a spectacular view of the Arabian Sea on the ninth floor of the NCPA Apartments that I began to enjoy living in Bombay.

It was not just because it was a relief to live in a bigger flat on a street that was the heart of the city – now going by the name of Mumbai – but because the isolation of the Beach Towers flat ended. Marine Drive then was not just a street on which rich people walked and jogged but a street on which everyone from the city's poorest citizens to the richest could be seen. It was not till Julie came into our lives, however, that I saw the city in all its contrasts, so this book is as much about how Julie changed my understanding of India as it is about how I discovered that the most important political problems in India were really economic. From the newsrooms of Delhi, in which I had spent most of my years as a journalist, other things seemed to matter much more, like secularism and communalism, and problems of caste and creed. But there was something about the very air of Mumbai that made me realize very quickly that India's most important and least discussed problems were to do with the economic policies that our political leaders had followed.

Of course living with Ajit, who is not just an industrialist but an economist, helped greatly, because on our travels in other countries he saw things that I had never noticed before. While I peered into cathedrals in Florence and marvelled at the shops on the the Rue du Faubourg Saint-Honoré in Paris, he would spend hours telling me how beautifully these cities were planned. While I noticed museums, he noticed motorways and railway stations, and soon I began to see things differently too, so that by the time we travelled to China soon after moving into the NCPA Apartments I had learned to marvel at things I had never noticed before.

Ajit was part of a business delegation, and I went along because it was my first chance to see a country that I had heard and read so much about. What fascinated me before I met Ajit were things like the Cultural Revolution and the great famines in which so many millions died. Or how Mao Tse Tung's vision of a country based on the idea of equality had translated into everyone wearing Mao suits and everyone living in poverty. What fascinated Ajit was the way in which

Deng Xiao Ping had lifted a broken, wounded country out of deep despair and turned it into an economic miracle. He talked about this so much that I went with a determination to see China through his eyes and not just my own.

As things turned out, I nearly did not make it as far as China. We stopped en route in Kuala Lumpur for a night because Ajit had business associates he needed to meet. While he worked I spent a languid day by the pool of the Shangri-La Hotel. In the evening when he came back he said he had booked us a table in the city's finest seafood restaurant. As someone with an insatiable appetite for seafood I was delighted. The restaurant happened that day to be celebrating a lobster festival. This pleased me as lobster tops the list of my favourite foods from the sea. What did not please me was that the lobsters sat in a glass box looking very sad and we were asked to choose the ones we wanted to eat. This was something I absolutely could not do because I thought the lobsters gave me long, sad looks every time I looked in their direction, so I said that I was going to go for a walk and let someone else choose for me. I returned when the tepanyake table was already sizzling hot. But when the chef put my chosen lobster on to cook, it seemed to still be alive and moved its limbs restlessly as it was cooked. This made me feel so awful that I did not enjoy eating it at all but ate anyway since I did not want to disappoint Ajit or the chef.

The consequence of this meal was a violent attack of food poisoning that began at midnight and kept me up all night, vomiting out everything I had eaten and more. Our flight to Shanghai was early in the morning. When Ajit saw the state I was in he suggested that we should perhaps take a later flight. But I was in no mood to give up a day on my first chance to visit China and somehow staggered on to the aeroplane with the rest of the delegation. I slept all the way to Shanghai.

And was quite recovered by the time we landed. My first impression of China was of dusk falling over a city whose skyline was a chequerboard of giant yellow cranes. Ajit noticed them instantly and gave me the useful information that the largest number of tower cranes in the world were at that moment believed to be in Shanghai. 'They are building a whole new city on the other side of the river,' he said.

He was as eager as me to get a feel of the city, and as soon as we checked into the hotel we left to wander down the city's main shopping centre that was walking distance from our hotel. India at that time had no shop at all that represented an international brand, so it stunned me to walk down a street that could have been in any European or American city. Lacoste, Guess, Ralph Lauren, Hugo Boss rubbed shoulders with Cartier and Bulgari. There was not a single Chinese shop as far as I could see.

It was only the next morning when we went for an early jog that I saw the Chinese side of Shanghai. Our hotel was on the edge of the old city that was in the process of being slowly replaced by shiny new buildings of glass and steel. But much of it still remained intact under the looming presence of those tower cranes. The older city that to my mind was more charming than the new one was a place of narrow lanes lined with small Chinese-style houses and shops. We found ourselves jogging down a sort of dhobi street in which men in vests and lungis were ironing clothes just like in India and in which there were grocery shops just like the ones you see in old-fashioned Indian bazaars.

We jogged past some fine government offices with distinctively Chinese designs and found ourselves in a large square in which men and women danced on the pavements to Western music. Never in all my travels, and I have travelled a lot, have I seen elderly people waltzing in the streets as if it were the most normal thing to do. Ajit spent that first day in business meetings with Chinese officials while I wandered about the city with the ladies. We went to temples and handicraft shops and ate a dim sum lunch in a restaurant that, other than the temples, was the only Chinese pagoda we saw that day. At night we went to eat dinner in the Peace Hotel that was built in the 1920s and first owned by Victor Sassoon. Sir Ellice Victor Sassoon was from a wealthy banking family that was known as the Rothschilds of the East and had huge interests in India and China. The Peace Hotel had somehow managed through the revolution to retain its colonial grandeur.

While I was taking in the old-fashioned elegance of the building, Ajit was explaining that the street we were on was called the Bund and that the river it ran along was called the Huangpu. 'Look at those lights on the other side. That is Pudong, which is the new part of Shanghai. They say it will be more modern than Singapore or Hong Kong.' At night it looked like just another construction site filled with high lights and dark pits but the next morning when I drove there I could hardly believe what I saw. There were buildings the like of which did not exist in any Indian city. It was not just their height and modernity that impressed me but the quality of their construction. I could not think of a single tall building in Bombay that was now Mumbai, and my new home, in which there were buildings that even half resembled those I saw that morning in Pudong.

If Shanghai left me bedazzled, Beijing came as a disappointment. From having seen far too many pictures of the Forbidden City and too many Chinese movies in which the China of old seemed very much alive and present, it was a terrible shock to see that Beijing was just an ugly, modern city. There was nothing Chinese about the hotel we stayed in, the malls we shopped in or the atmosphere of older parts of the city. Then I remembered a conversation with a foreign correspondent in Delhi who was an old China hand. He told me that Mao Tse Tung at the height of his delusions of grandeur had ordered the old city of Beijing demolished and rebuilt facing west. Of course he and his high officials had chosen to live in the ancient splendour of the Zhongnanhai on the edge of the Forbidden City, which mercifully was allowed to survive the Cultural Revolution.

If modernization had taken its toll on beautiful, ancient Chinese cities, it had brought with it magnificent new highways that were completely unheard of in India in the 1990s. We drove on one of these new highways to the Great Wall, and I gasped with amazement and found myself wondering if they had been around when Rajiv Gandhi came here as prime minister. Did he notice them if they had? Did he wonder as he drove to the Great Wall why we had been unable to build them in India? Or did he travel in foreign lands as most of my generation of Indians did, without ever thinking that India could become a modern country?

His visit to the Great Wall of China is commemorated in a photograph of him and his wife standing in the sunlight and gazing up towards the high wall. He wears a cap and a leather jacket and she wears a coat of brown sable – the most expensive of all furs – that matches the colour of her blow-dried hair. Those were times when Indians asked no questions about where political leaders got the money to buy fur coats for their wives. In any case, with the Gandhi family most Indians accepted, and continue to accept, that the family inherited such great wealth that Motilal Nehru used a laundry in London to have his suits cleaned and was so rich and generous that he donated his family home in Allahabad to the country.

3

STREET PEOPLE

Behind the Air India building on Marine Drive, in a narrow, cluttered street live the poorest people I know in Mumbai. At the busy end of the street is a Sulabh Shauchalaya almost hidden by handcarts that sell flowers, newspapers, tea, south Indian breakfast and street food. At the quieter end of the street is a car park and in one hidden corner of it lives a community of Pardhi people who came to Mumbai in the early 1960s. It was a time when tall buildings were being built on a portion of Marine Drive, newly reclaimed from the sea. A time when the Oberoi Hotel was still a twinkle in the eye of Rai Bahadur Mohan Singh Oberoi and a time when the mighty Tata group was planning to build for the city a theatre on the very tip of Nariman Point with acoustics fine enough for Zubin Mehta to conduct orchestras. Other buildings came up as well. Buildings that were disproportionately narrow. Buildings with ugly facades and tiny windows designed to keep out the heat in those days when air-conditioners were only for the few. It was to help build these structures that this community of Pardhi people migrated from Sholapur. Then they just stayed on because life on the pavements of the city was better than in the villages they left behind. They earned enough to live but never enough to afford even the rent of a room in a slum.

So they built a makeshift colony in a corner of the car park and it was here that they slept, ate, drank, lived and died. The little square of public land that is their home is on the edge of a small public park built in the memory of some forgotten leader. Before the public toilet came up at the busy end of the street they used the park as a lavatory. Now they use the Sulabh that gives them concessional rates because they are permanent customers, but that is the only real improvement in their standard of living. Other than cellphones. Everyone has a cellphone. And everyone, even very small children, has to try and earn a living. Children who come back with nothing at the end of the day get no food, so they spend long hours at traffic lights begging and beguiling those who go by in fancy cars because they know that if they come back with nothing they will get nothing to eat.

It was through the children that I came to know this pavement community. And it was through walking Julie that I came to know the children. Julie was a Beagle that I gave Ajit for his birthday in the summer of 2001. Ajit is without question the most difficult person to find a present for, so that year his daughter Shalaka and my son Aatish decided that the best present for him would be a dog. Shalaka said he had always longed to have a dog of his own but his mother hated dogs, so the Great Dane he bought as a boy had to be kept outdoors at all times and inevitably one day vanished. It broke his heart and he still talks of him with affection, but Julie became the love of his life from the moment he first saw her. She was three weeks old and a little black runt of a puppy, but when he picked her up she licked his face and put her paw in his breast pocket. When she was six weeks old I brought her to Bombay in an Indian Airlines flight in which Ajit had arranged for us to sit in the last row. She was meant to have stayed in her basket throughout the flight but I let her poke her head out to be fed a biscuit and soon she became the centre of attention. From the moment she arrived in Bombay on a humid day that reeked of rotting fish and diesel fumes she seemed to know she was home.

For the first few months she stayed mostly indoors with short trips to the garden downstairs for potty training. It was only when all her shots were done that she was allowed to be taken outside the compound for her morning and evening walks. The first people who became her friends were the street children who loitered about from the early hours of the morning in the hope that some generous walker would buy them breakfast or give them some money. From the moment they saw Julie they fell in love with her and she with them. I think what she loved about them was that they were not afraid of her, unlike the plump, rich children whom she met in the lift of our building and who always cowered and cried when they saw her. In her Beagle way she found this deeply offensive and took to growling at them, making a bad situation in small lifts much worse. But she never growled at the street children who formed a gaggle around us when we walked and quickly took to calling me Julie Aunty.

In this gaggle of raggedy children were Surekha, her sisters, their friend Mangala and two boys called Sahib and Sartaj. They were all dark and scrawny from malnourishment but Surekha and her sisters had fine features and a sunny temperament and this made them look prettier than the others. They also had enough charm to wheedle gifts, money and food out of the obese, middle-aged people who took their morning constitutionals on Marine Drive at a pace slow enough to be interrupted. It was my impression that they always managed to make enough money out of their morning expeditions on Mumbai's most famous street until many years later I asked Roopa, Surekha's much older sister, what the worst memory of childhood was for her. The question made her burst into tears. 'We were always hungry.' She had her small daughter in her arms and clutched her closer, controlling her tears with some effort. 'We were always hungry because if we came home at the end of the day without earning any money we would get nothing to eat.'

If I had known this when I first met these children I might have started Nashta earlier, but as things happened it was because of a small boy whom I only met once that Nashta came to be. While walking Julie one morning I saw a boy of about ten lying face down on the pavement. His small, dirty feet were rough with callouses as if he had walked a long, long way. He was so deeply asleep that he did not wake up even when ladies with sneakers on their feet and diamonds on their fingers jumped over him as they walked. One of them took pity on him and left a packet of glucose biscuits by his head. And I, noticing a young man selling idlis and dosas not far from where the boy lay, gave him some money and asked him to feed the boy when he woke up. Julie's gaggle of street children immediately set up a collective wail. 'What about us? What about us? Can't Ali feed us too?'

'Yes. Of course,' I said, giving Ali the extra money, and from this transaction Nashta was born.

Within days every child who lived in the car park behind the Air India building turned up at Ali's little pavement stall to eat breakfast. I soon discovered that they knew Ali well and knew even that the only day on which he would not be on Marine Drive was Eid. They told me that on Eid he went to Haji Ali and that he lived in Dharavi with his widowed mother and a sister who was physically handicapped and had to be carried everywhere. This made it impossible for his mother to work, so it was on what Ali earned that this family eked out its existence.

When I got to know Ali better I learned that his mother woke up every morning at four to make the food that he brought to sell on Marine Drive, and I learned that he had another sister whose marriage he worried about. Ali was more than grateful when Nashta began because his earnings tripled. He did not like Surekha and her friends much because they teased him constantly and usually made a mess around his little stall, but he told me that his life had changed because of the money he earned from Nashta.

Of the children who ate at his stall it was Surekha I came to know best. She was the leader of this pack of raggedy little people who were all adults before their time and she was the most articulate of them. She would have been no more than ten when I met her, and although she had the hardest life a child can have she seemed always to be happy and ready for any new adventure. That is any new adventure that did not involve going to school. When I tried to use Nashta to persuade its unschooled members to start going to the municipal school for at least a few hours the one who resisted most was Surekha. When I asked her why, she usually just smiled cryptically, and if I really tried to get an answer she would admit she saw no point in learning to read and write.

It was not as if the children had much time on their hands either. They spent all day trying to earn money in whichever way possible. If there were no policemen around they begged at traffic lights. Begging could get them arrested but if they were seen trying to earn an honest living by selling flowers stolen from graveyards or jasmine garlands when the season was right then they would be left alone. One evening a few days before Christmas, soon after I started Nashta, I saw Surekha and her little gang wearing red Santa Claus caps and trying to sell mistletoe and books of carols outside the newly built Inox cinema. They danced around people going into the cinema like crazed elves from a Christmas tale and when they spotted me even tried to sell me a few things.

'What are you doing?' I asked Surekha. 'Where did you get this stuff?'

'Someone came and gave it to us,' she said with a grin.

'Do you know what it's for?'

'Kismis,' they chanted in unison.

'Do you know what Christmas is?'

'No. But it's for kischuns.'

There was no point in pursuing this line of conversation, I quickly discovered, because I knew by then that although they knew a lot of words they usually did not know any more than the words. They had no religious beliefs but seemed happy to adopt any festival that came along, and since in the gang were Hindu and Muslim children they became whatever anyone wanted them to be according to the festival of the moment. On Diwali they were all Hindus because it was that one time of year when Hindus felt generous enough to acknowledge them as children that needed feeding, and on Eid they all became Muslims and lined up outside Muslim shrines to eat leftovers from Muslim feasts. The only place where they knew that they would be bathed, fed and clothed every Friday was the Pavement Club in an old stone church not far from the Oval Maidan.

I was introduced to this club by a friend of charitable disposition who discovered it through doing charitable work on behalf of the Rotary Club. 'If you are working with street children you should meet Mr Lawrence,' Jyoti said one day and so it was that I found myself one afternoon being introduced to a tall man with a kindly face and the gentle demeanour of a priest. When I called him Father Lawrence he told me that he was not a priest but helped the church look after street children. He then took me on a tour of the Pavement

Club. In one corner of the churchyard, schoolchildren in neat grey uniforms from the Cathedral School were bathing naked toddlers. After they were cleaned up, the children were led into the stone church, where they were given fresh clothes, donated by Mumbai's more charitable citizens, and then encouraged to sing and dance to Bollywood songs. Older children were given basic lessons in reading and writing.

The children I saw that afternoon in that old stone church probably had only that one day in the week when they could experience the joys of childhood and I remember thinking how wonderful it would be if there were a million Pavement Clubs in India. So imagine my horror when a few days after my first visit to the Pavement Club I read in the newspapers that rabid Hindutva groups had come together in a religious conclave in Ahmedabad to demand that Christian organizations be banned in India. More Hindus had become Christians since Independence, railed Ashok Singhal, than in all the decades of the British Raj. This he declared was a threat to Hindu culture. Singhal I knew was rabid even by the standards of rabid Hindutva but so sickened was I by this latest outpouring of religious bile that I wrote a column saying that Hindutva organizations should help set up a million Pavements Clubs.

'Imagine the difference a million Pavement Clubs could make. We wouldn't have to face the daily horror of seeing India's children scrabbling through the garbage heaps of our cities. We are almost the only country left where this kind of abhorrent sight still exists. What makes it even more repugnant is that our religious organizations seem so much more capable of spreading hatred and venom than compassion and knowledge.'

The more familiar I became with the lives of Mumbai's street children the more I realized that India's shameful, horrendous poverty would not disappear as long as this disconnect remained between policy makers and the people for whom they made their policies.

Since 1975 India has had what officials proudly claim is the biggest children's welfare programme in the world. It is called the ICDS (Integrated Child Development Scheme). It was started by Indira Gandhi when she most needed popular support during the Emergency. If it works at all, this programme works so badly that not a single street child I have met has ever heard of it.

In the years that Sonia Gandhi was India's de facto prime minister, if there was one thing she succeeded at, it was in creating the impression that she was the patron saint of the poor. The Mother Teresa of Indian politics. Even Surekha had heard of her. Surekha told me one day that she had been to Delhi to ask Sonia Gandhi to give her a house.

'You did what?' I asked in amazement.

'We went to Delhi – my mother and I,' she said with a smile, 'because someone told us that Sonia Gandhi was giving houses to poor people.'

'Who told you this?'

'I don't know who…but people talked about it, so we went.'

'Do you know who Sonia Gandhi is?'

'No.'

'Do you know who the prime minister is?'

'No.'

'Do you know who the president is?'

'No.'

'Do you know the name of your country?'

'India.'

'Good. So tell me why you believed that by going to Delhi to meet Sonia Gandhi you would be able to get a house?'

'Everyone told us that she was the only person who cared about poor people,' she said simply.

'So what happened when you got to Delhi?'

'At the railway station we asked people how to get to her house and they guided us so we got there but then they would not let us in. We waited all day and then spent the night in a gurudwara and went back the next day and the next and finally someone from her house came out and met us and gave us some papers that he said we should bring back to Bombay and we would be given houses.'

'And then?'

'We came back and took the papers to the mantralaya and the nagar palika and showed them there but still nothing happened.'

Surekha and Roopa were sitting in my study with their children in their laps for one of the many sessions in which we discussed their lives when she told me this. We had come to an agreement that I would pay them for these sessions and they were more than willing. As usual they came dressed up elegantly in shiny, synthetic saris with appropriate matching jewellery and with their hair tied up neatly in buns. When I asked how they always managed to be so well dressed, they laughed and said that they bought their saris from Crawford Market when there was the weekly bazaar. 'You can get a sari for Rs 100,' they said, 'and sometimes if they are second hand then for even less.'

'But where do you keep your clothes?'

'Everyone has their own plastic bag in which we keep our things and when the police come to make us move we have to hang on to them really tight.'

'And when it rains?'

'We have plastic sheets that we put over us and this keeps the rain out. Sometimes when it rains too hard we take shelter in one of the buildings.'

They said this casually, as if they lived in a city in which during the rainy season it did not rain for weeks and weeks, sometimes without letting up. Ever since I first met them when they were still children, I had found it hard to watch the rain from the window of my ninth floor apartment and not think how they managed. The monsoon is the only season in this city when there is a let-up from hot, humid days and dry, balmy nights. It is a season that brings so much relief, romance and magic that even in the most squalid slums there is a sense of relief, but for street people it is just a harsh reminder of the fragility of their lives and their livelihood. Those who can leave for their villages leave temporarily. There they live in even more extreme poverty and deprivation than they do in the streets of Mumbai, so they return as soon as the rains stop.

4

CHILDREN

Children grow up fast in the streets. One mild winter evening in 2004 or 2005, Mangala arrived with a baby in her arms. Mangala is a small, plain girl with big eyes and thick hair. She seemed to stop growing when she was about ten, so she never stopped looking like the little girl I first met in Surekha's gaggle of friends. When I saw her with the baby in her arms, I asked her whose it was and she said it was hers. 'But you can't be more than twelve,' I said horrified.

She did not answer but Surekha, who was with her, said, 'No, she is older than that.'

'So who is the father?'

'Nobody knows,' Surekha said calmly as Mangala looked down at her bare feet.

She was so small it seemed hardly possible that she could have produced a child, but there she was with a baby that was frighteningly small but had big round eyes and a sweet smile. After that whenever she came with jasmine garlands to sell, I gave her a little extra for the baby. One evening after dinner Ajit and I were walking our friend Albina du Boisrouvray back to the Oberoi Hotel when we met Mangala and her baby. Albina is among the kindest, bravest people I have ever met. She comes from an aristocratic French family and has inherited huge wealth. Her mother was the daughter of Antinor Patino, once considered the richest man in the world. Albina had what many may think of as the perfect life until she lost her twenty-four-year-old son Xavier in a helicopter accident. After going almost mad with grief she managed to bring meaning back into her life by channelling her wealth and all her energy into a charitable foundation in her son's name. This is what first brought her to India around the time when it seemed as if AIDS was on the verge of becoming the pandemic it had already become in Africa.

That evening I told her Mangala's story. Then I asked if I should adopt the baby since it would almost certainly die of malnutrition or disease if left in the charge of a single mother who was herself only a child.

'No. How many children will you adopt if you start?'

'Just this one. Because his mother has no way of looking after him.' I thought I saw the little baby looking at me as if he were listening to the conversation. Mangala paid no attention.

'You cannot afford to get emotionally involved in these situations,' Albina said.

'I totally agree,' Ajit said. So that evening when Mangala vanished with her child into the fumes and lights and traffic noises of the street behind the Oberoi Hotel was the last time I saw the baby. The next time Surekha and Mangala came with their jasmine garlands I noticed that the baby was not with them. When I asked what had happened to him Surekha said, 'Oh. He died.'

Mangala said nothing. But as I was to discover in the years that I got to know this street community better, there was no time in their lives for sorrow or pain simply because it was always with them in some way or other. Death was just part of life.

As someone who had spent half a lifetime covering politics and governance, I often asked them if they knew about the great schemes that have been created to 'alleviate poverty' by the people who ruled over them. Leaders who never failed to mention 'the poor' in their speeches inside and outside Parliament and policy makers who sat in exalted offices in Delhi appeared to think only of the poor. In Mumbai's mean, brutal streets hundreds of thousands of Indians who live there have never been able to benefit from these schemes and their only contact with the state is when some policeman comes and moves them off public land. Or when small children get arrested for begging and have to be released from state children's homes that are more brutal than Mumbai's streets.

5

INDIA GETS RICHER

The apartment building in which I live is at the very end of Marine Drive. At that point this most magnificent of Mumbai's streets disappears into the sea in an ugly clutter of concrete tetrapods. In my building live some of the richest people in India, and it was when my association with the city's poorest citizens began that I realized how much they hate being reminded of India's poverty. The building became for me an interesting and accurate barometer of India's growing prosperity. It became evident in different ways that some Indians were getting richer every day. Richer residents, some who had become NRIs to escape taxes, started buying more than one apartment and linking them together, sometimes interfering dangerously with load-bearing pillars and walls. They barely came to Mumbai once a year from their main homes in Dubai and Oman but felt the need anyway to live in big apartments.

Then there was the basement car park. When we first moved to the NCPA Apartments at the beginning of Vajpayee's first term as prime minister, the car park was filled mostly with Japanese cars. These came to be slowly replaced by more expensive German cars. BMWs, Mercedes, Porsches and Bentleys began to fill spaces where humbler Lexuses and

Toyota Innovas once stood. And in the place of Pajeros came Range Rovers and Audi SUVS.

Then there was the way in which the women of the building changed their accoutrements and accessories. In the gym on the twenty-second floor, I liked watching how the wives of India's millionaires and billionaires started abandoning Indian jewellery for that made by Cartier and Bulgari. Louis Vuitton luggage became ubiquitous. When Hermes set up shop in an old-fashioned heritage building in Horniman Circle, every woman I knew seemed to have a Birkin bag or two. Poverty was a long way away from this world of new global Indians who spent summer holidays in European resorts, autumn in New York and who could always be spotted on the promenade in Davos at the time of the World Economic Forum's annual meeting.

After I started living with Ajit, I started going myself on this annual trip to Davos and used my skills as a journalist to spot signs of change and prosperity. When I first went to Davos in 1995, there were no more than a handful of Indian businessmen at the forum. The men included some of the richest industrialists in India, dressed in ill-fitting suits that seemed to have been made for them by backstreet tailors in Delhi and Mumbai. Their wives made it such a point to dress in Indian clothes that an economist friend, who used his own barometer to gauge the prosperity of countries, said as a bevy of Indian women stumbled through the snow in saris, 'When they stop wearing costume abroad India will have arrived.' I saw the point of what he said. After two attempts at staggering through snow in moonboots and a sari I gave up, but the wives of Indian tycoons continued to keep the tricolour flying high sartorially much longer.

Then one day, at almost exactly the time that the world began to stop seeing India as an economic basket case, there was a revolution in Davos. Suddenly, Indian women were wearing Chanel suits and Gucci boots under coats of sable and mink and their husbands were dressed in Brioni and Zegna. Almost exactly the same thing happened in the NCPA Apartments at almost exactly the same time.

A consequence of this was that Indian poverty became something that newly rich Indians were increasingly ashamed of. It became a thing of such deep shame that it needed to be ignored or hidden away somewhere. Perhaps the contrast between their lives and those of Mumbai's street people, incidentally residents of the same neighbourhood, embarrassed them so much they could not bear to see them around.

The street people I knew did not help matters by being drunk and disorderly late at night on the pavement outside our building. So it was that one morning I got a call from a lady in my building who sounded very upset.

'You have to stop encouraging these people,' she said angrily.

'Which people?'

'Those poor people who live in the street...I have seen you talking to them.'

'Why? What happened?'

'Did you hear the noise last night? Do you know that woman I have seen you talking to was so drunk that she was shouting and making so much of a ruckus that we could not sleep?'

'Which woman?'

'That woman with the two little girls...I've seen you talking to her. You must stop encouraging them to hang around the building.'

'Where should I tell them to go?'

'Wherever they came from...I don't care. What I care about

is that they shouldn't be making a noise outside my window at night or I shall call the police and have them arrested.'

'Please don't do that,' I implored. 'Lakshmi has a tendency to drink too much and I will speak to her about this, but if you have her arrested what will happen to her children? Her son is less than a year old.'

'Well, she shouldn't have had so many children...in any case she has to go away from here.'

'She cannot,' I said, 'because she and her husband Hamid were born on the pavement and have been living here long before the building came up.'

'Ah, so now you are trying to tell me he is a Muslim so that because I am a Muslim you might get my sympathy. Well, you won't. You will have to tell them to go away.'

'They have nowhere to go,' I repeated and put the phone down.

I never heard from this lady again and I never met her. But I soon discovered that most people who lived in my building felt the same way about poor people and poverty. They affected refinements of all kinds. They organized ghazal evenings and concerts and spent huge amounts inviting famous people to come and give talks in the NCPA theatre and if there was a literary festival they patronized it passionately, but their servants were treated as if they were sub-human. They were not given even basic amenities like a room, a bed or a toilet.

As one of my ways of keeping fit was to climb the twenty-two floors of the building and climb down again, I routinely came upon servants sleeping on landings and using the walls of the stairwell as urinals. The worst employer was a close neighbour. When she next came to invite me for 'an evening of ghazals' I confronted her about the treatment of her servants. She stiffened her squat, fat frame as I broached the subject and said, 'As a woman you should understand that I cannot have strange men sleeping inside the flat at night.'

'Frankly, I don't understand. You should be ashamed that you cannot even give them a room of their own.'

'There is no servants' room,' she said.

'Of course there is...every flat has a servants' room and toilet beyond the kitchen.'

'We don't because we wanted a bigger kitchen. As for the toilet they can go downstairs and use the one that the drivers use.'

'Well, they don't use it at night,' I said, 'or the walls of the landing on your floor would not be covered in urine stains.'

It was pointless, I soon discovered, to have conversations of this kind because the people who lived in the NCPA Apartments quite simply thought of poor people as not quite human. Meanwhile, my associations with these sub-humans continued to grow. After the conversation with the irate lady I went down to have a word with Lakshmi. The rains were about to come and she and her two small daughters, Meghana and Rajyalakshmi, were helping Hamid (called Amit by everyone) build a shack on the edge of the sea. It was just above the tetrapods on a tiny space that reeked of urine, but the little girls took me proudly to see their new home. It was made of sticks and waste plastic but at least it offered shelter from the rain.

Lakshmi was a frail, dark woman who would have been pretty if she was not a drunk. Her two little girls listened carefully as I spoke to her about her drinking problem. Lakshmi cradled their small brother in her arms and listened attentively as I gave her a lecture on the bad effect her drinking could have on her children. When I finished she said, 'You are right. I shouldn't drink like this, but at the end of a day of sorting through garbage dumps to make barely Rs 50

when I come back and sit on the pavement, the only thing
that makes me happy is liquor.'

Between Amit and Lakshmi they made around Rs 150 a
day. This was enough to feed themselves and their children
and buy a quarter bottle of cheap liquor. But not enough for
anything else, and so when Lakshmi had one of her drinking
bouts and her liver began to give her trouble, I would have to
pay for her to be taken to hospital. My driver Jaywant, who
had to drive her there, would protest about her sitting in the
car because she smelled so bad. 'Last time I took her to the
hospital the doctors refused to touch her until she cleaned
herself up,' he said. 'Please tell her to wash before getting into
the car.'

It was something I never got around to doing because
Lakshmi had so many bigger problems to deal with. Of these
the two biggest problems were her little girls. She worried
about them being sexually abused more than anything else
and one day confided in me that she thought Amit was
abusing Meghna. 'These girls are going to be the death of
me,' she said wearily. 'Please take them away.'

'I can only put them in a home. Are you okay with that?'

'Yes. Yes.'

'And little Vijay?'

'No. Not him,' she said, holding him closer. 'I need to have
him with me.'

Once more I turned to my friend, Jyoti Doshi, for help,
and as she had with the Pavement Club she introduced me
to a home that was run by a Parsi trust in Matunga. The
head of the trust was a man she knew called Cyrus Guzder
and he was more than willing to help. A social worker called
Anagaha helped me with the procedural details of getting the
parents to consent to their girls being put in the home, but
part of the procedure was that they had to spend their first

few days in a government home that was so awful that they wanted to run away.

When I went to see them they wept and begged to be taken back to their parents and I thought I had made a terrible mistake until the warden said she wanted to speak to me in private. So the weeping girls were taken away and she said, 'Look, I know that the conditions in this home are terrible but it is only for a few days. You have to get the Matunga home to sign a paper saying they will take them and they can go immediately. But don't take them away from here as the older girl tells me that her father is always touching her in a funny way...'

'Sexual abuse?'

'Yes.'

Lakshmi did not want the girls to come back to the street either, so they were forced to endure the period they had to spend in the custody of the Maharashtra government's welfare system. They were beaten, bullied and given food that was more appalling than the food they ate in the streets of Mumbai. Then one day Anagaha called to say we could take the girls to the private home in Matunga. It was a long, long way away from the pavement on which they had spent their lives and the girls got increasingly nervous as the drive got longer. They stared with frightened eyes at the crowded, unfamiliar streets we drove through, and Anagaha had to reassure them in Marathi that they were going to a much better home than the one they had spent their first days away from their parents in.

The government home was so bad that children regularly ran away from it. Rajyalakshmi told us, with tears pouring down her face, that she was beaten every day by other children and that nobody helped her. She was seven years old but looked much smaller. Meghana seemed to have had an easier time, but their days in the government home had frightened them so much the last thing either of them seemed to expect was that they might like the new home. So when we drove through the gates of the Byramjee Jeejeebhoy home they were reluctant to get out of the car. It was Anagaha's gentle persuasion that got them into the office of the warden. Once inside they seemed to relax a little. There were children's toys in cupboards and happy pictures painted by children on the walls, and the lady they were introduced to talked to them in Marathi and told them they had nothing to worry about.

She took us on a tour of the sprawling home and told us that it had been built by a Parsi family in the 1930s. It looked like an old-fashioned Parsi house. We walked along sunny corridors that led to large rooms in which beds were neatly laid out. There was a girls' wing and a boys' wing and a kitchen in which children sat on the floor chopping vegetables. Meghana and Rajyalakshmi seemed to like what they saw and when I left them I did not feel so bad as I had on the drive to Matunga. I knew the girls would be better off in the home but still felt a little worried about the responsibility I had taken on. I got weekly reports on their progress from Anagaha, who said Rajyalakshmi had taken longer to adjust than her sister, but by Diwali when I next went to see them they were completely transformed.

They wore pretty frocks and clips in their shampooed hair and looked nothing like the waifs they had been when I brought them here. Lakshmi tried to see her daughters in the Byramjee Jeejeebhoy home, but she was drunk whenever she came, and this upset the girls so much that the warden discouraged her from coming. When she was stopped from entering the gates of the children's home because of being too drunk, she would make such a noise that it made her daughters too ashamed to come out and see her. Anagaha told me that she was banned from seeing them altogether finally because she kept trying to take them with her. This they were so reluctant to do that even when the home closed for vacations and children with parents went home they refused to leave. They were among the handful of children who lived permanently in the children's home.

On the street outside my building I ran into Lakshmi every now and then and she was nearly always drunk. Then came a phase when I would find her lying on the pavement even during the day. When I asked her what her problem was she would sometimes complain about pains in her legs and sometimes about her back. Whenever I sent her to the hospital the doctors said her only problem was liquor. One day she vanished altogether from the pavement on which she was usually to be found lying next to her small son under a raggedy blanket. When I did not see her for several days I made inquiries and found that she had broken her leg and had moved to an inner, quieter pavement behind my building. I never saw her again. I did not see her husband either, so it was many weeks after she died that I learned of her death. I immediately called Anagaha and asked how we should break the news to her daughters.

'We will go together,' she said, 'and find a way of telling them that won't be too much of a shock.'

'All right,' I said, 'but do you need me there? I am not sure if I will be any use.'

'No. You should come,' said Anagaha, 'because you are the one who brought them to the home, so they associate you with what may have been the last time they saw their mother.'

I had not seen them in five years. They had moved to a home for older girls when I went with Anagaha to tell them that their mother had died. On the way there Anagaha told me that Lakshmi had been banned from seeing her daughters.

'Did she see them when they moved to the new home?'

'I am not sure but I don't think she did.'

The new home was in a narrow, yellow-washed building on a busy street in a Mumbai suburb. I followed Anagaha up a steep staircase to the first floor that consisted of rooms that led off a narrow veranda. Anagaha took me into the warden's small neon-lit office and pointed to a painting on a wall and said that it was a painting by Meghana. 'She is such a good painter that she could easily get into the J.J. School of Art,' she said, 'and she has grown into an intelligent and confident girl.'

She had barely said these words when a tall, dark girl walked in. She wore her thick hair pulled back from her face in a plait and this emphasized her full mouth and large, dark eyes. I would never have recognized this Meghana as the frightened little girl from five years ago. Her younger sister's face had changed less and she retained the fine features she got from Lakshmi. They did not recognize me and barely remembered who I was even when Anagaha reminded them that it was I who had brought them to the home. I sat silently as Anagaha, with the ease of a trained social worker, asked them a lot of questions about this and that. How were they doing in school? What were their favourite subjects? Were they happy in the new home? I listened.

Meghana said her favourite subject was art and she hoped one day to become a painter. Rajyalakshmi said the only thing she liked to do was read. When I asked what she liked reading she said she liked to read story books. I asked what kind of food they got in the new home and they said they got good vegetarian food every day and now and then some good Samaritan would bring them chicken or fruit.

Anagaha kept up light banter about this and that for several minutes before she finally asked the girls if they remembered their mother. They said of course they did, but that they did not miss her much. They missed their little brother more, they said, but when she told them that Lakshmi was dead both girls began to cry. I felt terrible but found myself unable to find words that would comfort them, so I sat silently while Anagaha comforted them instead. It was only when we were leaving that the girls hugged me tightly and said they would like very much to see their father and brother again. I did not go with Amit when he went to see his daughters for the first time in five years but heard later that the reunion went well and that the girls were especially happy to see their brother.

6

SONIA

In the summer of 2004 I was among those who believed Sonia Gandhi had not the smallest chance of becoming prime minister. One rule of political commentary that I usually follow is to never be certain about anything but that summer there seemed good reason for certainty. Atal Behari Vajpayee had run a reasonably good government, the economy was in good shape and people seemed happy with the way the country was going. So when I was interviewed by Satinder Singh for CNN days before the results of the general election were due, I made a foolish prediction.

He decided that we should do the interview in the magnificent forecourt of Humayun's Tomb, newly restored by the Aga Khan Foundation. The restoration was so recent there was the smell of fresh paint in the warm, dry air of that May morning. And the smell of dry leaves and neem trees. I remembered that it was here that Bahadur Shah Zafar's sons had taken refuge after the British defeated the mutinous soldiers who declared India's independence in 1857. It was here that an ancestor of mine, Maan Singh, had found the princes and taken them to the Khooni Darwaza on Bahadur Shah Zafar Marg, where I had always believed that he personally shot them.

This story has come down in my father's family as a shameful one. Whenever my father showed us the yellow diamond ring that was believed to have been taken from the finger of one of the princes, this shameful incident would be recalled. So it made me very happy when William Dalrymple wrote his book on Bahadur Shah Zafar and absolved my ancestor. It was William Stephen Raikes Hodson who killed the princes, he wrote, and ever since we have talked of Maan Singh's role with a measure of pride because according to Willy's research he came to Humayun's Tomb to try and save the princes.

On that warm, dusty May morning Satinder and I walked up and down on one of the tomb's splendid sandstone terraces with the acrid scent of squashed neem pods in the warm breeze. The interview went something like this:

'Do you think Mr Vajpayee ran a good government?'

'Yes. I think he did.'

'So you think he is popular enough to win again.'

'Yes. I think he is.'

'Do you think there is any chance of the Congress party under Sonia Gandhi making an unexpected comeback?'

'No. I am certain there is no chance of this happening.'

If you had asked any other political journalist in Delhi the same questions you would have got the same answer and this is my only excuse for having stuck my neck out so foolishly. I have never done it since and certainly never so publicly and I am deeply grateful that CNN seemed to think the interview with me was too unimportant to run. At least if they did run it I missed watching me make a complete fool of myself.

It may have been that same evening or the next one that I went to a dinner party that my sister Kitto and her husband Oliver gave in their house in Sainik Farms. It was a hot, sultry evening and the dinner party stretched on endlessly, at least for some of us. Long after the other guests left, Gita Mehta, Swapan Dasgupta, his wife Reshmi and I sat around the dining table drinking wine and speculating about the results due the next morning.

Someone suggested that Kitto, an intuitive and remarkably prescient fortuneteller, bring out her Tarot cards. So she did and we asked the sort of questions to which Tarot cards usually find abstract and mysterious answers. What would be the future of Mr Vajpayee, one of us asked casually, and to our amazement the cards Kitto pulled up all indicated disappointment.

We were so taken aback that we asked many more questions and every time she dealt the cards there would be more indications of defeat and disappointment. Except that the cards also predicted that Sonia Gandhi would not become prime minister, which cheered us up slightly since like a lot of other Indians we were ashamed at the possibility that an apolitical Italian housewife could become Prime Minister of India. And so we concluded that the cards were deeply confused this time.

The next morning, 13 May, I began watching the results on television as soon as they started coming. Despite the very first ones making it clear that the Congress was leading in the most unexpected constituencies I continued to nurture the mistaken belief that early trends often failed to tell the whole story. But in my heart I knew that something had happened to upset everyone's calculations. By that afternoon it became clear that the Congress was going to emerge as the single largest party. The first person I rang was my sister to compliment her on the accuracy of her Tarot cards. Then I concentrated all my attentions on the political upheavals that turned that hot summer's day in Delhi into a moment in history: India was likely to get its first foreign-born prime minister. It was the biggest political upheaval I could remember since Indira Gandhi and her son Sanjay lost the 1977 general election so badly that they lost their own seats of Rae Bareli and Amethi. That time we had waited all night outside newspaper offices on Bahadur Shah Zafar Marg and afterwards there had been dancing in the streets.

This time to celebrate the extraordinary victory of Indira Gandhi's daughter-in-law there was dancing, firecrackers and drums outside Congress headquarters at 24 Akbar Road as a curtain of gloom descended over BJP headquarters on Ashoka Road. Senior BJP leaders vanished to hide their shame in solitude and Sonia Gandhi gave her first press conference.

As someone who had long campaigned in my columns against the idea of India having a foreign prime minister I found myself despondent. Thoughts of Indira Gandhi came to me over and over again that day, and I remember thinking that she would have been truly appalled that her Italian daughter-in-law should be taking her job as leader of India.

Sonia's vaunted closeness to her mother-in-law was apolitical and totally domestic. It was unlikely that even after Rajiv entered politics and became a general secretary in the Congress party she would have had a single political conversation with her. As someone who drifted on the edges of the circle in which Rajiv and Sonia moved I knew that her role in the prime minister's household was that of a dutiful daughter-in-law. She made sure that the kitchen produced good food, that the children went to school on time, and that when her husband or mother-in-law needed something she was always there. And here she was in a position to become India's prime minister.

Sonia knew nothing of Indian politics but what troubled me more on that morning of her victory was that I knew well that the India she knew, and I am not at all sure loved, was an India whose boundaries did not extend beyond the drawing rooms of Lutyens' Delhi. It was an India of memsahibs and sahibs, big bungalows and ayahs and holidays in Corbett Park or in the summer months somewhere in the hills. The vast, turbulent nation that lay beyond the framework of this dreary canvas she knew nothing of. In all the years that she lived in Delhi as a prime minister's daughter-in-law and wife I never once saw her show concerns that could be described as social, except if this word were to be used in the context of social secretaries and dinner parties.

After she agreed to become president of the Congress in 1998, I often ran into Congress friends who told me how much she had changed. 'People change, Tavleen,' Louise Khurshid said to me more than once. 'The Sonia of today is not the Sonia you knew. She is very different and has a real interest in politics and political things.'

This assessment was something I was unable to confirm with empirical evidence since in the years after she became a political leader I met her only twice. Both times, accidentally, and both times at the Taj Palace Hotel. The first time was when Prime Minister Vajpayee invited me to a lunch for Vladimir Putin. I arrived early along with other lesser guests, and we found ourselves having to wait endlessly in an enormous room that glittered with chandeliers and the whiteness of tablecloths laden with silver and crystal.

While waiting for the banquet to begin, we journalists gathered in an obscure corner and chatted about this and that. As we were talking, Renuka Chowdhury, then best known as an ardent devotee of Sonia, ambled over with an amiable smile on her face. For reasons I cannot remember she began a conversation with me about Sonia. 'You should really get to know her better,' she said, adding, 'Come with me. I'll introduce you to her.' It was then that I noticed that behind Renuka's ample frame stood Sonia in deep conversation with Sheila Dikshit.

Renuka appeared not to know that I knew Sonia and I was in no mood to enlighten her or take her up on her offer to introduce me, so I muttered some excuse and moved away. But the wait for Mr Putin continued for a very long time and at some point I needed to go to the ladies room. This involved walking to an exit that was beyond where Sonia stood. Renuka had now joined her and the two Congress ladies stood on either side of their leader with the docile demeanour of ladies-in-waiting.

I tried to scuttle past this group unnoticed but Sonia spotted me and said, 'Come and talk to me, Tavleen, you who hate me more than anyone else.' It was not the sort of remark that anyone can let pass without response, so I said, 'I don't hate you, Sonia. I hate the fact that you are in politics. Why are you in politics by the way?' Before Sonia could respond Renuka leapt in, embarrassed I think by the familiarity with which I had spoken to her leader, and said in her usual strident way that nobody could understand politics until they stood for election. To this I think I said something like how it must all be very new for her then since she had only won her first election some months ago, and she said with a flounce, looking less like a genial buffalo than usual, 'Don't patronize me, Tavleen.'

I ignored her and turning to Sonia asked about her newly born grandson. She told me his name was Rehan and then I took my leave.

My next close encounter happened mere months before the election that brought her first government to power. It was one of those meetings that the Confederation of Indian Industry routinely holds in that same enormous hall at the

Taj Palace Hotel and she was chief guest. I remember that she began her speech by saying with a dimple and a charming little giggle, 'When the leader of the opposition is invited as chief guest to a meeting like this it must mean that the times are changing.' The rest of her speech was unremarkable and after it was over a small group of important industrialists took her off to have tea in an anteroom. I remained in the big room with Ajit. Najma Heptullah joined us and after some minutes of the usual sort of social chitchat suggested that we also go and have some tea. This was many minutes after Sonia had gone into the anteroom where tea was being served and I thought that she would have left by then. But there she stood surrounded by sycophantic industrialists bowing and scraping shamelessly. If she had been the Maharani of India they could not have kowtowed more obsequiously.

I tried to avoid going up to her because I had nothing that I could think of to say and also I had made it more than clear in my column that the idea of India having an Italian prime minister was in my view deplorable and demeaning. I had often mocked her political moves, the most memorable being the way in which she brought down Vajpayee's government in 1999 with the support of Jayalalithaa. She did this convinced that Mulayam Singh Yadav would support her to form a new government and gave a triumphant interview to television reporters in the forecourt of Rashtrapati Bhavan in which, when asked how many MPs were with her, said, '272 and many more coming.' I was among those who had made fun of her for making such a big mistake in her first major political decision.

So, that morning in the small room filled with the scent of coffee and buttery biscuits I thought my best move would be to stay as far out of sight as possible. But Ajit noticed me trying to lurk behind the big tea and coffee dispensers at one end of the small anteroom and advised me not to be stupid. 'Go and say hello,' he ordered. 'It's rude not to.'

'But what will I say?'

'Introduce me to her.'

I went up to her and said, 'Sonia, I would like you to meet this man I have been with for the past fifteen years but I suppose you already know...'

'No...the only gossip I get these days is political gossip,' she said with a friendly smile.

'Ah...well. This is Ajit Gulabchand.'

'So you are Tavleen's partner,' she said, turning to Ajit with her most charming smile. 'God bless you. Tavleen and I have our political differences but underneath that there is friendship.'

This rendered me speechless. But luckily she was quickly engulfed in a scrum of captains of industry who thought I had already taken up too much of her time. This was the last time I saw her at close enough range to have a conversation.

My colleagues in the media did not share my gloom on that hot summer afternoon when it became clear that Sonia Gandhi could become India's prime minister. Television reporters could hardly contain their excitement as they waited in the cul-de-sac outside her heavily guarded home at 10 Janpath. She moved here after Rajiv Gandhi lost the election in 1989, and each year the walls grew higher until the house became invisible. After her brief, jaunty appearance at her first press conference, Sonia remained closeted in the invisible house with her children.

Meanwhile, senior leaders of the Bharatiya Janata Party gathered in other bungalows in Lutyens' Delhi to try and make sense of a defeat that had been the last thing on their minds. Vajpayee had been a competent and popular prime minister, so nobody seemed able to understand what had gone wrong. From friends who were in these gloomy conferences I learned that in the house of Lal Krishna Advani, who had hoped that it was now his turn to be prime minister, appeared an astrologer who predicted (like Kitto's Tarot cards) that Sonia would never become prime minister and from this was derived a brief moment of cheer. In times of political crises astrologers descend in droves on the fine bungalows of Lutyens' Delhi to offer comfort, advice and 'solutions' that range from the anodyne to the dangerous.

In the anodyne category falls advice to offer prayers in major temples and in the dangerous category falls advice to resort to black magic and tantric rites. Indian political leaders are easy prey in their moments of defeat and rarely ignore the solutions suggested to them. I have personally seen senior political leaders buy gold earrings for sixteen virgin girls, feed sixteen cows with their own hands and make offerings of liquor in temples where the gods are believed to have a taste for a tipple. From all accounts the astrologer who told Mr Advani that Sonia would never become prime minister offered only his piece of cryptic information. No bizarre solutions.

The next day we realized that he spoke the truth. Once she turned down the chance to become prime minister the newspapers raved about Sonia's 'sacrifice', with some editorials rapturous with sycophantic homage.

In a column that appeared in the *Indian Express* on 17 May I said this about them: 'Indian newspapers are replete with hacks of "secular" persuasion who have not stopped gushing about Rahul Gandhi's "youthful sincerity" and Priyanka Vadra's "gorgeous looks" and concluded that it was this dazzling combination that made the difference. One of our financial newspapers (*Business Standard*) passed this off as political analysis: "The gerontocracy did not stand a chance. Charisma works absolutely. Mix it with a liberal dose of Rahul Gandhi's youthful sincerity and Priyanka Gandhi's gorgeous fetching looks and the choice was unambiguous."'

The reason I quote this sycophantic comment is because it reflects perfectly the consensus in smoke-filled newspaper offices and in Delhi's television studios. And Sonia, reserved to the point of being uneasy with conversation of any kind, used this to her advantage when it came to handling the media. She evolved a policy whereby she refused to talk to journalists except those who were carefully vetted as supportive and obedient. The kind that may have asked her questions about India's stand on important international issues or big political and economic problems were never allowed near her.

The media was most helpful in this exercise. In newsrooms and TV studios I seemed always to run into some editor or columnist who had just come from 10 Janpath. You could tell that they had almost before they said anything in her support. No sooner did they get that invitation to tea in 10 Janpath than hard-boiled reporters would acquire so changed an expression on their faces that jokes began to be made about how 'one cup of tea with Sonia Gandhi could change the DNA of a journalist'. Later, years later, a famous editor who regularly took tea with Sonia and who became a close confidante of her daughter Priyanka had a story to tell.

We were having coffee together in the coffee shop of the Oberoi in Mumbai and I, as always, looked up to the eighteenth floor and paid silent tribute to those who were lined up against a wall and shot dead by the Pakistani jihadi terrorist, Fazlullah, on 26/11. And I was thinking of those who were killed in this coffee shop that same horrible night, when the editor said something that brought me instantly back into the present moment. This was not long after Tarun Tejpal was jailed for the alleged attempted rape of a friend of his daughter's in a lift in the Grand Hyatt Hotel in Goa.

We were talking about how astounding it was that he had made so much money from a magazine that barely sold a few thousand copies.

'The money didn't come from journalism,' the editor said.

'I am sure not,' I said.

'Well, let's just say that Tarun Tejpal had good reasons to be very, very close to 10 Janpath.'

In my head it was as if the pieces of a puzzle started to come together. I met Tarun through Vidia and Nadira Naipaul. Although he was always charming and friendly when we met, there was something about him that kept me from sharing their admiration of him. And I had always been sceptical whether his sting operations were sting operations or exercises in entrapment. His most famous sting operation was conducted in the third year of Vajpayee's government, and it so discredited Vajpayee that it turned his government into a lame duck. The two people caught on hidden cameras accepting money from fake arms dealers were the BJP president, Bangaru Laxman, and Jaya Jaitley, who had long been the closest aide of George Fernandes. George had to resign as defence minister and the scandal never died. But because I saw it more as entrapment than journalism I began to follow other *Tehelka* exposés closely and noticed that they seemed always to expose Sonia Gandhi's opponents.

Sonia's rise to the dizzying heights of political power may have been an accident of marrying into the right family but she soon proved that she was much smarter than most politicians at managing the media, democratic institutions and Delhi's drawing rooms. In the drawing rooms, conversations with glamorous socialites usually followed a pattern. Delhi is so political a city that even socialites like to talk about politics every time they spot a journalist. I am not sure why but they always seemed to have read my column, so they would accost me after their first glass of wine and insist on telling me their political thoughts.

This was the pattern.

'You know that I always read your column.'

'Thank you.'

'I think you write well but I don't like the way you attack Sonia Gandhi.'

'Oh?'

'Why do you write such bad things about Sonia?'

'I used to object to her political role because I did not want India to have an Italian prime minister but now that the people of India have accepted her I no longer do.'

'But you are always writing in your column against her?'

'My job is to write about politics and governance and so when she seems to be interfering in matters of governance I write about it.'

'Well, whatever you might say, I think she is the best thing that happened to India ever.'

Big businessmen and their diamond-studded, blow-dried, overgroomed wives became her most vocal supporters in Mumbai. An odd thing since she did everything she could to project herself as the patron saint of the poor and the enemy of the rich. The adulation of Sonia Gandhi for a while knew no bounds and was evident not just in fashionable drawing rooms in Delhi and Mumbai but in the dusty wilds of rural India. From notes in my journal six months after Sonia's first government came to power I have this one written on 2 January 2005: 'Politically the new government seems to have settled in so well that it's becoming hard to remember that the Congress (party) was ever out of power. The BJP has entered a sort of period of rapid decline that will become permanent unless someone can revive it and there are no signs yet of that someone. VR (Vasundhara Raje) says it's not going to happen.'

What puzzled me was how she had gone from being an Imelda Marcos-type figure and the hated foreign woman to being the Mother Teresa of Indian politics. When her political role was just as the prime minister's wife she was blamed for almost everything that went wrong, from the Bofors bribery scandal to his aloofness from party workers when he travelled in rural parts. And when he lost the election in 1989 the songs that people sang in the villages of northern India usually had some reference to 'you son-in-law of Italy'. So how did the transformation happen?

Delhi is a city in which conspiracy theories are never in short supply, so the transformation was rumoured to have been brought about with the help of a foreign public relations firm. The conspiracy theorists swore that they even knew the firm that had worked on her image makeover and named a famous one. Others said it was paid for by a foreign government which wanted her to become prime minister so that she could weaken India by weakening the economy. This is what she ended up achieving, and within two years of her chosen prime minister taking charge of India there were indications of trouble. Indian businessmen were the first to notice that government policies were going wrong.

The barometer of what was happening was the World Economic Forum's annual meeting in Davos. As I said earlier, I have been attending this dazzling conference since the days when it was a small, intimate gathering. For us in those days before the Internet opened up boundaries of all kinds, India was so isolated from the rest of the world that the annual WEF meeting was the best chance to catch up. It was in Davos that I sent my first email and in Davos that I first heard of the Internet. In the 1990s, when India's economic reforms had not fully ended the licence raj, there was no interest in India and very few Indians came to Davos. So few that when Deve

Gowda as prime minister brought his sons, daughters-in-law and grandchildren along at taxpayers' expense, hardly anyone in India noticed. He was hardly noticed in the conference either and I may have missed his presence totally if I had not run into his entire extended family in the Walzerof Hotel in Klosters one evening.

This small family-run hotel had the only Michelin restaurant in the vicinity of Davos, and Ajit and I made it a point to go there at least once during the annual meeting. This time, I remember staggering into the lobby on heels that were totally unsuitable to the icy conditions of the road only to find once I recovered my balance that the lobby was full of south Indians. There was a bevy of women in silk saris tending to a small army of children, while their men stood around in clothes more suitable to southern India than Europe in winter. Discreet inquiries revealed that this was the 'family of the Prime Minister of India'.

He seemed to have used the WEF annual meeting as a chance to give his family a winter holiday. And he was right to think of it as no more than this because the truth was that in the mid-1990s the world thought of India as an economic basket case if they thought of India at all. Then suddenly one day after the century changed and Indian software companies saved the world from the dreaded Y2K crisis, India began to be noticed in Davos. By 2005 India was the flavour of the season.

Indian fashion shows became the defining moment of the grand soirée on the last night of the conference, Bollywood music drifted out of Swiss cafes on the promenade, and in the bar at the Central Sport hotel it was Indians that made the most noise and had the most fun. Everyone you talked to said that India was a heartbeat away from becoming the new China. Who knows what may have happened if Sonia

Gandhi had not decided that the way forward was to go back to the economic ideas that once made Indira Gandhi the darling of the poor.

Indian industry grew and bloomed so rapidly after the licence raj ended that Indian businessmen were buying famous foreign companies like Jaguar and Arcelor and Indian names began to be counted for the first time in international billionaire lists. This could not have happened if the licence raj had still been in place, and Sonia decided it was time to bring it back. No sooner did she lend her special touch to government policy than businessmen began to be treated once more as profiteers and looters, and to keep them down all sorts of taxes and regulations were imposed, including a 'fringe benefit tax.' This was a tax on expenses just in case they disguised income. It was in 2006 in Davos that the first signs of the India story coming to an end began to become evident. I did a programme for NDTV at the time called India Inc. that came from an accidental suggestion to Radhika Roy over lunch in her office in Delhi. NDTV Profit had just started and she asked if I could think of any ideas for the new channel. 'Why don't we do a series on the Gujaratis and the Marwaris?' I said. 'They are the ones who have been the real pioneers in Indian business.'

'That's a great idea,' she said and soon I was interviewing more businessmen than I knew existed. India Inc. was popular, so after we had finished with the Gujaratis and the Marwaris I was obliged to come up with ideas for further seasons, and the seasons continued to multiply. I cannot remember what season we were in that year but I do remember doing many interviews with many big industrialists on the snowy promenade and many pieces to camera in freezing conditions.

It was in the course of doing these interviews that I discovered from almost everyone I talked to that a gloom was beginning to descend on the economy. Growth rates, they predicted, were likely to start dropping soon because the government was pursuing policies that encouraged cronyism instead of free markets. There is almost a reversal of the economic reform process, one major industrialist said to me in sombre tones, adding that nobody was more aware of this than the prime minister but he seemed incapable of stopping the slide because he had to listen to his boss.

Dr Manmohan Singh, who as finance minister had initiated the dismantling of the licence raj, acquiesced unquestioningly to the diktats that came from Sonia's National Advisory Council. This kitchen cabinet was made up of NGO do-gooders, leftist economists and a sundry collection of well-meaning activists who had gained fame and celebrity in the annals of activism by espousing some worthy cause or other. Sonia's patronage made them think of themselves as experts in the area of 'alleviating' poverty. Often when their policies were implemented by the Government of India, I wondered why they never made any difference in the lives of the street people I had come to know so well.

Everyone knew that Sonia Gandhi was India's real prime minister right from the moment in 2004 that Dr Manmohan Singh was chosen as her proxy, but her friends in the media – and their ranks were legion – continued to perpetuate the lie that she never interfered in policy. Ministers openly defied the prime minister and still they pretended that India had a real government instead of one appointed by someone whose only political qualification was that she married into a certain family. Editors who would tear government policies to shreds in their columns would never blame them on 10 Janpath. Sonia became as powerful as she did, and without any accountability, with the media playing an insidious, irresponsible role.

When I asked famous TV anchors and colleagues in the print media why they accepted so compliantly her absolute refusal to give interviews they had no answers, but later I discovered that they had private access not just to her but to her children. This was enough to keep them quiet. In my own case I continued to point out every instance of direct interference by Sonia in government policy and was reviled for it. And because I was in a minority of one I soon became a target. After Shekhar Gupta resigned from the editorship of the *Indian Express* he told me that she had personally asked him to stop my column on the grounds of what I wrote against her.

7

CHILDREN'S STORIES

It is in the eyes of street children that you see the true brutality of the Indian state. The blank adult gaze that meets your eye is hard to look at if you are Indian and have even a modicum of compassion. But it is important to look. The next time your car stops at a traffic light and a child's small, dirty hand appears outside your window in a gesture of supplication, look into the child's eyes instead of turning away. If you look you will see fear, hunger, sadness, confusion and cynicism. Then if you try talking to the child it will point to its stomach and make hungry gestures and it will make a whining noise and you will most likely be put off and turn your face away. And you will never discover that every Indian street child has a story of India to tell and it is nearly always a sad, sad story.

From walking Julie on Marine Drive and from Nashta I learned to never look away when a street child begs outside my window at a traffic light or tries to sell me something, and so it was that I met a little boy called Suresh. My car had stopped at a light somewhere between Haji Ali and Worli when a large pile of pirated books appeared in the window, underneath which was a boy too small to be carrying such a heavy load. The first thing I noticed about him was that he wore a school uniform and looked cleaner and healthier than most street children. So when he asked if I could give him a lift to Prabhadevi I readily agreed. When he sat on the seat next to me I wondered how someone so little – he looked no more than seven years old – could be sent off by his parents to do so dangerous a job.

When I asked him about this he turned his small face towards me and said, 'But if I don't earn some money then how will my mother manage?'

'Doesn't your father work?'

'He died two years ago. Now my mother works and I work in the afternoons when I come back from school.'

'What does your mother do?'

'She washes dishes in people's homes.'

'Where do you live?'

'In a jhopadpatti in Worli.'

'Do you have any brothers and sisters?'

'I have a sister. She is small.'

'Where do you get the books from that you sell?'

'A seth comes and gives them to us.'

'So why do you want to go to Prabhadevi?'

'There is a traffic light there at which cars stop longer, so people have more time to buy books. My commission depends on how many books I sell.'

When we got to Prabhadevi he thanked me for giving him a lift and I bought as many books as I could and said goodbye, thinking that by the standards of Mumbai's mean streets Suresh was one of the lucky ones. The children who come to eat breakfast through my Nashta club would have considered themselves the luckiest people in the world if they had a roof over their heads. And a school to go to. I soon noticed that in Surekha and her gang of friends it was the boys who grew up first and went off to work. So Sahib and

Sardar disappeared one day. They were lively, naughty little boys. When I did not see them for a few days I asked where they had gone and the answer I got was, 'They are working now.' I never saw them again as little boys. But accidentally some years later I ran into Sahib in the Oval Maidan. When a wiry construction worker with his hands and face covered in cement dust greeted me I was taken aback. Then he bent over and gave Julie a hug and told me who he was.

In the street it is not just boys but girls who have no idea what the word childhood means. If they did they could become India's most valuable citizens because despite the adversity of their lives they retain a sense of honour that never ceases to amaze me. One morning, soon after Nashta began, Julie disappeared. I was having my hair washed in the Oberoi beauty salon when I got a frantic call from Ajay, a young Bengali man, who worked for me at the time as a butler.

'Julie has vanished,' he said. He sounded close to hysteria.

'What? How could she have disappeared from the ninth floor?'

'I don't know. Someone must have left the kitchen door open. I was inside doing the bed and when I came back into the kitchen she was gone.'

'But she would have had to take the lift down to the ground floor. How is that possible?'

'I think she may have gone down the stairs.'

'Have you checked in the garden? She may be there.'

'No, she has gone out... There is a new security man at the gates and he says he saw her walking out and didn't think he needed to stop her.'

'Saab will kill you and me,' I said, now quite close to hysteria myself.

'I am going out to look for her,' Ajay said.

'All right. But let Yuvraj (the cook) stay near the phone. She is wearing a dog tag with our phone number on it, so if someone finds her they will call and someone should be there to answer the phone.'

After telling Ajit what had happened my first reaction was to get in touch with Surekha and her gang. They spread the word through their network of street children and soon everyone who was not at work was recruited to find Julie. What was really sweet was that all of them were as worried about her as I was. They told me that they knew of gangs of dog thieves who stole dogs and then sold them at a place near Crawford Market, so we needed to act fast. In the end we found her about a kilometre away from our building. Someone had noticed her sitting on a pavement near the local fire station and lured her into a building called Vidhi, where I found her calmly eating her way through an entire packet of Marie biscuits. She did not seem pleased to see me and resisted getting into the car until she had finished the last biscuit.

Within minutes of my finding her, one of the children's search parties appeared in the street outside the building. And when I tried to thank them for their help they looked at me with their big adult eyes and said that they wanted to find Julie as much as I did. So there was no need for thanks. After Nashta became a breakfast club for street children we gave each child an identity card that they produced when they were arrested by the police. This helped a little but not nearly enough as it should have. I was routinely summoned to the children's home in Dongri to bail out the children who had been arrested from Surekha's gang. Street people in Mumbai have ration cards, identity cards, Aadhaar cards and all sorts of other cards. They never make a difference because the police and municipal authorities do not see them as citizens with a right to life and livelihood.

The officials who make the rules seem to make them with the idea of keeping very poor people mired in poverty so that they vote unquestioningly at election time.

My most poignant experience of this was in the remote Nandurbar district of Maharashtra when during the tenure of Sonia Gandhi's first government a terrible drought caused children to start dying of hunger. In long years of reporting the one thing I hoped never to see ever again was a child dying of hunger. I first saw children dying of hunger in a village in Orissa during a famine in the late 1980s. There was no road to the village, so I had to walk for more than an hour on a dirt track that went uphill. Along with me was a doctor who cursed the government in Bhubaneswar all the way to the village because all he had been sent by way of aid was medicines. 'I have told them that the children need food and all they do is send me more medicines. What use are medicines to children who have lived on birdseed for months?' After walking for an hour we came to the first village. It was a small collection of mud huts inside which children lay on dirt floors, unable even to move or talk. I have been haunted by those images to this day.

So whenever I hear of 'malnutrition deaths' I rush off to wherever they are happening and try my best to draw attention to them. So it was that I found myself in the drab little town of Akkalkuwa on a grey September day some months after Dr Manmohan Singh began his first term as prime minister. My reason for being there on this particularly humid day was that Sonia Gandhi was coming personally to see if children were really dying of hunger.

To welcome her they painted the hospital in Akkalkuwa because it was here that children were being treated for starvation. In a nearby field they built a helipad. They poured fresh tarmac onto the dirt road that led to the village of

Gangapur, where she was meant to go since it was not as far from Akkalkuwa as the more remote villages in the hills beyond. Gangapur was a village of mud huts and extreme poverty. The hut of Vesta Bawa was the first one you saw when you entered the village. So local officials prepared the Bawa family to meet Sonia Gandhi. But in the end she did not come. Dark monsoon clouds and strong winds made it impossible for her helicopter to land. It was my TV crew and I who went to Gangapur instead.

Bawa and his wife Pramila lived in a small, bare hut with their seven children, all of whom were starving because the only meal they got all day was a breakfast of watery khichdi for the smaller children and dry rotis for the older ones. None of the children had ever eaten vegetables or drunk a glass of milk. They lay about listlessly on the mud floor of Vesta Bawa's hut. The smaller ones whimpered feebly as malnourished children do. Vesta and Pramila looked as if they themselves had never eaten a proper meal. Vesta told me that he could only afford to buy Rs 10 worth of food for the family every day because his daily wage as a farm hand was Rs 20 and he rarely got more than fifteen days of work in a month.

His poverty was severe enough for his children to qualify for help under the ICDS, Indira Gandhi's children's welfare programme that boasts of being the biggest in the world, but only if they could prove they were on the verge of dying of starvation. This decision was made by doctors in the hospital in Akkalkuwa, and although all his children were starving only his smallest daughter was admitted. In the hospital, ICDS provided for her to be given Rs 40 worth of eggs and nourishing broths three times a day. But no sooner did she stop showing signs of dying of hunger than she was sent home to start starving again. When Pramila and Vesta told me this story it made me angry enough to ask why they had seven children in the first place. Vesta looked at me as if I had asked a really stupid question and said softly, 'I took my wife to the hospital to have a hysterectomy after the second child but they could not do it because they said my wife was so malnourished that the operation could endanger her life.'

His answer shamed me into silence. In the tiny hut there was nothing but a small mud stove with a pot on it and a bottle of brown liquid that looked like edible oil that had been used and reused many times. In one corner lay a pile of tattered bedclothes on which the smaller children sat. Their eyes were dull, snot ran down their faces and they whimpered all the time. I wished with all my heart that Sonia Gandhi had been able to come and meet this family and then realized that it would have made no difference. She would have seen this kind of poverty many times before and been inspired to put even more money into schemes like the ICDS that required children to nearly starve to death before helping them. I sat for a few moments more on the mud floor of the hut, staring into the vacant eyes of Vesta and Pramila. They said nothing and I was too ashamed to continue asking questions. Finally, I asked if anyone else was helping families like theirs and Vesta said, 'They bring us food once a day from the madrassa.'

On my way to the village I had driven past an imposing Islamic religious school that had come up with a simple, effective solution that had not occurred to India's socialist rulers. The way to prevent children from dying of hunger was to provide them with one nutritious meal a day. If the vast funds spent on schemes like the ICDS had been spent instead on ensuring that every village council had the money and provisions to set up a free kitchen in times of need, malnutrition in children would probably have ended decades ago.

That year alone more than 10,000 children were believed to have died of 'malnutrition' in the Nandurbar district. Gangapur was the most fortunate of the villages in the area because it was close to Akkalkuwa and because it had a proper road that led to it. When I tried to get to more remote villages in the small, rust-coloured hills that lay beyond Gangapur, I found myself on a broken road that petered out completely as the drive became steeper. So to get to Dabgaon, the first of the Adivasi villages, we walked for nearly an hour along a path overgrown with nettles and weeds. In this village I met a man whose three-year-old daughter had died a week earlier in the Akkalkuwa hospital. When her condition deteriorated he borrowed a vehicle to take her to the hospital but the drive took an hour and a half. 'When we got to the hospital they gave her seven "salines", but when the seventh one was finished she was dead,' he said emotionlessly.

At the end of a long, depressing day I found myself in the fine new secretariat of the collector of Nandurbar. It was a modern building of glass walls and marble floors and the collector himself sat resplendent in a large air-conditioned office. In keeping with the interior design preferred by Indian officials, there were faux-leather sofas and tables covered in shiny laminates. There were pictures of leaders on the walls and plastic flowers in brass vases. At first Sanjay Khandare was quite welcoming. Indian officials love being on television, so while my crew set up lights and cameras he ordered for us sweet, milky tea and biscuits. None of us had any appetite after the day we had spent in the villages around Akkalkuwa but I was grateful for the tea.

As I remember it I may not have taken more than a couple of sips before the mood in the collector's office turned ugly. No sooner did the camera begin rolling and I started asking questions about starvation deaths than Mr Khandare told us to turn the camera off. He did not want to talk about 'rumours' of malnutrition deaths, he said rudely, and when I told him that I had just returned from villages in which these deaths had happened he told me that I understood nothing about the problem.

He proceeded to enlighten me. He said that the real problem in this district was that Adivasis married their children off when they were still children and by the time they were teenagers they were already producing children of their own. When I asked what he was doing to prevent child marriages he virtually threw me out of his office. Sanjay Khandare was not especially evil or especially lacking in compassion. He was typical of the kind of officials in whose charge the Government of India has for decades delivered vast sums of money under schemes that guarantee jobs, land, cheap food grain and subsidized housing.

After Sonia Gandhi became India's de facto prime minister these schemes multiplied in the name of 'alleviating poverty.' These were named after Mahatma Gandhi and members of the family she had married into. This is done in the hope that the semi-literate beneficiaries of these schemes will respond with gratitude and votes at election time. If anyone really benefits from these schemes it is officials.

8

THE POET

The election that made Atal Behari Vajpayee prime minister for the third time in three years came at the end of 1999. I was among those who hoped he would bring real change with him as well as last a full term, but within days Vajpayee settled comfortably into the Congress mould. This showed in small things. On the death anniversary of Jawaharlal Nehru he went to pay his respects at Nehru's samadhi. Sonia Gandhi and her children were present, looking royal and disdainful. Later I asked Pramod Mahajan why a BJP prime minister needed to follow the Congress tradition of paying homage on the death anniversaries of the Nehru-Gandhi dynasty.

'This is protocol,' he said. 'We cannot change protocol. They tell us it will look bad.'

'By they you mean the bureaucrats?'

'Yes.'

'Why do you have to listen to them?'

'This is how it is done.'

'What about the stupid practice of cabinet ministers lining up to bid him farewell at the airport when he goes on a foreign trip? This happens only in third-world countries.'

'He wants us to do this,' Pramod said. 'He likes it.'

It made me wonder if this need for needless reassurance

had anything to do with his humble origins. He grew up in genteel, middle class poverty in Gwalior when it was still ruled by a maharaja. It was then a town of narrow lanes and small bazaars built in the shadow of a mighty fort and on the edge of a vast whitewashed palace where the maharaja lived in decadent splendour. In his palace were chandeliers so heavy that elephants were made to walk on the roof of the durbar hall to see if it could sustain their weight. And on a dining table that could seat a hundred people were engraved the delicate tracks of a silver train that carried liquor bottles in its toy carriages.

In the 1984 general election that Vajpayee lost to the young Maharaja of Gwalior, whose father had been his benefactor, Vajpayee liked to tell the story of his humble origins and compare it with Madhavrao Scindia's privileged upbringing. I was staying with my friend Vasundhara Raje in her mother's palace, the Rani Mahal, and the rajmata as a passionate BJP leader was keen to know how Vajpayee was doing. The estrangement between the rajmata and her son over his support to Indira Gandhi after she jailed his mother during the Emergency had now become permanent. The Rani Mahal was walking distance from the main palace, from which Madhavrao Scindia was conducting his campaign, but there was no communication between mother and son at all.

The rajmata knew her son well and was certain that he would defeat Vajpayee but was still eager to know how Vajpayee was doing. So on cold mornings in that winter election I would leave the warmth and comfort of Vasu's suite in the Rani Mahal to follow Vajpayee into the narrow lanes and alleys of his hometown as he knocked on people's doors and asked for their votes with his hands joined together in supplication.

He was forced to campaign door to door because he had

taken too casually Rajiv's decision to order Vasu's brother to contest against him. It was part of his strategy to use stars to defeat major political leaders. Since Scindia was contesting for the first time from the capital of his former kingdom he was a formidable candidate. But Vajpayee had ignored Gwalior and campaigned elsewhere, thinking that he was a tall enough leader to not need to campaign in a constituency he had won easily before. When he arrived and found that Scindia was likely to win, he decided to try and get voters to remember that he was one of them and that his opponent was a prince. At small street corner meetings he reminded them of the poverty of his childhood. He told them how he had studied under streetlights for his exams. While his opponent had lived his whole life behind the walls of that palace over there and could not understand what it was like to be poor and needy. The maharaja won.

When ten years later Vajpayee became prime minister he forgot easily that he had once lived in poverty. No sooner did he move into the three houses on Race Course Road that make up the Indian prime minister's residence than he began to behave just like Congress prime ministers had. His ministers did the same. In the colonial bungalows that sprawl across the expanse of that part of Delhi that Edwin Lutyens built, the only thing that changed was the occupants. In the best traditions of the democratic feudalism that defined the Congress party, traffic was blocked every time ministerial convoys drove through the streets. Sirens screamed, lights flashed from the roofs and ministers fell over themselves trying to get the highest levels of security so that they could saunter into the lobbies of five-star hotels surrounded by commandos in black fatigues.

The lack of change was so worrying that I spoke of it to a BJP friend on an evening in a garden redolent with the scent

of early summer flowers. My friend was a junior minister in
the new government. It was his first taste of pomp and power
and he loved it, and my questions that evening irritated him.

'Why are you guys behaving just like the Congress did?
Don't you know that people want things to change?'

'Like what?'

'Like the fact that you shouldn't be living in a government
bungalow since you have a huge house of your own in this
city.'

'Oh, come off it,' the minister replied. 'Now that it's our
turn you keep writing those silly pieces about moving us out
of Lutyens' Delhi. Why should we? It is our right to live here.'

'And your right to pay almost no rent, almost nothing for
electricity and water and your right that taxpayers should
pay for you to travel by air?'

'Yes. That is the system. We cannot change the system.'

'But don't you see that the wrong kind of people are
coming into politics because of these perks? Don't you see
that political leaders are bringing their children into politics
only to hang on to their bungalows in Lutyens' Delhi?'

'Stop being so idealistic. Like journalism is your business
and what you make a living out of, politics is our business…
it is how we make our money.' He grinned as he said this and
poured himself a large whisky.

'Cheers.' He raised his glass and winked.

Cynicism, arrogance and disdain for their constituents
were despised Congress traits that Vajpayee's ministers
quickly acquired. Nothing changed, nothing at all. So India
remained the broken down, decrepit country it had always
been while a new political elite made sure to take good care
of their own families. Vajpayee's granddaughter was sent
to the Sanskriti School in a part of Delhi where not even a
whiff of ugly poverty floats in the polluted air, and soon every

minister and MP pulled strings that ensured their children went to this elite English-medium school. If the real India intruded into its wide corridors and shining halls it was only as a subject to be studied in history classes.

In the summer of 2002, soon after he became editor of the *Indian Express*, Shekhar Gupta asked me if I would do some reporting for the paper in addition to the column I had written since 1987. The Fifth Column moved briefly to *India Today* but moved back to the *Express* that year. Like Shekhar I believe that journalism must fundamentally be about reportage and not commentary, so I readily agreed and asked if he had any particular stories in mind. 'Why don't you go to UP,' he said, 'and do some pieces on the state of schools and hospitals.'

I set off with a photographer along roads I had taken many times before to cover riots, elections and other political events. We drove towards Meerut and I noticed how little things had changed in any real way since I first started travelling in these parts as a young reporter in the 1970s. The difference was that the small towns of my earlier reporting years had about them a decrepit charm that had now faded.

Where there had once been rural bazaars that reeked of spices and fried food there were now shopping centres selling televisions, computers, cell phones and electrical goods. Above shop fronts hung boards advertising computer classes, English-medium schools and private clinics. But because the towns had grown organically out of villages, no attention had been paid to infrastructure like roads. So we seemed to move on a wave of traffic through the main streets of every filthy, crowded, ugly town we drove into.

When we spotted a hospital or a school I would stop and make a random inspection. Nearly every time, I found myself in hospitals so ruined that trees grew out of wards and medicines rotted in cupboards that seemed not to have been opened in ages. Ambulances without wheels rusted in overgrown grounds and sometimes there were hospital buildings without doctors or patients. When I asked local people why this had happened they told me that local politicians made money out of construction, so they liked building new facilities and then abandoned them because they could not care less. Most people used private health services because public hospitals were so bad.

In one village I saw a man lying on a string cot by the edge of the road with his broken leg held together by a metal brace. When I asked him what had happened he said that he had been injured in a car accident and the leg was wrongly set by a doctor and had to be broken and reset again so many times that he had run out of money and lost his job as a driver. It was stories like this that I heard in almost every village in which I stopped to make inquiries about public health services. Everywhere I met families who had spent all their savings trying to save the life of a sick child or relative, and everywhere I met people who said they were forced to use private doctors because government hospitals were so bad.

But it was the condition of the government schools that really broke my heart. Technically they were well appointed. There were playing fields and school buildings and even toilets set at the edge of the fields, but the classrooms resembled bombed-out ruins from the inside. The handful of children who studied in them sat on mud floors, with grubby textbooks beside them. Teachers sat on the only chair in the room, usually knitting or mouthing a lesson indifferently for children to repeat after them.

When I asked questions about the dismal condition of the classrooms I was told that there was never any money for maintenance. 'But it's only very poor, low caste children who come to government schools,' one plump middle class teacher told me without lifting her eyes from her knitting. 'All the others go to private schools.'

'Where do you come from?' I asked.

'I live in Meerut,' she said.

'So you come from there every day?'

'Yes.'

'How long does it take you?'

'An hour.'

'Why don't you live here in the village?'

'How can we be expected to live here without any facilities? It would be impossible.' This time she looked up from her knitting and gave me a look of horror.

'But don't you get paid quite well for your services?'

'So what?' she said, giving me a filthy look.

As I walked out through the heaps of broken furniture and other rubbish that lay in the wasteland that should have been a playing field, I stopped to talk to a group of older children. They had English textbooks in their hands, so I asked a girl with big intelligent eyes if she would read me something. She opened her book and read a random passage fluently. Impressed, I asked her the meaning of what she had read and she said, 'I don't know what it means. But I can read English.'

My final stop in the schools I visited was always the toilets, and it was a sickening experience. In every case these toilets were narrow cabins behind whose broken doors lay such indescribable filth that it was clear that nobody had either used or cleaned them since the day they were built. It was the same everywhere.

After a long, dismal tour I arrived late that afternoon in Saifai in the constituency of Mulayam Singh Yadav, who was then the chief minister of Uttar Pradesh. He was proud of the town in which he had spent his youth as a part-time wrestler and a part-time teacher. And had spent a lot of money tarting it up. The roads were wide by rural standards and looked as if a fresh coat of tarmac had been laid on them. The bazaar looked clean and modern and there were hints of planning in the way residential colonies had been built. When I asked local people where I could find the school I was directed to the Amitabh Bachchan School.

This school, named after India's legendary movie star, was set in a fine whitewashed building surrounded by manicured playing fields and gardens. The children wore clean uniforms and sat at proper desks in proper classrooms. It was the kind of school that I had hoped would come up all over India under Vajpayee since he was himself such a learned prime minister.

It was not as if he did not know that there was urgent need for new policies. In an interview I did with him before he became prime minister he told me that when he first came to the Lok Sabha he had taken part in a debate in which Prime Minister Nehru was explaining the reasons behind his government's decision to build hotels. This was an idea copied from the Soviet Union, where vast state-owned hotels like the Rossiya in Red Square were once upon a time the only hotels in Moscow. Vajpayee said he intervened in the debate to say that it should be the government's job to build hospitals not hotels. 'And Panditji reminded me that I was newly elected and did not understand that it was possible for the government to build hospitals and hotels. But look at India today (this was 1997). Look at the state of our government hospitals.' And yet in the six years he was Prime Minister of India he did nothing at all to change the healthcare policy founded in Nehruvian times or ever indicate that he considered this a priority.

Vajpayee left educational reform in the hands of his minister of human resource development, Murli Manohar

Joshi. He started a literacy programme called the Sarva Shiksha Abhiyan that was very successful in enrolling large numbers of children in schools and hopeless at teaching them anything. That morning in Saifai when I was on my inspection tour of the Amitabh Bachchan School's fine grounds and classrooms, I got a call from Shekhar Gupta, who asked if I was in 'Mulayam territory'. I was surprised that he should have discovered this sitting in the *Indian Express* chief editor's office in Delhi, and when I asked the secret of his omniscience he said with a laugh, 'I've had a call from Mulayam Singh saying he will break your legs if you go anywhere near Saifai.'

'Too late. I am already in Saifai.'

Shekhar used his powers of persuasion and restraint to prevent Mulayam acting on his threat and even extracted from him an apology, so I continued my tour of dilapidated schools in villages and towns that were ugly, poor and dirty. Etawah and Bhind had once been my old stomping grounds. I came here often in the early 1980s looking for Phoolan Devi. The story of her lethal revenge on the men who imprisoned and raped her fascinated me, so just after she massacred twenty-two upper caste men in the village of Behmai I set off in search of her. I wandered about villages that lay along the borders of Uttar Pradesh and Madhya Pradesh and always seemed to just miss her. My cousin, Karamvir Singh, as the SP (superintendent of police) in charge of Mainpuri, had killed another famous dacoit, Chhabi Ram, and knew the dacoit story well and so threw clues my way about Phoolan's whereabouts.

But as things turned out I did not meet her till the night before her surrender when a senior police officer arranged for me to come to the inspection bungalow in Bhind in which she was kept before she surrendered to the chief minister of Madhya Pradesh. The other journalist who had managed to get here was Sunil Sethi, who reported then for *India Today*. It was February, freezing weather, and Sunil and I had to spend the night in the open because Phoolan, her family, and her gang had occupied every room in the inspection bungalow. Her gang was so very raggedy that one of the conditions she made before surrendering was that police tailors sew new uniforms to replace their shabby, torn ones.

All night as we sat beside a fire in the garden trying not to freeze to death we heard the clatter and rattle of the sewing machines of tailors who sat on the dimly lit veranda churning out police uniforms. Every now and then she would emerge from one of the rooms and turn on us like a wild cat. She looked like a wild cat with her slim, wiry body and her flashing eyes. Her hair fell to her shoulders and looked as if it could use a good shampoo, and her police uniform hung loose on her frame and seemed as much in need of a good wash.

Forget about either Sunil or I getting an interview, she snarled every time we tried to talk to her and uttered imprecations in a Hindi dialect we could not understand. The police officers guarding her told us that even in these last hours before the surrender she was not sure that she was doing the right thing. They looked weary and tense whenever they came to warm their hands at the small fire in the garden beside which Sunil and I spent the night.

The next morning we set off for Bhind town in a police bus. And the officer who had helped me all along arranged for me to sit beside Phoolan so that I could interview her. But it was hopeless. She spoke a rural dialect that I could not understand and she had no idea what I was asking her questions for. She was more interested in the rival gang that was also surrendering that day and travelling in the same bus. Ghanshyam Singh, a burly, bearded bear of a man had a more impressive gang and much more impressive weapons.

Phoolan did not like this one bit. So instead of listening to my nervous questions she spent her time glowering at him and muttering insults.

The surrender rites of dacoits include a ritual in which they stop at a Shiva temple and fire the last of their ammunition into the air. We stopped at a small whitewashed Shiva temple and watched Ghanshyam and his men fire their weapons into the pale-blue sky of a winter dawn. They did this with a dancing movement that was mesmerizing, but Phoolan was displeased and made her last attempt to draw attention to herself by jumping off the bus and trying to run away. She knew she could not go far but it caused a distraction.

When she finally got to the surrender ceremony she was without question the star with her red bandana, long hair and wild eyes. This cheered her up but not nearly as much as it cheered the policemen who handed her over with an audible sigh of relief. As for me, this adventure ended with a black and white picture of Phoolan Devi and me that appeared in *Sunday* magazine along with my story of her surrender. In the picture I look sleepless, exhausted and dishevelled, and Phoolan wears a police uniform. A friend rang me the day the magazine came out and said, 'Do you want to hear something funny…(and he laughed) some people who saw that picture thought you were Phoolan Devi and that Phoolan Devi was a policewoman arresting you.' In those times before YouTube and twenty-four-hour news channels, nobody was ever really sure what anyone looked like.

Etawah had changed a lot since that time. Where there had then been villages of mud huts and open fields, there were now small, ugly towns with bazaars, open drains and narrow streets clogged with traffic. The bazaars sold cell phones and fancy electronics. They advertised computer classes but these were signs of private enterprise. When it came to public services they were either non-existent or existed only because someone had made money out of construction.

My tour happened during the SARS epidemic of 2003 in Southeast Asia, so the hospitals I visited shamed me even more because on television I had seen pictures of a hospital in Vietnam that were better than any that I saw in Uttar Pradesh that day. In the Vietnamese hospitals there were clean wards with neatly arranged beds. And other things like stretchers to carry patients to efficient, clean, modern ambulances. Things that I did not see in any of the hospitals I visited in UP that day. Healthcare and primary education are areas in which state governments have primacy, but the central government has a vital role to play in making policy. If Vajpayee had wanted he could have initiated a new direction.

Was it his awe of the Nehru-Gandhi dynasty that prevented him from doing more to rectify the Congress party's abysmal failures in the social sector? I think it was. After he became prime minister he seemed never to miss a chance to be present when Sonia and her children gathered at the memorial sites on the Yamuna to remember some dead member of the family. And like them he paid almost no attention to other dead leaders except the Mahatma. His family was even more obsequious, as I discovered at a banquet in Rashtrapati Bhavan soon after he became prime minister. I happened to be talking to Vajpayee's daughter Gunnu when Sonia walked in and was astonished that no sooner did Gunnu spot Sonia entering the gilded doors of the banquet hall than she raced off to greet her. When I asked her later why she had behaved so deferentially, she said 'just out of courtesy'. There was too much courtesy through Vajpayee's first full year in office, and Sonia took full advantage of this. She got rid of him as soon as possible.

He had been prime minister less than a year when Delhi's

corridors of power began to buzz with rumours that the government would not last a full term because J. Jayalalithaa planned to bring it down. She was Chief Minister of Tamil Nadu and a vital ally in the fragile coalition that was that first version of the National Democratic Alliance. She understood her importance well and behaved so imperiously when she came to Delhi that it sometimes felt as if she was prime minister and not Vajpayee.

March in Delhi is a season for weddings. Not just because the stars always seem to be in auspicious positions but because the weather is usually perfect. The days are neither hot nor cold, and the evenings are mild enough to allow garden parties. I was at the wedding of a cousin when a colleague rang from a newspaper office to tell me that Jayalalithaa was having tea with Sonia Gandhi and hinting at a 'political earthquake'.

We were in the courtyard of my aunt's old-fashioned house in Tughlak Road and the bride was having her hands and feet decorated with henna. We, the ladies of the family, dressed in traditional Punjabi clothes, chose bangles from multi-hued bundles tied up with gold and silver ribbons that shone in the sunlight. Lunch was about to be served and a bar was set up in a corner of the courtyard at which ladies with hennaed hands delicately poured themselves glasses of chilled white wine. But I had to excuse myself and rush off to Jayalalithaa's press conference. When I arrived, banks of TV cameras surrounded the raised stage on which she sat, smug, large and resplendent. She was clearly enjoying herself thoroughly and answered questions in cryptic riddles.

Before departing for Tamil Nadu she declared that she had asked the prime minister to agree to her 'reasonable demands'. One of these was that the defence minister, George Fernandes, be sacked or transferred to a 'less sensitive' ministry. She should have known that no chief minister had the right to decide these things or even talk about them but she was so blinded by hubris that she went ahead and withdrew support. The Vajpayee government lost a vote of confidence in Parliament by a single vote.

9

CHILD PROSTITUTES

You can live in a city for years and not know it at all. It is not that I did not know that Mumbai was a major centre for trafficked children. I did. But I did not know that it happened so close to where I live that I could walk from my apartment on Marine Drive to the brothels near the Kennedy Bridge where little girls are bought and sold every day to brothel owners who use them as sex slaves till they become too old or too sick to be of any use. I would not have known any of this if a senior police officer had not casually asked me one evening if I was interested in going with his team on a brothel raid.

'Of course,' I said. 'I do a television programme for NDTV called Indianama and it is exactly this kind of human story that we try to tell.'

'All right. I shall arrange it in a few days. We are conducting regular raids to stop child trafficking, and you people in the media hardly even give us credit for this.'

So it was that I found myself in Mumbai's police headquarters some days later, waiting with my crew at the foot of a very grand staircase. Its walls were lined with pictures of former chiefs of police, some of whom had served in the days of the British Raj. My cameraman, Ajmal Jami, was enthralled enough by the ascending portraits and the grandeur of the staircase to start taking pictures even if they would have no relevance to the story we were about to film. I waited in an orderly garden with the usual municipal flowers planted in so regimented a manner as to create the impression that they were on parade. As I wandered about the garden waiting for the police officer who was to lead the raiding party, I noticed a man standing quietly on his own on one side of the grand staircase. We smiled at each other and he introduced himself as Ian Dowling. He was in charge of a rescue home where girls were taken after being freed from the brothels, he said, and pointed to a group of girls who waited with an older lady nearby.

The raid involved detailed planning, and while the police officers did this we took the girls to a restaurant opposite the police headquarters to give them some breakfast and to give us a chance to talk to them. They were very young girls and so cheerful and chatty that I found it hard to believe that they had until recently been sex slaves servicing ten men a day. When I started asking questions about how they had ended up in brothels I found that they had either been brought to the city by distant relatives who sold them to brothel owners or been kidnapped. One of the girls who had been kidnapped was called Rubina. She said she was fourteen years old and had been kidnapped two years earlier from a pavement near the shrine of Nizamuddin Aulia in Delhi. She had been playing with her friends, she said, when some men dragged her into a car and gave her something that made her unconscious. When she woke she found herself on a train, and when she tried to make a noise they threatened her with violence.

Rubina had thick shoulder-length hair, skin the colour of sandalwood and big, beautiful eyes. 'What happened when they brought you to Bombay?'

'They took me to this brothel where the owner bought me for Rs 10,000 or at least I think that is what she paid.' She sipped her tea and ate her slice of bread, falling silent as she remembered what had happened. The restaurant had narrow tables set in a long room that looked like a corridor, its walls were painted in a gaudy shade of red and it was filled with the smell of fried snacks. There were other people at tables near us who seemed in a hurry to eat their breakfast and get to work. It was an odd place to listen to Rubina's story.

'Then what happened?' I asked.

Rubina looked me straight in the eyes and answered without being slightly emotional about what she said. The other girls listened without interest. They had clearly heard the story before or had stories of their own that were only marginally different. They ate their breakfast hungrily, with barely a glance in Rubina's direction.

'Then for the first few days I tried to resist going with the men...but every time I did, they beat me and locked me up without food or water in a dark room. So in the end I had to do what they asked.'

'How many men used to come every day?'

'Many...ten, fifteen. But all I want now is to try and find my parents. I have a telephone number of the people who live near where we used to live.'

'Where is it?'

'I hid it in my makeup box. It's in the brothel and I am coming with you so that I can try and find it.'

It was late afternoon when the raid finally began. A light drizzle had started to fall. We went with the police party to a spot under the Kennedy Bridge from where we walked towards a dilapidated, ordinary-looking building that could have been just any other block of flats. We followed the police and Ian Dowling as they entered a dank, dark stairwell in which a stray bitch had taken refuge with her litter. When we started walking up the stairs, the police officer leading the raid turned around with his finger on his lips to warn us to be as silent as possible. 'If they hear that we are coming,' he whispered, 'they will hide the underage girls.'

When we got to the top of the stairs we found ourselves on a rickety balcony that looked onto a tiled roof that was covered in a blanket of garbage. There was rotting food, plastic bags, condoms, rags and waste paper, and they formed a layer so thick that you could barely see the red tiles that made up the roof. A crow picked at a dead rat whose intestines had spilled out in a small pink pile. Jami silently focused his camera on this scene of unspeakable squalor, and I silently retched because the stench of festering garbage and dead animals was beyond belief.

The policemen crept in a single file down the narrow balcony, and we followed till we reached a blue wooden door. It was locked. They knocked and a woman's querulous voice answered from inside. Without answering they knocked harder and someone opened the door slowly. The police officers rushed in shouting, 'Police.' We followed in their wake, with Jami taking pictures and me gasping at the smell of boiled rice, women's dirty clothes and cheap scent that this den of vice emanated. In the small, windowless room we came face to face with a plump, blowsy woman who looked like a retired prostitute. She wore a shapeless frock that barely concealed the sagging rolls of tired flesh that made up her corpulent body. She was so unperturbed by our arrival that I got the feeling she was used to this kind of raid. The only other person in the room with its blue walls and dim yellow lights was a woman with a painted face who was definitely not underage.

On either side of this squalid pleasure house were cubicles so small they barely accommodated the single bunk bed that they contained. I counted four or five cubicles on either side. While the policemen questioned the fat woman about 'young girls' and she wailed out her denials, Rubina rushed into the first cubicle on the left of the room and pulled out a blue vanity case from under the bed. She turned it upside down to empty cheap lipsticks, talcum powder, a comb and small boxes of makeup onto the soiled sheets of the narrow bed. She searched in the lining of the bag and shook it to empty it completely and then turning to us said, 'It's not here. I know I left it here.' She had tears in her eyes.

On the way to the next brothel Ian whispered, 'The sad thing is that she is HIV positive.'

'That is horrible. Does she know?'

'She knows that she has a sickness but has no idea what AIDS is. None of them does.'

We went back down the dank, dark staircase, got into our cars and drove a short distance to another building not far away. It was as rundown as the one we left but was taller and looked even more like just a block of flats. We entered another dark, dank staircase that was wet and slippery. There was a strong smell of urine in the stairwell, and I feared that the stairs were lined with it. Jami was ahead of me as we walked up and suddenly stopped as we reached a small landing at the top of the first flight of stairs. The policemen had gone on ahead, ignoring the woman who lay comatose on the landing.

She had very dark skin, her lips were painted dark red, there was chipped red nail polish on her fingernails and on her feet were shiny plastic slippers. She wore a yellow salwar-kurta and cheap jewellery and lay in a foetal position with her head covered by a spangled yellow dupatta. 'Is she dead?' I asked Jami as he took his pictures. 'No. I don't think so.'

'Probably drunk,' one of the policemen said contemptuously. He said it as if he could not have cared less if she were dead, but Jami and I were mesmerized by the way she just lay there as if she were a stray bitch.

At the top of two flights of stairs we found ourselves in a passage with a warren of small rooms leading off on either side. Unlike Rubina's torture chamber, these rooms were brightly lit and filled with the sounds of music and women's voices. It was nearly evening and the women were combing their hair and painting their faces in readiness for customers. When we talked to them they said cheerfully that they were all in the trade willingly.

'But we have heard that in most brothels there are very young girls,' I said to a woman with a painted face and long oily hair.

'No. There aren't,' she said and I noticed that in the mirror before which she combed her hair she glanced at the policeman who stood outside the open door.

'We know there are young girls who have been forced into prostitution,' I said firmly.

'I haven't met any here,' she said. 'Women in this brothel have come because circumstances forced them to. My husband threw me out of the house. I had nowhere to go but here.'

'How old are you?'

'I should be about twenty-five,' she said. She looked at least ten years older.

Other women I talked to in this brothel denied that they had ever seen child prostitutes. They all said that it was circumstances that had brought them into this line of business. Some said that they had been thrown out by husbands and others that they came from families in which girls were brought up to continue in what they call the oldest profession in history. They laughed and chatted with us as normally as if they were secretaries in a respectable office or salesgirls in a department store. But beneath the surface of the chatter and the music there was an indefinable sadness that got reflected in small things. Like in the glossy pictures of Bollywood stars and Hindu gods on the walls and in the scenes of mountains and forests that interspersed them. Scenes and people from a world unattainable to the women who passed lifetimes in these dismal rooms until they were too old or too sick. Then they ended up like discarded garbage in dank stairwells.

Some days later Jami and I drove to Ian Dowling's rescue home in New Bombay. We were meant to have gone the very next day but by the time I got home that evening I had a high fever. I was too depressed to go to dinner with Shankar Sharma and his wife, Devina, but Ajit said it would look rude if I did not make the effort. Shankar was one of the original investors in *Tehelka* magazine, and when he was jailed for this by the Vajpayee government I tried to help him in every way I could. I thought it was wrong that he should be targeted but did not realize then that there was a mysterious connection between Sonia Gandhi and *Tehelka*. Or that Tarun Tejpal was one of a handful of journalists who was extremely close to Priyanka Gandhi.

On the drive to Nerul to see Ian Dowling's rescue home, Jami and I talked about the horror of what we had seen in the brothels and agreed that this was one of the most horrible stories either of us had ever covered. At the end of a drive that took us through rundown suburbs and dumping grounds so poisonous that fumes rose out of them, we crossed the bridge on the sea that connects the island of Mumbai with the mainland of India. The roads grew wider and the buildings were new, ugly and half-finished, but there was less squalor and the air seemed cleaner. We drove past train stations and a huge stadium and orderly, soulless residential estates before turning into a lane that led us to the rescue home.

Ian Dowling and his wife waited at the entrance to receive us. The house was not particularly large but there was a reception area that opened onto a large room in which a lot of neatly dressed young girls sat in a circle. On the walls of the room were pictures of Jesus, a large cross and other Christian symbols. The girls greeted us with the words, 'Jesus is our saviour.' Ian explained that he was a born-again Christian and that he had come to religion after years of drug abuse and crime. 'I feel for these girls,' he said, 'because I was like them, homeless and abused, and that what was what my life was for years and years until I found Jesus.'

The girls listened with the attentive air of schoolgirls in a moral science class. In their freshly washed clothes and with their neatly pinned-back hair, they looked more like schoolgirls than rescued prostitutes. It was only when they began to tell us their stories that the whole horror of their young lives unfolded before Jami's camera and my questions. The first person we talked to was a girl with a serious injury on the top of her head. Half her hair had been shaved to dress a raw, bleeding lump. Her face was swollen and she had the eyes of a frightened deer. Ian told us that she was one of their most recent arrivals and that they had found her half-dead on the doorstep of a brothel during a recent raid.

She told us her name was Shama and that she thought she was about thirteen years old. When I asked her how she had come to Mumbai she started crying. With a constant stream of tears washing down her bruised face she said, 'My mother died. We were three sisters and so an aunt brought us here and separated us. I don't know where they took my sisters but I was made a servant in the house of a family in Chembur… they made me work naked all day and beat me and forced me to drink urine. If I made a mistake they poured boiling water on my hands and hit me with iron rods and wooden rolling pins. When they hit me this time I became unconscious, so they threw me in the street. And the next thing I remember is being rescued.'

The story horrified me so much that I actually tried to get in touch with the family that had done this to the young girl. But they were an NRI family who lived only some of the year in Mumbai and most of the time in Dubai or Abu Dhabi, so I never managed to trace them. We talked to the girls in a room that looked like a chapel under a poster that said, 'One night he dreamed he was with the Lord...' I asked the girls if they had become Christians after coming to the home and they said they had because Jesus had given them the only happiness they had ever known. The girls had names like Babita, Rashna and Lavanya and in every case they had been trafficked.

The stories were typical of the one a girl from Kolkata told me. She had short hair, a heart-shaped face and looked ten but said she was thirteen. She had spent two years in a brothel before being rescued. She said, 'A friend called Asha took me to the railway station and said it would be fun to ride on the train. We got onto the train and it started moving and I got scared. I told her I wanted to go home. She said, "All right, I'll take you home but here eat this paratha." When I ate it I became unconscious and when I woke up I was at a big station with lots of people and they told me it was Bombay.

'Asha took me to a house and there was this gharwali (brothel keeper) who gave me food and nice clothes and put makeup on my face, and then I was put in a room with a man. When I screamed they hit me and after that they gave me something to drink, and then this happened every day for I don't know how long until I got sick and then they threw me out.'

'Were you allowed out of the house?'

'They would make me stand outside in the evenings…but I couldn't go anywhere on my own.'

There were girls who had been sold by their parents when they were seven and eight, girls who had been kidnapped, girls who had been thrown out after being raped by male relatives and girls who came to Mumbai with someone who promised to educate them. The one thing they had in common was that nobody came looking for them and that the safety net that the Indian welfare state was supposed to have provided had holes so big that they had simply fallen through them. They were happy to be in the rescue home and they said they were happy to believe in Jesus because nobody else had ever helped them.

After talking to the girls, Ian and his wife led us upstairs to show us neat dormitories, a dining room and a clean kitchen. He was doing his best, he said, but he did not know how long he could carry on running the rescue home because he was always short of funds. He made sure the girls learned a skill or went to school if they were young enough and that they had decent clothes to wear and food to eat. But there were more than forty girls in his charge and he was not sure if he could handle any more.

When we finished filming this episode of Indianama, I tried very hard to help Ian Dowling raise funds for his rescue home but failed completely. Oliver Musker, my English brother-in-law, introduced me to Marguerite Litman, a rich and glamorous socialite in London who was on the board of the Elton John Foundation. She took me to lunch in a fashionable restaurant. Over grilled sole and white wine I told her that Ian would probably have to close his rescue home if he was not able to raise the money to keep it going. I told her that he was doing more to help victims of AIDS than anyone

I knew in India and she said she would try and help. I never heard from Marguerite again but did hear that she had got the Elton John Foundation to donate a substantial amount of money to a socialite in Delhi whose work for AIDS victims was inspired mostly by Hollywood stars like Richard Gere.

Where then was the great Indian welfare state in all this? After coming back from the rescue home in Nerul, Jami and I went back to Mumbai's police headquarters and up the grand staircase with its portraits of former police chiefs to ask the man who had helped me do the story this question. Anami Roy sat behind an enormous desk in a vast room filled with shiny new furniture and police memorabilia. He was determined to stop the trafficking of little girls but admitted that their real problem was that the government rescue homes were so awful that rescued girls usually ran away and went back to the brothels because they had nowhere else to go. The solution, he said, would be to give NGOs like the one run by Ian Dowling the funds to run the government welfare homes, but this was not something that the government permitted. It would amount, he pointed out, to an admission of failure.

10

MEETING VAJPAYEE

It was in 1977 that I first met Vajpayee. He had just been released from jail in the final weeks of the Emergency and was the star campaigner in the election that brought the Janata Party to power and ended the Congress monopoly on ruling India. He lived at the time in a small government bungalow on Delhi's Feroze Shah Road that was walking distance from the *Statesman* newspaper office where I worked. I first went to see him to talk about a verse of poetry he had recited at a rally at Ramlila Maidan. It was this rally, and possibly his speech, that turned the tide of the election against Indira Gandhi. After this first meeting I went to see him every now and then to chat about politics and poetry. He was a youngish man then with a thick head of greying hair and a dreamy poetic expression in his eyes. When he talked about the political changes he would like to see in India he always sounded passionate and sincere, but it was when he talked about poetry that I could see what his real love was.

After he became minister of external affairs in the Janata government I saw him less. But one occasion remains imprinted so vividly in my memory that I often repeat what he said that evening whenever my friends bring up the subject of Vajpayee. The occasion was a reception for poet Hafeez

Jalandhari at the Ghalib Academy in Delhi. This poet, whose most famous poem was about youth and loss, chose to go to Pakistan when India was partitioned and this was his first visit back to India. Vajpayee was invited as chief guest and this was the only reason why the *Statesman*, still very British and quite uninterested in 'native' poetry, agreed to let me cover the event. Having grown up with ageing aunts singing '*Abhi toh main jawaan hoon*', I longed to see the poet who wrote this wistful, sad, beautiful song that spoke so longingly about youth.

So on a hot, steamy evening I found myself walking through the streets of Nizamuddin. They smelled more pungently than usual of kebabs and open drains because of the heat. Inside the auditorium it was stuffy and boring. An endless list of dreary speakers droned on in complicated Urdu, and I noticed that Hafeez, a small, frail old man, looked as if he could have done without this welcome ceremony. Then Vajpayee arrived, and no sooner did he start to make his speech than the atmosphere became electric with nostalgia and emotion.

He began in his usual way by standing at the podium and closing his eyes as if thinking deeply about what he wanted to say. Then he opened his eyes, greeted the poet, welcomed him to India and turning to the audience said, 'I have been invited here today not because I am a politician but because I am a poet.' Then he stopped and there was a dramatic pause before he said, 'It is true that I was a poet once (pause, eyes closed) but in the desert of politics the stream of poetry has dried up.' There was huge applause from the audience so he paused again and closed his eyes. Then turning to Hafeez, and with an actor's perfect timing, said, 'We were the same people once, we belonged to the same country, but politics has raised between us a thick wall. I am not saying that this wall can be brought down easily, but can we not remove a few bricks in it so that we can at least get a glimpse of each other's lives?'

In Urdu the words were magical and moving. 'Main nahin kehta deevar gira di ja sakti hai par kyon na ek do eenthein khiska di jaayen...taank-jhaank toh ho.' Hafeez, who after becoming a Pakistani proved his loyalty to his new country by writing its national anthem, was moved to tears and there was hardly a dry eye in the audience.

Twenty years later I travelled with Vajpayee to Lucknow to interview him for my television programme, Ek Din, Ek Jeevan. We met at Old Delhi railway station to take an overnight train that left at 10 p.m. We were in the same first class carriage, but other than catching a glimpse of him to say hello and goodnight I did not get to speak to him. I slept uneasily, as I usually do on trains, and must have woken up at every station where we stopped on the way. This gave me a chance to work on the questions for my interview, and I think I must have still been working on them when we pulled into Lucknow as dawn was breaking over the city. The station was crowded and full of the usual railway station noises, but a small group of BJP workers had formed a cordon around our carriage and there was a reception committee of garland-bearing local politicians. Vajpayee greeted them and told us that we should meet him at the house of Lalji Tandon, the chief of the Uttar Pradesh unit of the BJP.

He lived in a large house with courtyards and verandas, and it was on one of these verandas over breakfast that I got my first chance to talk to Vajpayee that day. He seemed more relaxed than I had ever seen him in Delhi and was as comfortable in front of the camera as a trained actor. He talked about life, politics and poetry, admitting that he may never have become a politician if Syama Prasad Mukherjee had not died the way he did in a jail cell in Kashmir. He was leading a movement to end the special status of Kashmir, and Vajpayee had been with him in this struggle.

What would he have rather been, I asked, and he said he would have preferred to be a journalist. But added quickly that now that he was in politics he would like to do something for the country so that he would be remembered as 'a good man'. I asked what his priorities would be if he did become prime minister, and he said it was hard to say because there were 'so many things that needed to be done' but he thought the most important of these was to regain the trust of the people. 'People have lost faith in political leaders and in the democratic process and this is not good…and it is the fault of political leaders that there has been this loss of faith.'

He did not seem to have a clear idea what his economic priorities would be as prime minister but said that it had been wrong for India to copy the Soviet model of development. It was because of this centralized economic control, he said, that the most basic needs of the people had not been met. It was shameful that so many decades after Independence something so basic as clean drinking water remained unattainable for so many ordinary Indians.

Later that day we drove out of the city along dusty, broken roads to a village of shabby homes. A shamiana had been erected on a patch of waste ground for a public meeting that he was due to address. When he spoke he continued with the themes we had talked about and emphasized the shame of India not having been able to give her people something as fundamental as clean water after fifty years of Independence. 'I am the MP from Lucknow and I cannot understand why it is so hard to provide water to the people of this city. I cannot understand why a city built on the banks of the Gomti river should face a shortage of water.'

There were other meetings and events all day of various kinds: the opening of a small water-pumping station, a gathering of local gentry and conversations with political workers. And in between these meetings and events we continued with the interview and continued to talk of things as diverse as religion, poetry, politics and history. As we talked I realized for the first time that when it came to economics he was not guided by ideology but by instinct and by disappointment that so many decades after colonial rule ended, India had failed to give her people proper schools, hospitals and basic infrastructure.

Vajpayee was an admirer of Nehru but not so blind an admirer as not to be able to see that the foundations he had laid for India's economy had been weak. He saw that the direction India had taken had led us nowhere, and that it was because of this there was a general sense of despair among ordinary people and a loss of faith in political leaders. What would you say were your biggest achievements as a political leader, I asked, and he said, 'I think I have managed to live by my principles.'

'And your biggest failures?'

'The failures that we see in this country are my failures... I was first elected in 1957 and now it is 1997 and what has been achieved?'

Disappointment was the leitmotif of the day I spent with him and regret that he as a political leader had not been able to do more to take India out of the morass that she was in. For me this return to Lucknow brought back memories of what this once-beautiful Muslim city had been like before socialist leaders like Mulayam Singh Yadav imprinted upon it their ugly stamp. I remembered from school holidays when my father's regiment was posted here that Lucknow had once been a city of old ornate houses set in gardens of flowering trees. I remembered the orderly streets of the cantonment and romantic bazaars filled with shops that sold bangles, fine embroideries, muslins from Dhaka, silks from south India and 'attar' in crystal bottles. These bazaars had vanished and in their place had appeared hovel-like shops that sold plastic buckets and cheap electrical goods.

The Gomti river described with so much romance in old books about Lucknow was now no more than a drain. The absence of beauty and aesthetics seemed to affect Vajpayee as well, and by the end of that day he talked of poetry as if she were a lost lover. 'Poetry is gone from my life. Poetry needs solitude. It needs a certain atmosphere. It needs to rise out of a deep creative process just as clouds need to build up their reserves before rain can be made.'

At the end of the interview I asked him to recite one of his poems for the camera, and he chose one in which a poet is so filled with despair that he can no longer write poetry. The poet sees around him broken dreams and gloom and knows that from these things cannot come poetry. Then the poem changes from despair to hope and the poet talks of writing a new song and finding new inspiration in his country. He recited it with that actor's timing he used so well in his political speeches, and it made such good television that long after his time as prime minister was forgotten people looked out for this interview on YouTube and wrote me letters saying that he was the greatest prime minister India ever had.

The truth is that he was not. As prime minister he seemed to lose confidence in his own instincts as a politician and even in his extraordinary gift of oratory. He gathered around himself dreary people who wrote dreary speeches that he read in dreary tones so that when he made his first speech from the Red Fort on Independence Day he sounded like a tired old bureaucrat. Of his entire time as prime minister I remember only one brief shining moment, one truly great speech, and ironically this moment occurred in the sunlit garden of the governor's residence in Lahore.

What brought him here that February day in 1999, weeks after becoming prime minister for the third time in three years, was his old dream of making peace with Pakistan. It was a dream he had nurtured since he became minister of external affairs in the Janata government in 1977. This government did not last two years and the dream remained unfulfilled, so that winter when he took charge of a government that looked set to complete a full term, almost the first thing he did was drive across the Wagah border in a bus. It was a gesture that was both extraordinary and unexpected and caused so much excitement that a special Indian Airlines flight was arranged to take a small army of journalists from Delhi to Lahore. I was on that flight despite a nasty attack of dysentery that had started in Benares the week before. Shivratri celebrations took me to this city that Hindus believe is protected from Yama, the God of Death, by Shiva himself. The festivities were magnificent but a Benarsi bug settled deep into my gut, making it impossible for me to risk drinking a glass of water without ensuring that there was a lavatory in my immediate vicinity.

In Lahore the evening before Vajpayee was due to arrive I dined with friends, and instead of eating anything I drank only red wine. Islamism and jihadi terror had not yet taken hold, and it was possible to drink in this lovely Punjabi city's elegant drawing rooms without fear of attack by the morality police. The wine seemed to bind my stomach a little, but once I got back to the hotel I spent most of the night in bad shape. It did not help that I was staying in one of Lahore's lesser hotels and the lavatory smelled awful.

The next morning I had as little breakfast as possible and went off to see my old friend Aitzaz Ahsan, who was home minister in Benazir Bhutto's first government. I had known him from the days when he was just a lawyer. He was excited about Vajpayee driving across the border in the bus but more excited about a new book he had written on the Indus civilization that he said was totally different from the Gangetic civilization that defined Hindu India. He told me that I was a daughter of the Indus and not the Ganga, and I saw our conversation as a continuation of the endless quest that sensible, secular Pakistanis have set themselves to find a real reason for Pakistan's existence. It is as if they have a deep need for constant reassurance that they are better off not being part of India. Our conversation and the weak tea I drank caused me to spend another longish period in his elegant and spotlessly clean toilet, and his wife Bushra realized that I needed medical assistance. She gave me a strip of Immodium and warned me not to eat anything in Wagah. 'The toilets might not be very usable,' she said.

I drove to Wagah with my friend Ahmed Rashid. He was a correspondent at the time for the *Telegraph* in London and not yet as famous as he was to become after 9/11 when his book on the Taliban came out. The book became an instant bestseller because its timing was perfect. Until then almost nothing was known about the Islamist group that had offered the hospitality of Afghanistan to Osama bin Laden.

When I called Ahmed and told him he should come to Wagah with me, he was initially reluctant. It was a pale, misty winter morning, and he seemed to think it would be more worthwhile to spend it at home working on his book. But when I reminded him that we could be seeing history being made, he agreed to come along. We drove through fields and villages that looked just like fields and villages on our side of the Punjab. So familiar did they seem that it was almost puzzling that the shops had signs written in Urdu and that instead of temples and gurudwaras as the main adornment of villages there were mosques.

When we got to the border we were directed to a press enclosure in which green wooden benches had been laid out – of the kind used for witnessing parades, with varying gradients all the way up. Ahmed and I settled down on one of these and listened to the chatter of fellow journalists, who were mostly Indian and had come with me the day before on the special Indian Airlines flight.

We waited hours for the bus to arrive and got tired of waiting, so when it did not come till late afternoon the press enclosure began to resound with jokes about the unreliability of Indian buses. 'It has probably broken down halfway between Amritsar and Wagah,' someone said.

'And there probably isn't backup available since it's meant to be a special bus and not just one from Punjab Roadways.'

'Or there could be a puncture and there isn't a mechanic available so close to the border.'

'Or maybe it broke down between Delhi and Panipat.'

Then just as we were beginning to take our own jokes seriously, Nawaz Sharif appeared on the red carpet that had been laid out for India's prime minister. A posse of officials surrounded him. He was dressed in an ajkan that seemed just a little bit too tight for him, so his balding head bulged out at the top and his stomach formed a bigger bulge lower down. There was no sign of the military men who we knew were the real controllers of foreign policy. Pakistani journalists told us in low voices that the army chief, General Pervez Musharraf, was so angry about Vajpayee's bus journey that he had refused to come to the border to receive him. We did not know then that even as we spoke he was plotting to send troops disguised as freedom fighters across the Line of Control in Kargil.

Even after Sharif and his consorts arrived nothing happened for a long time. They walked up and down the red carpet and seemed as bored with the waiting as us. Ahmed was beginning to get impatient and started to mutter about trying to get a ride back to Lahore when suddenly there was a flurry of activity and across the border came Indian women dancing in silk skirts and colourful dupattas and the sounds of Punjabi bhangra music. Ahmed's jaw dropped when he saw the dancers. 'Do you know that we haven't seen women dance in public in Pakistan since Zia-ul-Haq started his Islamization in the 1980s?' he said. Behind the dancers came a group of turbaned Punjabi men playing drums. And behind them came a man carrying a basket of sweets on his turbaned head and behind him came the bus. It was painted a dull gold and had the words Sada-e-Sarhad written on its sides. As it came closer I spotted the prime minister seated right in front with Jaswant Singh and other senior ministers. Behind them sat actors from Bollywood, sportsmen, writers and journalists.

Vajpayee made his crossing with the drama and emotional resonance of a better-quality Bollywood film. And it was with drama and emotion that he delivered his speech in the sunlit garden of the governor's mansion the next day.

The whole event had about it an unreal quality. Here we were, a huge contingent of Indians and an Indian prime minister in the heart of enemy territory, at an occasion that resembled an English tea party. The governor's mansion was whitewashed, splendid and more British in its architecture than Punjabi or Islamic. And in its manicured lawns, edged with beds of English flowers, stood tables covered in white tablecloths. At them sat members of Lahore's gentry, among whom I spotted not a single one of my many, many friends in this city that I first visited in 1980. The people invited to hear the Indian prime minister were mostly retired bureaucrats and army men and their wives.

The sun shone down on a perfect winter afternoon that could have been in Delhi except that the women at this event were more demurely dressed. As if to make up for their lumpy, fully-clothed bodies, their faces were more heavily made up and their hands more bejewelled than necessary. Since the Indians were mostly journalists they darted between the tables trying to interview people, or stood, as I did, with a small group of officials near the podium where Vajpayee was due to speak. Beside me was a high official from the ministry of external affairs who seemed worried and nervous. When I asked him why he was so jumpy he said, 'I hope the prime minister doesn't read the speech they've written for him.'

'Why?'

'Because it's boring and unimaginative.'

'Who would have written it?'

'Well, we gave our inputs from the ministry but someone in the PMO writes his speeches.' This got me worried because I knew that the 'someone' was a failed journalist who had been instilled in the PMO by L.K. Advani along with some other of his acolytes. Advani never forgot for a minute that really it was his turn to be prime minister since he was responsible for reviving the BJP and taking it from the two seats it got in 1984 to eighty-six seats in 1989. There is no question at all that this happened because of the frenzied atmosphere of Hindu nationalism that was created by Advani's rath yatra to Ayodhya and the anti-Muslim rage that built up around it everywhere it travelled. When the BJP found itself in a position to form a government in 1996 (this lasted thirteen days) and then again in 1998, he did not demand to be made prime minister because he sensed that Vajpayee was more acceptable, but he never forgot this sacrifice and used his position as the second-most important person in the government to surround Vajpayee with his favourites. One of them was the failed journalist.

When the high official expressed his fears about the written speech, I shared them. Having heard Vajpayee at his best I knew that if he spoke extempore he would make the sort of speech that could bewitch his worst enemies. This was a moment that needed such a speech. From where I stood with the high official I had a clear view of the wooden podium and noticed that papers were laid on it that would have been the written speech. Vajpayee arrived at the podium, surveyed the sunny lawns, the tables with their white tablecloths, the silence that fell over the gathering as they waited for him to speak and then he closed his eyes. It was only when he spoke from the heart that he did this, so I whispered to the official that I thought he would be making his own speech. 'Thank God,' the official whispered back.

Seconds later we heard Vajpayee say, 'I came yesterday and I will leave tomorrow. This is the rite of all travellers. But what I want to remind you of is that the one change that will not happen is that we are neighbours and that we will always be neighbours because we are bound together by geography.' He then quoted a verse of poetry by the Indian poet, Ali Sardar Jafri, that had been on the front page of one of Lahore's newspapers that morning. Loosely translated the verse says we will bring you from India the light of a Benares morning and you can bring with you the scent of Lahore's gardens and then let us ask who the enemy is. 'Tum aao gulshan-e-lahore sey chamanbardosh, hum aayengey subah-e-benares ki raushni leykar...uskey baad poochchey key dushman kaun.' He could not have chosen a more appropriate line of poetry to set the mood.

What followed was a speech that was vintage Vajpayee –

full of big ideas about peace and shared history but woven together with words so beautifully chosen that by the end of the speech half the audience was in tears. It happened that almost the first person I met after the speech was Vajpayee's daughter, Gunnu, and I think we were sharing our relief at his not reading out a prepared speech when an old gentleman came up and said in a voice trembling with emotion, 'I am a former chief justice of the Lahore high court and I just wanted to tell you that I have heard many speeches in my time and I have never heard one that moved me so much.' He had no idea who Gunnu was, only that we were Indian.

Peace was not to be. In less than four months came a war in Kargil between the Indian army and Pakistani troops disguised as 'freedom fighters'. But we did not know this in Lahore that day. That evening when I had a very nostalgic dinner with Pakistani friends, we talked with dreamy romanticism of how we might see open borders and real peace in our lifetime. How wonderful it would be, we said, if we could drive from Delhi to Lahore whenever we wanted. How wonderful if the Wagah border could stop being the hideous barrier of barbed wire and walls that it now was and become instead just a check post of the kind that exists between countries in Europe. My friend, Jilo Jamil, reminisced about childhood journeys to Delhi from Lahore.

'My parents would just load us all into the car and we would arrive in Delhi and stay with Hindu friends for days on end. Lots of other people did this kind of thing in those early days after Partition. Do you think there will ever be that kind of peace again?'

'Who knows,' I said.

'It's so sad,' someone said, 'that when Pakistanis and Indians meet in other countries they become close friends, and yet when we come home there is an impregnable border between our countries. And we have more in common with each other than any two other countries.'

'Not any more,' I said, 'not since Zia-ul-Haq made you start thinking of yourselves as part of the Middle East. Now we are more divided by Islam than by borders.'

'Rubbish. Nothing has changed in any real sense. Look at us speaking to each other in Punjabi. We are united by language if nothing else.'

So on that night that Vajpayee spent in Lahore we drank red wine in the high-ceilinged drawing room of an old-fashioned house and talked of love and friendship, poetry and politics. Javed Akhtar was at this dinner party and was the star of the evening. He sat surrounded by an adoring audience as he told us of the ride on the bus with the prime minister, and it seemed for that brief moment in Lahore that Vajpayee could succeed in doing what no Indian prime minister had done before. We believed he had a better chance than others because as India's first BJP prime minister he did not need to prove his nationalism to hardline Hindus who always came in the way whenever there was talk of peace. Vajpayee was sincere in his desire for peace, but he seemed not to know what he was up against: Pakistan's military.

In all the years I have travelled in Pakistan I have never met a military man who did not think of India as an implacable, eternal enemy. And nobody believed this more than General Pervez Musharraf. Like many others who gave up India for Pakistan in 1947, he seemed to feel the need to prove his loyalty to his new country by spewing venom against India every chance he got. Years after he lost power he continued to give interviews in which he described India as an 'existential threat' to Pakistan. He must have really believed this because there is no other way to explain the foolishness of his Kargil war. In an almost exact emulation of that old invasion of

Kashmir by so-called 'tribal' fighters in 1947, Musharraf sent soldiers across the Line of Control in Kargil disguised as Kashmiri militants.

Kargil is a desolate outpost on the road that links Srinagar to Leh. It is such a bleak, forsaken town that after spending one night there while driving from Leh to Srinagar in the 1970s, I vowed never to come back. This was when all that there was in Kargil was a collection of decrepit houses on the edge of a border that was the sole tourist attraction. 'There is the Line of Control,' people liked to say, pointing to a mountain on the other side of a narrow valley. It is so undefined a border that it was no surprise that it was not the Indian army that first spotted the infiltrators but Kashmiri goatherds. They look for grazing grounds wherever they can find them and move backwards and forwards across that uncertain Line of Control.

When the news reached Delhi, Vajpayee responded with war. It was a brave decision since news of the infiltration came weeks after his government was brought down by that single vote in May 1999 on account of the machinations of Sonia Gandhi. When war began on the Kargil border, he conducted himself with the resoluteness that people like to see in leaders in wartime. This war happened to be the first that took place after private television channels had spread their influence across India, so it was beamed live into Indian homes by intrepid TV reporters, and this caused a wave of nationalism that filled the sails of the hyper-nationalistic BJP. When the general election came in October that year, Vajpayee managed to get his National Democratic Alliance more than 300 seats in the Lok Sabha. But within weeks of becoming prime minister for the third time in three years, he faced a crisis that seriously tarnished his reputation.

It began on the last Christmas Eve of the twentieth century.

I was having Christmas dinner in the home of Swapan Dasgupta and his wife Reshmi. Swapan is an unashamed Anglophile, and so it was a proper English Christmas dinner with turkey, Christmas pudding and punch. The other guests were Prabhu Chawla, who was editor of *India Today* then, and journalist Ashok Malik. I remember that we had just sat down to dinner when someone called from the *India Today* office to tell Prabhu that an Indian Airlines flight from Kathmandu to Delhi had been hijacked. Reshmi's beautifully prepared Christmas dinner was ruined by this awful piece of news, and we all headed home earlier than we would have. I sat glued to my television screen till late that night, watching the dark images that came from Amritsar airport, where the plane landed after being refused permission to land in Lahore. They were pictures taken from a distance of the stationary aeroplane, so the images were shaky and badly lit, but for a long while we could see the aeroplane. And then suddenly it was allowed to take off.

It was a crucial, cowardly mistake that led to a series of other crucial, cowardly mistakes. Afterwards security experts and political pundits agreed that IC 814 was doomed as soon as it left Amritsar airport. I met K.P.S. Gill some weeks after the hijacking and asked if he thought IC 814 could have been prevented from leaving Amritsar since the hijackers had already started killing passengers. He gave me a long, disdainful stare from his very great height before saying firmly, 'There were a hundred ways the plane could have been prevented from leaving...the tarmac could have been torn up, a road roller could have been put in its path...'

When it was all over and analysts began to piece together what had happened and why, they concurred that the key mistake was that the crisis was not put in the hands of someone with experience in counter-terrorism like Gill. Instead it was

Vajpayee's man for all seasons, Brajesh Mishra, who took charge of the crisis. He was national security advisor but had come to this post from a career in the Foreign Service and without any experience in handling trained terrorists. So within days the Vajpayee government was brought to its knees and forced to meet all the demands the hijackers made, and they met them in the most pathetic manner. Afterwards high officials in his government blamed their cowardly conduct on pressure from the relatives of passengers on IC 814, but even at the time this sounded like a really lame excuse.

Mishra's first mistake was to order the Punjab police to do nothing till commandos arrived from Delhi. Why he did this is a mystery since no police force in India had more experience of dealing with terrorists than policemen who had dealt with two decades of Khalistani terrorists. Before the commandos could get to Amritsar, the hijackers started attacking people. They got nervous when they saw a fuel truck move towards the aircraft too fast and began stabbing passengers with knives to show that they meant business. A bridegroom returning with his bride from their honeymoon in Nepal was the only one to die of stab wounds. Rupin Katyal died in the three hours it took for the flight to get to Dubai.

After the bungled attempt to stop them in Amritsar, the hijackers forced the pilot to take off for Lahore again. He convinced them that he did not have enough fuel to go further. Once more Lahore airport switched off navigation aids and tarmac lights, but the pilot knew he had to try and land the plane somehow, so when they saw him bringing it down in desperation the lights were turned on. After it was refuelled it went on to Dubai and then Kandahar, and after seven days of dithering and confusion the Government of India agreed to all the hijackers' demands.

Vajpayee began with tough talk and a declaration that the

Indian government would never bow before terrorists and then did exactly this and more. Maulana Masood Azhar, Omar Sheikh and a Kashmiri terrorist called Mushtaque Ahmed Zargar were escorted to Kandahar by India's minister for external affairs as if they were honoured guests and not violent fanatics.

Nobody, not even Jaswant Singh, has ever explained satisfactorily why he needed to go to Kandahar himself. His personal humiliation was made complete when Masood Azhar wrote proudly in his memoir that the minister had offered him food and drink on the flight to Kandahar but he had refused because he did not want to touch even a drop of water if it was Indian.

When I read this I found myself picturing exactly what must have happened. Jaswant Singh, or Jassu Uncle, has always had a needlessly high opinion of what he likes to call Rajput honour. It is a characteristic I remember noticing when I first met him as a young girl in Ambala in the 1960s. He was an army officer then and 2IC (second in command) to my father who was then commanding the Central India Horse. It would have been this Rajput honour that made him offer food and drink to a man who despised India so much that he was ready to kill innocent people in acts of terrorism whose only objective was to harm India. After it was all over I tried to ask Jassu Uncle why he had been so kind to this monster, but he never gave me a clear answer. The best explanation is that the Government of India needed to send someone senior enough to Kandahar who would have been able to negotiate on behalf of the prime minister if the deal to exchange terrorists for the passengers of IC 814 fell through.

It did not. The passengers of IC 814 were freed on New Year's Eve after an ordeal that lasted a week. As the world welcomed a new century and millennium celebrations were held across India, the twenty-first century began for Vajpayee's government with humiliation and defeat. The hijacking was the first major instance of jihadi terrorism. But for inexplicable reasons, as the twentieth century died and the new one began, the world seemed more concerned about Y2K disruption in computer systems than what was to become the most dangerous threat to civilization in the early years of the twenty-first century. Had the hijacking of IC 814 been seen as an ominous portent of worse to come, perhaps the United States could have been better prepared to prevent 9/11, and India for the attack on Parliament that came weeks later.

11

MUMBAI'S MEAN STREETS

It was some days after 9/11 that Surekha took me to see her home. She took Julie and me to a little street behind the Air India building where in one corner of a car park stood a collection of blue plastic sheets on bamboo poles. Under these fragile structures lived a collection of families in which everyone had to work every day of every year just to stay alive. As soon as children could walk they were taught to beg or sell flowers at traffic lights.

Surekha's mother was a small, dark woman with large green eyes that had about them a mean quality. Had she told me that the reason she had given birth to so many daughters was that she hoped they would start selling their bodies at an early age to supplement her income, it would not have surprised me one bit. She never actually said this but hinted that Surekha was very popular. 'There is a gentleman who comes every day in his car and he always gives her Rs 100.'

'Why does he do that?' I asked.

'Because he likes Surekha,' she said with feigned innocence. 'He sometimes takes her for a drive in his car.'

'She is very young,' I said. 'You shouldn't let her go anywhere with a strange man.'

'Oh, but he pays her so well and he always brings her back,' she said.

Surekha would have been no more than thirteen at this time but seemed already to have developed womanly wiles. One day she asked me if I could lend her Rs 1,000. 'What for?'

'I want to get myself some grey contact lenses,' she said. 'There is this woman who says they will look very nice on me.'

'What? You barely have enough water to wash and you think you will be able to look after contact lenses?'

'Why not?'

'Because you have to wash your hands before you use a special liquid to wash the lenses. You won't even be able to afford the liquid.'

No more was said about the coloured contact lenses, but I noticed that the little girls I knew were suddenly very interested in dressing up. Sabrina Holkar, a friend of Aatish and a princess of Indore, was whiling away some months in Mumbai before going to college and asked if she could help with Nashta. I told her she was more than welcome, and Surekha and her friends were delighted to have a young girl in their midst. They stared in fascination at her blue eyes and pale skin and soon took to marvelling at how little jewellery she wore. 'Sabrina, you aren't wearing any earrings?' I remember Surekha asking as Sabrina rolled her eyes skywards and said to me in English that she could not believe that a street child was giving her fashion advice.

The more I got to know Surekha and her friends the more I found myself wondering about how they could be safe from sexual exploitation in Mumbai's mean streets. Whenever I tried to ask the girls about this they would pretend not to understand what I was talking about. My impression from talking to the girls was that none of them had any idea what sex was or how children were born. Till a few days before Mangala arrived with her baby I had seen her skipping along Marine Drive with the gaggle of other street children, seemingly oblivious to the fact that she was pregnant. And she returned to being a young girl after the baby died. Later, when Surekha's own babies came I was to discover why someone like Surekha needed to learn at a very young age that babies die easily and there is nothing anyone can do about this.

Devraj was the most disabled person I saw on my morning walks with Julie. Nobody came close. Not the crippled man who pushed himself around on a wooden skateboard and not the humpback whose deformity was so grotesque it looked as if he were carrying his back on his shoulders like a sack of potatoes. Devraj had a huge head and a bulky torso, almost useless arms and flippers for legs. He could neither feed himself nor move without help but somehow managed to get to Marine Drive every morning before five. He would then spend the entire day seated in his rickety wheelchair, smiling cheerfully at everyone who went by. He never begged but people of compassionate disposition usually gave him something as they walked by. On his wheelchair he hung packets of chips and other small items of food that he sold with the help of an assistant. The assistant was often someone with disabilities of his own.

What intrigued me about Devraj was his ability to smile in the face of such obvious misfortune. He smiled all the time. I longed to ask him how he got to Marine Drive and where he slept at night but did not summon up the courage to do this until late one night when I was walking back with my sister and brother-in-law from a nightclub called Jazz by the Bay. It was after eleven at night and he was still seated in his usual spot on Marine Drive, so I stopped and asked him if he spent the night there.

'No,' he said, smiling his toothy smile, 'my friend will come soon and take me to his shop. That is where I sleep at night. Then he brings me here in the morning.'

I wanted to ask him more questions but my sister and brother-in-law were impatient to get home, and it was not till a few days later, while walking Julie, that I managed to talk to Devraj again. He told me that his name was Devraj Shetty and that he was from Karnataka. Then he told me his story. 'When I was small I got polio and that is how I became like this. My parents were too poor to look after me, so they left me in the street in Bangalore.'

'What? Just like that?'

'They were very poor. They couldn't afford to look after me,' he said without rancour.

'Who looked after you then?'

'People in the streets...they gave me food and a place to sleep. They taught me how to beg.'

'So how did you get from Bangalore to here?'

'Someone told me that I should go to Chennai, where there was an institute that donated wheelchairs to people like me. I went there and I met someone who told me that I would be much better off in Mumbai, and they put me on a train.'

'Did you know anybody in Mumbai?'

'No. And when I got off at the railway station there were so many people, such huge crowds rushing around, that I got really scared and just stayed there on the platform for several days until this shopkeeper who looks after me asked if he could help me. Since then I have spent the night outside his shop. He brings me here and takes me back at night.'

I was astounded by his courage, resilience and the sanguine manner in which he told such a sad story. But he did not seem to think there was anything unusual about the extraordinary journey he had made to get to this spot on Marine Drive. The way that he saw it was that there was always someone to help a person like him.

Devraj said he usually made enough during the day to pay for his food but not much more. I was so moved by his story that I asked if I could help him in any way. 'Yes,' he said, 'there is a government scheme I have heard of that gives disabled people telephone booths to help them make a living. I find it humiliating to beg and would love to have my own telephone booth.'

'So who would I need to contact?'

'I know where to get the application forms so I can apply. But if you know somebody in the government then they will consider my case on a priority basis.'

'I'll see what I can do,' I said, not wanting to raise his hopes.

When I got home that morning the first thing I did after scrubbing Julie with a warm towel, brushing her and giving her a soya biscuit as her pre-breakfast snack was speak to Ajit. He was a friend of Pramod Mahajan. It was the summer of 2002, Vajpayee was prime minister and Pramod was a powerful minister in his cabinet. Ajit called him and Pramod put one of his aides in charge of ensuring that Devraj managed to get his phone booth.

Meanwhile, I wrote about Devraj in my column that at the time appeared in *India Today*, and Pramod's aide read the piece and became determined to help. He was good enough to speak to senior officials in the Maharashtra government and arrange for me to meet the general manager of the Mahanagar Telephone Nigam Ltd (MTNL), the agency directly in charge of implementing the scheme of giving telephone booths to disabled people. The general manager was charming and helpful and said that he was ready to give Devraj a phone connection immediately but to set this up he would need to find an appropriate spot to place the booth.

After this, seven months went by. Every time I met Devraj he asked what was happening to his dream project, and every time I told him that I was still working on it. He was so excited that he had already started to see for himself a wonderful new life that would take him off the streets. Meanwhile, I went on almost a daily basis to the MTNL offices, where I met high officials who told me that they could give Devraj the phone immediately but the problem was space.

If he has a home, the high officials said, they would be happy to install the phone in his home within a week. When I told them that he was homeless, they said I would need to ask the police for permission to install the booth on a suitable spot of public land. Once more I sought the help of Ajay Singh in Pramod Mahajan's office and once more he did his best. But more months went by and nothing happened, so I started to make some inquiries of my own and discovered that nobody in Mumbai had been given phone booths under this scheme. Telling Devraj that he was not going to get his phone booth was one of the hardest things I have ever done. He looked so sad that I wished with all my heart that I was in a position to build him his phone booth, but after a few days by he came up with a new project.

'If you can pay the rent to get me a jhuggi in the slum at the end of Nariman Point,' he said, 'then I can start a video theatre for the local people.'

'Don't you need permissions? A licence?'

'Well, if I am living in the house and showing people movies on my own video machine then how can the police stop me?'

For someone with such severe disabilities he was remarkably resourceful and managed to locate a large shack in a slum on a wasteland by the sea sooner than I expected. The wasteland was in fact a garbage dump and the reek of rotting garbage and open sewers hung heavily in the air, but Devraj was delighted with his new home and invited me to the inauguration of his first show. A small group of women and children sat on the dirt floor of his hut and sweets were passed around in a soggy box as the first moving images flickered on the TV that I had bought him. I also bought him a special scooter for disabled people and soon he was whizzing around with the grandeur of a duke. But his new success went instantly to his head, and I soon started to hear tales of bad behaviour that worried me.

From being the Lord of this Slum on the Sea Devraj soon became the most hated person in it. Before I could get a chance to ask him if the stories were true, I got a frantic call from him one day saying he was in hospital. The police had brought him to the hospital after he was beaten up by local people for allegedly abducting a young girl. When I went to see him in hospital he denied that he had done anything wrong but could not explain why the police were after him. That was the last time I saw Devraj. When he vanished I asked people where he had gone and they said that he had left the city because he was in serious trouble with the police, not just because of the girl he was supposed to have abducted but because he was involved in other shady deals. There are rarely happy stories from the streets of Mumbai.

12

ROADS AND A ROADTRIP

Vajpayee's record in securing India against jihadi terrorism was unimpressive. After 9/11 the American government created a Department of Homeland Security and made it almost impossible for another act of jihadi terrorism to take place on American soil. After the Christmas Eve hijacking the Vajpayee government did nothing. The hijackers of IC 814 drove across the border into Pakistan and continue to live happily as free men. Two of the men they released went on to commit hideous crimes in the name of Allah. Omar Sheikh was jailed for involvement in the beheading of American journalist Daniel Pearl and Maulana Masood Azhar was the alleged mastermind of the attack on India's Parliament. Vajpayee's government did not even bother to investigate why these two men had remained in Indian jails for more than five years without being tried and punished. Had he done more to strengthen India's defences it is possible that the attack on Mumbai that came to be known as 26/11 would not have happened.

Vajpayee is remembered as the first prime minister who was not from the Congress to have lasted a full term and for being a good man but for little else. His legacy could have been infinitely more glorious if he had made more effort to govern less like a Congress prime minister. He inherited a country that had failed to provide the vast majority of her people with such basic public services as clean water and electricity and at the end of his term little had changed except a few highways. If there was one dream he had for India other than peace with Pakistan it was to connect her with highways as part of a project that was called the Golden Quadrilateral.

It was at a Delhi dinner party that I first heard of the Golden Quadrilateral from Brajesh Mishra. The dinner party was in the garden of Prabhu Chawla's house. Since Mishra was the second-most important man in India at the time everyone was paying court to him, and this seemed to make him more arrogant than usual. With the air of someone who believes they have come up with a visionary plan, he explained to his fawning audience the new highway programme. India will be linked from north to south and east to west, he said proudly, and this will transform the country. Ajit listened more carefully than the rest of us to what he said. His company, the Hindustan Construction Company or HCC, is in the business of building infrastructure, so when Mishra finished he asked, 'Will these highways be access-controlled...will they be modern motorways?'

Mishra seemed to take offence from Ajit having dared to question his 'vision' and answered rudely that access-controlled highways were impossible in a country like India because ordinary people would resent them. When Ajit suggested that instead of building so vast a network so quickly it might be wiser to build a single access-controlled motorway between Delhi and Mumbai that would reduce travel by half, Mishra said, 'Well, if you cannot dream of big things I cannot help you.'

In the end Vajpayee's highway dream remained only half fulfilled. His government speeded up the pace at which roads were built but the highways were of poor quality and would not be considered modern roads in most countries. What made them less than relevant was that the necessary link roads never got built, as I discovered during one of the most horrific road trips I have ever taken.

The story of Ajmal Jami's broken arm in a chopper crash in Bagalkot is a typically Indian story of how public services fail even those who can afford to pay for them. It is also a story of the uneven prosperity and uncertain development that defined Vajpayee's time as prime minister, and this makes it more than a story about a horrendous road trip. Jami and I were in Bagalkot in the wilds of rural Karnataka to do a television programme on the political campaign of Vijay Mallya for Indianama, my show for NDTV.

Mallya was famous for being famous, for being very rich, and for being very flamboyant. He travelled in private planes and yachts to his mansions on different continents, he owned an airline, parked his yacht in the Mediterranean in the South of France for the season and partied with the jet set in New York and London. For him to abandon this life of lotus eating for the relentless grind of a political career made no sense. But it made for a great episode for Indianama.

It was by accident in Mumbai while shooting an earlier episode that I had discovered Mallya's plans to become an independent politician. The episode was on the links between Bollywood and the city's underworld, and one of the people we happened to interview was the actor Sanjay Khan. While the lights, camera and action were being set up in his glitzy, Bollywood-style drawing room, we chatted of this and that and he mentioned that he was going to Bangalore in the next few days to travel with Mallya. 'You should come too,' he said cheerfully. 'He is going on his first political campaign and it should make a good story.'

'But will Vijay Mallya give me an interview? Because without an interview there is no story,' I said.

'Of course,' he replied, 'and if you are coming to Bangalore I insist that you stay at my resort.'

So it was that I spent the night before the chopper crash at Sanjay Khan's wildly lavish Golden Palms resort. I knew it from pictures I had seen some years earlier when Sanjay Khan's daughter married Bollywood heartthrob Hrithik Roshan. But the pictures did not prepare me for the eccentricity or the scale of the resort. It stretched over endless acres on the edge of Bangalore, and the best way to describe it is that it resembled a Bollywood film set on a vast and wondrous scale. Abbas (Sanjay's real name) had decorated the grounds with plaster sculptures and fountains that could have come straight out of an old Raj Kapoor film about Bombay when it was still Bombay. And in fairness to him he achieved the impossible by turning kitsch into a thing of style. Where this was most evident was in the Bollywood bar. He filled it with life-size plaster cameramen, fake cameras and cinema lights. Hindi film songs from old movies played in the background to add to the ambience. It was here over a drink that we discussed the logistics for our trip with Mallya.

'We will go to Hubli in Vijay's plane,' Abbas said, 'but from there to Bagalkot only four people can go in the chopper, so it will have to be either you or your cameraman.'

'Not me,' I said firmly. 'I hate choppers because they crash much too often. And in any case I cannot interview Mallya without Jami's camera, so let him go with you and I will go by road ahead of you and meet you there.'

It was a decision that filled me with terrible guilt when the chopper crashed. But the story began well. Jami and I spent a day in Bangalore shooting in Mallya's staggeringly luxurious home. We gawped like peasants at silver pool chairs and rooms filled with crystal objets d'art, Persian carpets and curtains of finest silk and agreed that we had never seen such extravagance. The economic liberalization that began under P.V. Narasimha Rao after Rajiv Gandhi's death in 1991 encouraged Indian industrialists to be less coy about their wealth than they were during the dour socialist decades. And in any case Mallya needed little encouragement.

It was said that each one of his homes, whether in London, San Francisco, Johannesburg or Goa, was lavish beyond belief. Naturally, in this one, his ancestral home, he had spared no effort. After spending more than an hour shooting pictures of the silver furniture by the swimming pool we shot pictures of Mallya's vintage car collection, his ornate, gilded temple, his office filled with memorabilia from the liquor trade (his main source of funds) and of his drawing room with its south Indian paintings and glittering furniture. Back at the Golden Palms that night I did interviews with Bangalore friends of Mallya who came to attend a dinner party Abbas organized in a vast ballroom. There was loud music, disco lights, millionaires and movie stars.

The next morning I left early for Hubli in Mallya's aeroplane along with a contingent of flunkeys. Jami was to come in the second shift with Mallya, Sanjay Khan and Mallya's private secretary. After we landed in Hubli I was transferred to a maroon Mercedes van equipped with Internet, a bar and a music system. It was without question the most luxurious vehicle I had ever travelled in and felt almost ludicrously so because from its windows I gazed upon countryside that became bleaker, more barren and more desolate the farther we got from Hubli.

We drove past villages so poor that to see a structure that was not built of mud and thatch became a detail to be recorded in my notebook. Malnourished children with spindly limbs and yellowing hair sat listlessly outside mud huts on land paved with animal and human waste. If I had needed to make a loo stop I would have had to go in an open field because between Hubli and Bagalkot I did not see a single restaurant or petrol pump offering toilet facilities. By the time I got to Bagalkot the story had acquired for me a surreal quality, made more so when I was ushered into Mallya's deluxe campaign bus. It had a bedroom, a drawing and dining room, a toilet (to my immense relief) and a satellite dish that enabled television and Internet services.

It was in this bus, parked on a hill overlooking a makeshift landing strip, that I waited for the chopper to arrive. I would have waited outside but this was late July when monsoon winds were so strong that I had no choice but to wait inside the bus. Late in the afternoon, after what seemed like hours of waiting, the chopper came into view. I watched it circle the landing strip twice and then disappear. When it did not land the second time I assumed that this was because the pilot had realized that the winds were too strong. But before I had time to think, the bus started up noisily and raced off behind the maroon Mercedes van that shot ahead of us out of nowhere. When I asked where Mallya was, someone in the bus told me he was in the maroon van, so I called his secretary, Tushita, who was travelling with him, and asked if I should join them for the interview. She said I could and we stopped in Bagalkot's main bazaar that consisted of a row of rundown shops on the edge of an open drain.

When I got into the van I found Mallya, looking shaken and drinking beer with the air of a Pasha. Tushita, a plump, small woman with a pleasant face and blow-dried hair, sat on the arm of his chair, muttering words of comfort while a man who said he was his media manager sat beside them looking obsequious and overawed. They kept praising him for his valour and he accepted their praise silently over sips of beer. Abbas sat opposite Mallya, looking more shaken than anyone else, drinking vodka greedily from a long glass. Puzzled by the atmosphere in the van I asked what the matter was and Tushita said with a wounded look, 'Don't you know? The chopper crashed. We are lucky to be alive.'

Abbas said in a trembling voice between big sips of vodka, 'What a black tongue you have. You almost predicted this would happen.'

'But nobody was hurt?'

'Only your cameraman. His arm is broken.'

'What? Where is he?' I asked, horrified by the casual manner in which this information was delivered.

'Oh, our people are taking care of him,' said Tushita calmly. When I asked to be taken to him forthwith she looked surprised. The media manager, who should have been with Jami, looked even more so, but they found me a vehicle that took me to a small, rundown building somewhere in Bagalkot. It turned out to be the main hospital.

Jami was on a narrow bed in what looked like a railway waiting room but was in fact the hospital's emergency ward. His arm was in a sling and doctors hovered around him as if they were seeing something they had never seen before. When Jami saw me he smiled but admitted that he was in considerable pain. The doctors said that his arm was definitely broken but they did not have the facilities to fix it and I should get him to Bangalore as soon as possible. I had by then already called Radhika Roy, my old school friend and co-owner of NDTV, and told her what had happened. She said that the winds were too strong for a rescue helicopter unless I could get him to a town that was about a hundred kilometres away.

Bangalore was a better option, the doctors said, because there was a new highway. When I asked how far the highway was from Bagalkot, they said a 'short, one-hour drive' and assured me that this was a distance of no more than forty kilometres. 'Is the road good?' I asked, thinking of Jami's broken arm.

'Yes. Yes. Very good,' the doctors treating him said.

'OK. Jami, that's what we should do.'

Jami's answer was his usual radiant smile as his assistant cameraman, Govind, went off to buy the painkillers the doctors prescribed.

Then I called Tushita to ask if I could take the SUV in which the crew had travelled with the equipment from Bangalore and she said, 'I am sorry I can't spare the Pajero. But I can find you a taxi.' Considering how many vehicles there were in Mallya's cavalcade her answer astounded me, as did her complete lack of basic concern. If she had been standing in front of me I think I might have slapped her.

The only help I got from Mallya's mighty entourage was that a flunkey arrived with a battered Qualis taxi and Rs 5,000 for the 'journey back to Bangalore'. I threw the money in the poor man's face but would have preferred to throw it in Tushita's.

My medical knowledge is limited, but even I knew that if Jami's arm was broken there were chances of a minuscule bone fragment travelling in the blood stream and causing harm to a vital organ. I was acutely aware of the need to get him medical attention as soon as possible. The doctors were certain that the nearest 'good hospital' was in Bangalore more than 450 kilometres away. This was typical of Indian health services: excellent healthcare in the cities where ministers and high officials could use them and nothing in the vast rural hinterland where the majority of India's poorest, most helpless people live.

Furious with Mallya and his minions for their refusal to

help, Govind and I loaded the camera equipment into the boot of the battered Qualis. Govind was from Bangalore but totally unfamiliar with this part of Karnataka. We settled Jami in the backseat as comfortably as possible and set off for the new highway around five o'clock in the evening, believing that we would reach it in less than an hour. Then began the nightmare. The road was so bad that the forty-kilometre journey took us till midnight, with Jami groaning in agony every time we hit a bump. Govind had misread the prescription for painkillers, and it was only the next day in Bangalore that we realized Jami was being given Coldarin and not a strong painkiller.

On the long, dark, horrendous drive to the highway we passed through a landscape so forsaken that there was not even a shop from which we could have bought a blanket or a pillow. Two hours before we got to the highway we saw the first sign of what can be very loosely described as civilization. Out of the darkness appeared a small teashop with a thatched roof and clay ovens, but at least the thick, sweet tea it served made Jami feel a little better.

When we finally got to the highway I felt like jumping out and kissing the brand new tarmac. A comfortable Japanese car waited for us there with pillows and blankets and food. All arranged by Ajit's office in Bangalore. Jami barely ate a morsel before falling asleep. I stayed up all night and was still awake as a pale pink dawn lit up cloth banners and hoardings on the highway that had pictures of a smiling Vajpayee and the information that the highway upon which we travelled had been built under the aegis of the Prime Minister's Golden Quadrilateral programme.

❋

Then came Tehelka. Was it a carefully planned plot by the Congress to destroy the credibility of the Vajpayee government?

Was it really investigative journalism or just entrapment? These were questions that nobody asked then. Tarun Tejpal and his team of 'investigative journalists' became heroes for supposedly revealing deep, dark corruption in defence deals.

The story looked good at first. Here were these intrepid reporters disguised as arms dealers who on their hidden cameras recorded the president of the BJP accepting Rs 1 lakh and stashing it away in his drawer. And there they were in the house of the defence minister of India, recording a conversation with the minister's closest aide (and alleged girlfriend) as she told them to hand over the money to a party worker. He is organizing a rally, she said on camera, and will need the money. I knew Jaya Jaitley well and found the story hard to believe because it was hard to think of her as someone who would make money out of an arms deal. Had she not been in politics and had she wanted, she could have made huge amounts of money out of being the tsarina of Indian handicrafts and handlooms. Others did but she did not. In all the years that she had roamed in the highest echelons of political power she had shown no sign of sudden new wealth. She wore ethnic, elegant but inexpensive saris, her jewellery remained of the costume genre and she drove around in a very small car.

After entering politics her closeness to George Fernandes was often talked about in not a very nice way but she maintained that their relationship never went beyond friendship. When he became defence minister, she worked out of his vast, rambling, unadorned government bungalow, where I often went to have lunch with her and at no time saw evidence that George had given up his socialist ideals for capitalist greed. The bungalow was more party office than home with one room at the back that served as his bedroom and an adjoining room that was his shabby library. There were books everywhere in government-issue cupboards and on government-issue tables and it was here that he spent his days when he was at home.

It was in this room that I often came to chat to Jaya about political developments and it was in this room that *Tehelka*'s fake arms dealers found her. They told her they wanted to sell arms to the Government of India and offered her the money which she took, and this looked so bad on camera that George had no choice but to resign as defence minister. Other victims of *Tehelka*'s Operation West End were army officers caught accepting offers of whisky and prostitutes. It was more entrapment than investigative journalism and Tarun Tejpal was more Congress acolyte than investigative journalist, but nobody knew this till much, much later. The first sign of his political affiliations came for me when Sonia Gandhi's first government came to power and *Tehelka*, the supposedly rebel magazine, had a piece by Tarun welcoming the rise of Sonia and looking forward to the arrival in politics of her 'luminous' daughter.

When they were in Delhi on one of their visits, Vidia and Nadira Naipaul took me along to dinner in his home. This was before he became famous. It was a humble sort of home at the time, and Tarun seemed like a journalist truly dedicated to making a difference by exposing corruption and venality in high places. So when the Vajpayee government went after him and his financiers, I was fully on his side. I knew for certain that Jaya was incapable of corruption and that George Fernandes was as honest a politician as any, but being the daughter of an army officer I knew that there was huge corruption in defence deals. And I knew arms dealers in Delhi whose houses and lifestyle were more opulent than those of maharajas of yore. It was no secret that corruption in arms deals went all the way up to the highest levels of the army and the political establishment.

It was no surprise that at the time of Operation West End, Tarun Tejpal became an international hero. Vajpayee and his government were the villains of the piece. The dishonour that the *Tehelka* story brought upon his government seemed to affect Vajpayee personally. He seemed almost to lose interest in politics and government and to totally lose that inner fire that had caused him to spend so many long, hard years in public life. These were years in the opposition and, after losing his Gwalior seat to Madhavrao Scindia, years in the wilderness, but in all that time he managed to remain passionate about doing something for India. It was this that he seemed to lose after Tehelka.

I interviewed him once more for Ek Din, Ek Jeevan after the scandal and it was a saddening experience. The passionate, angry poet had been replaced by a tired old man who did not care much for high ideals or the future of India. I spent a day with him in the prime minister's residence. We talked as he ate breakfast, with his powerful aide Pramod Mahajan hovering in the background. Mahajan himself had the reputation for being a political fixer and not a political leader, and I remember thinking that his intimacy with the prime minister's household sent a bad signal. By then Delhi's political grapevine was already buzzing with gossip of how rich Vajpayee's son-in-law had become and his name found its way in the fake deal that *Tehelka*'s fake arms dealers were trying to expose.

That day when I interviewed him as prime minister I noticed that the only time Vajpayee seemed to come alive was for a few moments when in his sunlit garden he watched his little granddaughter play with a fluffy white dog. The interview was not memorable.

13

DYNASTY 2.0

When Sonia Gandhi's government came back to power for a second term, nobody was more delighted than the denizens of Delhi's drawing rooms. They pretended that their support for Sonia was because of their 'secular' and 'socialist' convictions. But as someone who understood this milieu well, I knew it was really because the Dynasty represented for them a vindication of their class and confirmation that the people of that India that lay beyond their tiny, elite, English-speaking world was as certain as they were that India was ruled best when it was ruled by its natural-born ruling class. Prime ministers from the wilds of Gandhiji's 'real India' like Deve Gowda, Charan Singh and Chandrashekhar had shown that they did not have the mass appeal that the Nehru-Gandhi dynasty did. 'You see, dear, Sonia may well come from a humble background, but you have to admit that she is more like a maharani than most maharanis. She has learned how to rule.'

'And you notice that she has been so clever about shaking off the Imelda Marcos image.'

'And, dearest one, since she isn't prime minister herself, nobody can blame her for things that may go wrong.'

'The main thing is that in the past five years India has been ruled pretty well by the man she chose as prime minister.'

Dr Manmohan Singh had much to do with the Congress winning a second term. He had been a dignified, clever prime minister who had kept the economy running on all cylinders. He had brought India into the nuclear club through a carefully concealed back door by making his deal with the United States. And above all he looked much, much more prime ministerial than his opponent, Lal Krishna Advani, who looked during this election campaign like a pathetic old man trying to look young. The most absurd of these efforts was when he allowed TV cameras to take pictures of him doing weights training in a gym. But Dr Manmohan Singh was given little credit for winning a second term for Sonia's United Progressive Alliance.

All credit went to Sonia Gandhi and her 'charisma'. She had the total, unabashed support of the media, and this helped create the larger-than-life image that she had by the 2009 election. She achieved this rapport with the media through her strategy of private tea parties. She gave no interviews, or almost none, but every major TV anchor and every major editor was invited to tea as often as possible.

High officials were as much to be credited for the support they gave her but it was in Delhi's drawing rooms that you heard the real paeans to Sonia and her son. It became hard to go to dinner parties without some socialite or some high official praising her political skills and 'charisma'. She was definitely a better leader than her husband, they gushed, but she might even be a better leader than her mighty mother-in-law. Those leading the charge were nearly always high officials who concealed their ordinariness by speaking English better than most. Often they had learned this in the Doon School, and it was this that was their ticket to the drawing rooms.

'She is more diplomatic,' they would say as bejewelled socialites hung on their every word, 'more likeable and look how good her Hindi has become. India is lucky to have such a leader.'

'It is so nice to know that India's future is secure,' the bejewelled lady would usually reply.

Of these conversations, and there were many, the one that remains etched unforgettably in my mind was with the inimitable, indefatigable socialite – let's call her Madam Lutyens. Her political ideas changed when the people in power changed, but because she was such a skilled courtier she nearly always managed to find her way into the inner recesses of the new court. Her parents were Marxists and close friends of Indira Gandhi, and it was through them that she came to know Sanjay Gandhi when she was young and comely in a plump, blowsy fashion. They became friends and she used this as her social currency for decades. Years after Sanjay died she regaled drawing rooms with tales of how she could have married him had she wanted.

Then came a phase when she became violently anti-Dynasty. Jayanthi Natarajan recounts how she walked out of one of Madam Lutyens's dinner parties because a political discussion got so fraught that she was ordered to 'go and lick the soles of Rajiv Gandhi's Gucci shoes'. This phase lasted only till Rajiv Gandhi became prime minister, when she persuaded Naveen Patnaik and me to introduce her to Arun Singh's brother, Mapu, whom she proceeded to court assiduously. But since Arun Singh himself fell out of favour, Madam Lutyens's plotting failed to bring her into Rajiv's inner circle. But this failure was rectified when through careful cultivation of Sonia's close friends she managed to worm her way into her court. And her success came in double measure when her son managed to become so close to Rahul Gandhi that he routinely dined in his apartment. Madam Lutyens ensured that word of this spread through the closed-circuit world of Delhi's drawing rooms so senior ministers in the government mysteriously found out every time Rahul was coming to dinner and showed up eagerly to pay court to the Congress party's Dauphin.

By the time I met Madam Lutyens on that impossibly hot evening in the bohemian drawing room of a young publisher, news of her closeness to the Gandhi family had spread far and wide. The publisher, Chiki Sarkar, was an heiress but appeared to like hiding this. This seemed to be the reason for the absence of air-conditioners in her apartment in Jor Bagh in a summer month. Hot Delhi winds blew through open windows, making cold white wine lukewarm and polite conversation really hard. The only person undeterred by this was Madam Lutyens. She fatly plonked herself down beside me after working the room tirelessly. We were not friends in any real sense, so it surprised me that she should seek me out as I sipped my lukewarm Prosecco. Then I quickly realized that it was not me she wanted to talk to but the Brazilian friend I had brought with me that evening, Vera Santo Domingo. With the unfailing honing instinct of a skilled socialite, she recognized her as the sort of celebrity whose pictures appear in international gossip magazines. Vera had no interest in Indian politics but this also did not deter Madam Lutyens. She began to talk about politics from the minute she sat down, as Delhi's power-broker socialites are given to doing. And naturally she talked about her closeness to the Gandhi family.

In the sycophancy department she surpassed her own high standards when she began to recount Rahul Gandhi's virtues. Even I, who knew her eternal need to be counted in Delhi's highest echelons of political power, nearly fell off my chair when she said, 'Do you know I believe that Rahul Gandhi has the best of Rajiv in him and the best of Sanjay?' I recount this remark here to draw attention to how much support dynastic democracy has in the drawing rooms of Lutyens' Delhi. And it is not just socialites who endorse this distorted form of democracy but bureaucrats, journalists and men and women who like to think of themselves as public intellectuals.

Mighty editors and TV stars of Lutyens' Delhi virtually became Sonia's public relations agents. So the picture created by the media was of a highly intelligent, compassionate political leader whose only reason for being in public life was her desire to do something for India's 'poor'. They knew that she was India's de facto prime minister but nobody ever wrote this, just as nobody ever wrote that her National Advisory Council was more powerful than poor Dr Manmohan Singh's cabinet. They knew that Rahul was apolitical and confused about economic and governance issues, but they kept quiet about these things and accepted him as the heir by birth to the democratic throne of India.

This is why it has been so astonishingly easy for the Gandhi dynasty to turn India's oldest political party into a family firm. And once dynastic succession became acceptable at the highest levels of political power, it became impossible to prevent dynastic democracy spreading like a slow poison into the very soul of India. It spread horizontally at higher levels of leadership in every political party and vertically down to the lowest levels of grassroots democracy. It has now become almost impossible to find a village council that is free of this debilitating disease.

The worst example of how democracy was diminished because of the dynastic disease came when Lalu Yadav handed Bihar to his semi-literate wife, Rabri Devi, when he was sent to jail on charges of corruption. It was an outrage for one of India's poorest states to be handed over to an apolitical housewife but somehow we in the media accepted what happened as if it were quite normal. As for me, ever hungry for people to feature on Ek Din, Ek Jeevan, I saw that the rise of hereditary democracy in Bihar had the potential for a riveting episode. So within months of Rabri Devi becoming chief minister I found myself in Patna with a crew and producer from Mumbai who had never been to Bihar before.

Patna never fails to shock me every time I go there. Indian cities are not models of urban planning or sanitary living, but Patna beats anything you see elsewhere. Its finest streets stink of open drains and rotting garbage. Abandoned vehicles rust and crumble in bazaars that have as many stray pigs and dogs as shoppers. On this visit my first shock came even before I ventured out into the streets. It came as I checked into the Maurya Hotel and saw that it had been transformed in the five years since I last stayed there from an elegant ITC hotel into a squalid dosshouse. The lobby stank of urine and rancid cooking oil. The furniture was dark with grime and food stains. And there was no sign of the beautiful gardens and fine restaurants that I remembered from five years ago. The swimming pool had disappeared without a trace.

It did not take long to discover that the ITC group had sold the hotel to a local businessman who allowed it to become a den of vice. Rabri Devi's brothers, who were both rumoured to be of mafioso bent, turned the hotel into a private club for themselves and their cronies as their former chief minister brother-in-law indulged their bad habits. But there was nowhere else to go, so we took the rickety lift to the floor on which we had been allotted rooms and walked down a corridor filled with the squawks of a chicken having its neck wrung and the smell of cooking.

When I tried to register a protest with the man who was showing us to our rooms, he said with a look of genuine surprise on his face that he could not stop anyone from cooking in their rooms. 'If guests want to cook in their rooms they can do so. It is quite legal.'

'Isn't it a fire hazard?'

'Maybe,' he said, 'but they are guests who have paid for their rooms, so how can we stop them from doing what they want?'

When I got to my room the smell from the toilet nearly made me throw up, and when I saw that the bed linen was layered with grime, hair oil and other residue from past occupants I resolved to spend the night seated on the armchair. It was not clean but cleaner than the bed. My cameraman, sound recordist and producer had never seen a hotel like this and wandered about with dazed expressions on their faces. So we could not get out of the Maurya Hotel fast enough. We dumped our luggage in the foul-smelling rooms and went straight to the residence of Mr and Mrs Lalu Yadav for a recce.

The chief minister's official residence is a lovely old colonial house, whitewashed and double-storied, but it now had the distinct stamp of the Yadav family. In once lovely gardens there were stables for cows. Mrs Yadav was a keen dairy farmer before she became chief minister. And there was a fish tank from which fish were routinely extracted for the Yadav dinner table. Behind the old house a new annexe of glass and chrome had been built, and it was on the veranda of this annexe that we found Lalu (out on bail) in a vest and pyjamas, with his legs folded under him on the chair as if he were squatting peasant style in some village square. On plastic chairs around him sat senior ministers and officials. He did not even try to hide the truth. He was still running the Bihar government.

He greeted me with a genial smile and an offer of lemon tea. 'It's much better for you,' he said, 'because it doesn't leave a bad taste in the mouth.' We had tea and chatted of this and that while the cameraman took some shots. When I asked where we could find his wife he directed us into the main house, where a servant led us to a room on the first floor so filled with bric-a-brac it felt like a junk dealer's shop. The chief minister duly arrived in a parrot green sari. Her hair was neatly oiled and plaited and she wore no makeup except for bright red nail polish on her toenails. Rabri Devi was charming, friendly, refreshingly honest and seemed pleased to be interviewed on camera. I think this may have been one of her first TV interviews. She told me how she was so terrified when she heard that she had become chief minister that she had burst into tears. She had been in the kitchen, she said in Hindi with a strong Bihari accent, cooking lunch for her nine children when the news came. 'I just burst into tears. What could I do? I knew nothing about politics or government... but then I thought if he wants me to do this then I must do it.'

My cameraman recorded this impromptu interview and we parted on very friendly terms. She agreed to meet us the next day at dawn so that we could take shots of her when she did her puja. We planned a full timetable for the shoot that included taking pictures of her inspecting her dairy farm, as she did every day, of her cooking her children's food as she continued to do and then of her in the chief minister's office. She agreed happily to the plan. But the next morning when we arrived after a sleepless night in Patna's equivalent of the Ritz we found that we were no longer welcome in the Yadav residence. Forget about shooting the chief minister at prayer we were not even allowed into the house. Nobody explained why, so we spent several minutes hanging about under a magnificent neem tree, where the evening before we had watched Lalu cook meat curry on an outdoor stove.

After many minutes of waiting, my producer, Ashwini Malik, started to get impatient and asked me whether we should not try to find out what had gone wrong. She would have done her puja by now, he reminded me as dawn's pale colours were slowly replaced by the harsh white light of a summer morning. So I went off in search of the official who had invited us to Patna to do the programme in the first place. He looked flustered and uncomfortable and seemed not to find the right thing to say to me. When I persisted with my questions he said in a nervous whisper, 'Someone has made trouble for you. They have informed the chief minister that you are the journalist who wrote a column in *India Today* saying it was wrong for a semi-literate woman to be chief minister of Bihar.'

So what do we do, I asked, we have come all the way from Mumbai and cannot go back without interviewing her. He asked us to wait while he tried to find a way to persuade the chief minister that she should do the interview. We waited for more than two hours under the neem tree, watching the Yadav sons playing cricket. We took pictures of flowerbeds and cowsheds and of the fishpond and observed Lalu holding his informal cabinet meeting on the veranda. He was cold and unfriendly when he saw us and told us curtly that he was not going to give us an interview. Finally, after an interminable wait, we were summoned to the chief minister's office, a large room on the ground floor. She was dressed in a starched cotton sari that spread out around her, making her look fatter than she was. Her hair was neatly oiled and plaited and she pretended not to notice us for several minutes. She continued to examine the files on her desk as if the future of Bihar depended on this exercise. Finally, she looked up and said, 'Yes.'

The interview went badly from the start. It began with the chief minister asking coldly if I had written that the 'Bihar ki mahila' (woman of Bihar) was illiterate. And if it had not been for divine intervention I may not have remembered that I had also written that she was the Sonia Gandhi of Bihar. When I told her I had written this she looked very pleased and agreed to allow the interview. When the cameras started rolling I asked her several innocuous questions and she answered in a slightly hostile way but at least she answered. But this armistice did not last long. The interview came to an abrupt and unpleasant end when I asked if she thought it was important for political leaders to be educated. She froze before saying archly, 'Can illiterate people not see? Can they not hear? Can they not understand what is going on? Besides governance is not my job, it is the job of bureaucrats.'

Bihar was not the only state in which democratic feudalism came to be accepted as normal. Soon there were the Abdullah and Mufti dynasties in Kashmir, the Badal dynasty in Punjab, the Mulayam Singh dynasty in Uttar Pradesh, the Scindia dynasty in Madhya Pradesh, the Pawar and Thackeray dynasties in Maharashtra, the YSR and NTR dynasties in Andhra Pradesh and the Karunanidhi dynasty in Tamil Nadu. Once Sonia Gandhi became de facto prime minister she encouraged the practice of parliamentary constituencies being passed on in the family like private estates. So by the end of her ten years in power, nearly every young Congress MP in the Lok Sabha was a political heir of one kind or other.

We in the media totally accepted dynastic succession as a normal parliamentary practice. I cannot remember anyone seriously questioning this diminution of Parliament. The occasional article appeared from time to time but mostly we accepted that in India if a doctor's son could be a doctor and a lawyer's son could be a lawyer then a politician's son could be a politician.

The *Indian Express* began a column when Parliament was in session called 'Young Turks'. I made it a habit to read it regularly in the hope of finding one 'young Turk' who was not a political prince or princess. I nearly always failed. This new generation of Indian political leaders have mostly come into public life not because they want to serve the people but because they like the power, pelf and easy celebrity. These things come with becoming a Member of Parliament. In the words of a political friend who shall remain nameless, 'Parliament has become a very exclusive Diners' Club.'

It has been my dubious privilege to know well many political princelings and princesses not because of their public role but because some have been the children of friends. And whenever I have asked them why they wanted to be in politics they have come up with sham excuses about their desire to serve India, but occasionally one or the other has admitted privately that the real reason is money.

India's 'tryst with destiny' could more appropriately have been called India's tryst with dynasty.

14

NEHRU

My hazy early memories of Nehruvian India come from Ahmednagar in the early 1960s. I was nine or ten years old and on holiday from Welham School. My father was a major in the Central India Horse and his regiment was posted here. We lived in a house full of big, high-ceilinged rooms that led onto large verandas with sloping tiled roofs. We spent a lot of time on these verandas reading books by Enid Blyton and playing in a small, neat garden with small, neat flowerbeds. The house was at the corner of a street that led to the club. I remember that the streets were so quiet that if a car went by we looked up to see whose car it was. Usually it was someone we knew.

When we were not idling about on the veranda we were playing some sport or other. We woke early to go riding in a riding school that we could walk to and that adjoined a golf club where my father played every afternoon. My sister and I cycled around the small collection of English-style cottages that made up the cantonment. And we cycled every day to the club, where we played table tennis and swam in a children's pool. Everybody seemed to know everybody not just in the cantonment but in the small civilian part of the city that appeared to be no more than a bazaar made up of small shops and rickety buildings in which the shopkeepers lived.

The only entertainment in town was the weekly movie night in the outdoor cinema. We sat with our parents in the officers' enclosure and the jawans sat in a larger enclosure on the other side of a cordon. It was in Ahmednagar in this open-air theatre that I saw my first Hindi film. I have tried hard to remember what it was and failed but what I do remember was that it was 'partly in colour' and that in the story the heroine became pregnant after hugging the hero under a tree on a stormy night. I remember asking my father how she had got pregnant and I remember him looking very embarrassed. I got no answer to my question.

Memories of my childhood in the glory days of Nehruvian socialism are of a country that was makeshift, mediocre and muddling along. Everything about it seemed half-finished and unsure, and in this landscape of uncertainty the only things that seemed well made and solid were the things that the British Raj had left behind. In Delhi it was the vista between India Gate and Rashtrapati Bhavan that remained the most spectacular part of the city long after Jawaharlal Nehru started building ugly Soviet-style 'Bhavans' along its edges. And even before he banned private builders from building new residential 'colonies' like Hauz Khas and Greater Kailash, these new parts of the city looked like shanties compared with the leafy avenues of Lutyens' Delhi. In smaller Indian cities it was old British cantonments that offered an orderly and planned contrast to the chaotic, filthy civilian parts in which most citizens lived.

When we travelled to states ruled by former princes, the buildings and monuments that rose imperiously out of the dross of socialistic architecture were the palaces and forts that the maharajas built before merging their kingdoms into the Union of India. My father seemed always to get posted to somewhere else every time we came back from boarding school for holidays, so we travelled a lot and seemed to travel always to some new half-finished town whose only concession to civic needs were the bazaar, the club and the cinema.

The club was always an old British club whose musty bars, ballrooms and halls were slowly acquiring indigenous smells from spicy kebabs and scented hair oil. In the ramshackle bazaars of my childhood, if there was one proper shop it usually had an English name like Spencer or Martin and had been left behind by the Raj. Was it this contrast between new, socialist India and the India of the Raj that made us grow up in awe of all things foreign? I cannot say for sure but what I do know is that we craved all things foreign because Indian goods in Nehru's glory days were so horribly sub-standard.

My first memory of Nehru himself is of him coming to Wellington in the Nilgiri Hills. We moved to Wellington from Bangalore, and what I mostly remember of this hill station is that my sister, Udaya, nearly died from eating poison berries and had to spend some nights in the children's ward of a very English military hospital. And that she nearly died of shock another time because when she was dewormed she saw dead worms in the potty. I remember blue hills from the eucalyptus forests that covered them and I remember hunts in which my father and his friends rode wearing very British 'pink' jackets that were actually red. The hunt was so famous that my mother's brother, Pritam Singh Sandhu, who was a far keener horseman than my father, came to ride with it.

I must already have had inclinations towards political journalism because amid these memories of blue hills, British hospitals and hunting, one memory more vivid than the others is of Prime Minister Nehru coming to Wellington. There was a military parade and because my mother was such a devotee of Nehru, she took me and my sister along to see the prime minister in real life. We must have sat quite close to the podium from which he spoke because I have a distinct memory of a small man, with a slight stoop and a fine face. He wore a dark-coloured sherwani and a white cap. I cannot remember what he said but have a faint memory of people saying afterwards that he had made a wonderful speech. This was before the war with China in 1962, after which it was hard to find an army station in all of India where anyone had a single word of praise for him. Even my mother who made us listen endlessly to a scratchy recording of his 'tryst with destiny' speech went off him a little. 'It was really Krishna Menon's fault,' she took to saying, 'but then he shouldn't have made Menon minister of defence and he shouldn't have made General Kaul army chief.'

In most of the years that Nehru was prime minister I was in boarding school. My sister and I were taken to Welham Girls School in Dehra Dun when she was seven and I was eight. We did not know what a boarding school was until our parents left us in the charge of a very tall, very thin Englishwoman called Miss Linnell. The first thing she did was hand us tightly rolled cloth tapes with the number 99 written over and over again in small squares on mine. And the number 100 written over and over again on the tape she gave my sister. 'You are number 99,' she said to me, 'and your sister is number 100.' We did not know what the numbers meant until we discovered them stitched on our school uniforms and underwear some days later.

My sister took to boarding school easily. I had a difficult and unhappy first year, but by the time of the China war I was as happy a boarder as any. We did not know what the war was about or why China was the enemy, but Miss Linnell filled us with patriotic sentiment and ordered us to knit socks and sweaters and make cards and gifts for 'our brave soldiers'. It was an excuse to escape classes, so we spent sunny mornings on the hockey field, gossiping, giggling and ostensibly doing our bit for the war.

The only girl in Welham School who had some political sense was Subhashini Ali (Sehgal in school), as I discovered in a fashion show organized to raise funds for the war. She became the star of the show because she minced on to the ramp with her lips painted yellow and explained, with a yellow pout, that she was modelling a lipstick called Yellow Crush to inspire our soldiers to defeat the Chinese. I did not know then what she meant but the remark has stayed with me. And so has a memory of Nehru coming to Welham School to see his grandnieces who were sort of my age. I remember that there was huge excitement among the teachers on that day. And Nonika and Geeta, his grandnieces, acquired a new celebrity.

Welham School was as makeshift as the rest of India. It functioned out of two old-fashioned, quite beautiful houses that once belonged to a Nawab who may have abandoned his home to go to Pakistan. The houses were surrounded by vast gardens on the edge of which were planted mango and litchi groves. They slowly disappeared under ugly school buildings, dormitories and playing fields. In the time I spent there we lived under the permanent shadow of new construction, and this half-finished quality about everything became the leitmotif of my childhood.

My father's family were refugees from Pakistan, and in all the years of my childhood they seemed to be living in half-finished houses and in a half-made sort of way. On the land they were 'allotted' near Karnal to compensate for the estates they left behind in Pakistan, there were fields that were mostly jungle. We used to go partridge shooting with my father and learned to recognize the sound that the titar made. I shot a bird for the first and last time. It put me off shikar for good to see the little dead quail I shot. And in the ugly fly-blown town that was Karnal then, there was a half-finished structure called Rajkot House. Rajkot was the village my father's family came from near Gujranwala. My great-grandfather, a tall, thin man who always wore a white turban, lived in Rajkot House, as did my grandmother and my father's younger brother, Jindo Chachaji.

When we came visiting from one or other army station we saw Rajkot House being built room-by-room, so always over it hung the smell of wet cement. When it was fully built it looked uglier than when it was still being built, but it was for my father's family a palace compared to Hasan Manzil. This is the house they were allotted as refugees when they first came to live in India. I remember that Hasan Manzil was in a narrow, smelly alley in the old city of Karnal. It was built in the style of Muslim havelis, with rooms rising up, one on top of the other, around a small inner courtyard.

On the lowest level lived buffaloes, and my strongest memory of this house is the smell of dung wafting up into our bedrooms and mingling unpleasantly with the smell from the single lavatory. This smelled worse than the dung because it consisted of a cement platform with bottom-sized holes that opened on to metal pans that some unfortunate person cleaned once a day. So Rajkot House with bedrooms that had attached bathrooms with flush toilets was for my father's family a truly grand house.

India in the 1950s was not so much a country as a place that was trying to become a country. But it was a place of great hope and deep patriotism that allowed us to overlook the serious flaws that Nehru was building into the foundations of modern India. Foundations that would later cause many walls to rise up crookedly and many institutions to remain half-built decades after Nehru died in 1964.

He was a romantic, a writer and a dreamer, and these are excellent human qualities but not useful for running a country the size of a continent. So although he built fine institutions of higher learning he appeared not to notice that only a small, upper-caste elite would have access to them unless there was investment in mass education. He did not make this investment and this ensured that East Asian countries that had literacy levels as low as India in 1947 raced ahead of us in the next twenty years. By the time his Italian granddaughter-in-law became president of the Congress party, government schools were so bad that even poor Indians tried to send their children to private schools. Not investing in mass public healthcare was another serious mistake. Why did Nehru, a man so deeply influenced by European socialist ideas, not take some of the best things that socialist economies offer?

Why did nobody tell him that he was making a mistake? I have put this question to people who worked with him and nearly always got the same answer, put best in the words of Jagat Mehta, who was one of India's most high-minded bureaucrats. 'We loved Nehru so much that we didn't dare tell him when he was doing the wrong thing.' The result of nobody telling Nehru when he was making a mistake was that there were as many poor people in India when he became prime minister as when he died. His 'temples of modern India' – the massive public sector factories he invested in – failed to create sufficient jobs or wealth.

Nehruvian India was no place for rich Indians either. When his policies made it impossible for businessmen to do business a group of industrialists went to see him in

Delhi. In the group were K.K. Birla, J.R.D. Tata and S.L. Kirloskar. The version of this meeting that I have heard is that these mighty industrialists tried to convince Nehru that his economic policies were making it impossible for them to make profits and without profit there would be no investment. Nehru listened carefully and when they had finished said quite simply that for him 'profit' was a dirty word. This was so clearly the opposite of being what later came to be called 'business friendly' that they realized there was no point in saying any more. So they remained silent as Nehru built a licence raj so punishing that private factories making more than their allotted quota were penalized. Government factories made everything from milk and bread to guns and tanks, and they made them so badly that the enduring memory from my childhood is of how we longed for foreign toys.

The first foreign toy that I remember being given was an American golliwog. That is what it was called in those times before political correctness. And when some foreign-returned uncle brought us dolls or clothes from abroad we gasped at how beautiful they were. In Welham School the most envied children were those whose parents could afford to go abroad and bring them stuffed toys from Harrods. Not only was it a time when we craved foreign goods, it was a time when most Indians who could afford it tried to emigrate to America or England. When they came home for occasional holidays they brought back tales of cities with spotlessly clean streets and countries in which people did not 'defecate everywhere', as V.S. Naipaul so cruelly described in *An Area of Darkness*.

To us who thought of filthy cities and open defecation as normal, it seemed as if these tales of clean cities and wondrous shops came from another planet. A joke I remember from my childhood was about how Nikita Khrushchev on his visit to Delhi says to Nehru that he liked the city but was shocked at the sight of men urinating in public. The joke goes that this so upset Nehru that when he goes to Moscow he makes it a point to look out for men urinating in public. Finally, he spots one man and gleefully points him out to Khrushchev who orders his policemen to find out who the man is and they come back with the information that he is an Indian.

So are there any good things I remember about Nehruvian India? Yes. For those of us who lived in our small cocoon of privilege, life was wonderful. We knew there were millions of poor people in India but we never came into contact with them except when they came to work in our homes as servants. Everyone I knew lived in a big house filled with lots of servants, and everyone I knew spent long summer holidays in hill stations that in those times were not teeming with thousands of middle class honeymooners. There was no middle class to speak of and nobody seemed to mind this much, because although feudalism was slowly being replaced by Nehruvian socialism it was a socialism that was really very feudal. The only difference was that instead of princes and landed aristocracy it was politicians and bureaucrats who lived like feudal potentates, and at the very top of this grand new edifice of democratic feudalism was Nehru himself. He was more powerful than any leader of India had ever been, undefeatable in elections and believed by many to be the glue that held India together.

It was many, many decades after his death that Nehru's policies began to be questioned. Even then there were more people ready to stand for him than against. And when he was criticized it was always with a degree of prevarication. So in the 1990s when P. Chidambaram was finance minister in the fragile, fractious government of that 'simple farmer from Karnataka', Shri Deve Gowda, I talked to him at some length about why India continued to pour vast amounts of money into public sector companies that provided no more than a few thousand jobs and never made a profit. He conceded half-heartedly that the public sector had failed.

'You see, the idea behind investing in the public sector was that it would make the money we needed for investment in the social sector. This never happened, but the original idea was a good one.' Nehruvian socialism became a sacred creed for Indian political leaders, so it was the same sort of answer that you got from even those who had never been in the Congress. For Congress prime ministers it was impossible to openly say anything against Nehru's economic policies even after P.V. Narasimha Rao was forced by India nearly going bankrupt to start dismantling the licence raj in the 1990s. Narasimha Rao's policies were openly opposed by 'socialist' Congress politicians and by the leftist parties. They called them 'neo-liberal' economic policies and continued to attack any move away from Nehruvian socialism long after the Soviet Union collapsed and China became a capitalist country albeit with 'Chinese characteristics'.

Was it just hypocrisy or a real belief in Nehruvian socialism? It is hard to say. But on my first visit to China in 1997 I met a minister from the Marxist government of West Bengal who conceded that there was some amount of hypocrisy involved. Ajit and I met this minister in Shanghai in the house of an Indian diplomat. We had arrived just two days earlier, and I had spent the two days bedazzled by almost everything I saw. When I met the minister from West Bengal I asked him if he thought that China's economy was still Marxist. He laughed so much at my question that his belly shook under his white dhoti-kurta. 'Well, you could say it is Marxism with Chinese characteristics,' he said.

'Or capitalism with Chinese characteristics?'

'Call it what you like,' he said with another hearty laugh, 'but it works. Look at the difference between India and China.'

'I am looking,' I said, 'and cannot understand why Calcutta doesn't look like Shanghai or why your party opposes foreign investment in India but supports it fully in China.'

'These are complicated issues,' he said. 'Very complicated.'

'Or just hypocrisy?'

'Maybe,' he said and laughed once more till his belly shook. Then he changed the subject.

So completely had Nehruvian socialism entered the soul of India that Hindi films of the 1950s usually had in their black and white images and their romantic lyrics the message that it was wrong to be rich and noble to be poor. Feudals and businessmen were invariably greedy, ruthless and evil, and poor people filled with endless virtue. So romantic and picturesque was poverty in the eyes of the urban middle class filmmakers of those times that they somehow always worked into the plot a village or forest scene with tribal people in beads and feathers, dancing rapturously.

Bollywood, in those days when it was not called Bollywood, made films with middle class themes for the small handful of middle class people who could afford to go to the British cinemas we inherited from the British Raj. They were very grand buildings, those cinemas, with names like Regal and Eros, Odeon and Plaza. Their interiors were decorated with mirrors and art deco furniture that looked more European than Indian. But nearly all the films made in those times were about patriotism and the nobility of fighting evil oppressors like rich businessmen and blood-sucking landlords. And of course the British. So Nehruvian socialism may have served to keep the vast majority of Indians mired deeply in poverty but it was fully in consonance with the mood of India.

Bollywood was a beacon for poets and writers in Nehruvian times, and every one of them was either a card-carrying member of the communist party or a socialist. Many of these 'progressive' people came from rich feudal families, but when they came to Bollywood they chose to live in genteel poverty in communes. Everyone lived in genteel poverty in Nehruvian times and nobody seemed to mind because of that hope and patriotism that permeated the very air we breathed. Nehru's admirers, and there continue to be millions, concede grudgingly that he made serious economic mistakes but never admit that he also made some very serious political mistakes for which India has paid a heavy price.

There may never have been a Kashmir problem if Nehru had not made some very bad decisions. The first of these was to take the Kashmir issue to the United Nations, and the second was to arrest his old friend Sheikh Abdullah and keep him in jail for almost the entire time that he was prime minister.

When I started going to Kashmir as a reporter in the early 1980s I began asking questions about why Sheikh Sahib was arrested and discovered that most of the reasons were flimsy. With Partition as a raw wound in India's memory there was paranoia about the country breaking again, so it may have been easy to believe then that the Sheikh was plotting with the Americans to take Kashmir out of India. In retrospect it seems hard to believe. I met Sheikh Abdullah only once and it was the first time I went to Kashmir as a reporter and not just for the usual summer holiday.

It was in the late summer of 1981. I wrote at the time for *Sunday* magazine but on a part-time basis since Aatish was less than two years old. I was staying with my sister in her house in what was then still Curzon Road, and Farooq Abdullah came to a dinner party there. He was not a politician then. His greatest successes were in the drawing rooms of Delhi, where he was hugely popular. Black and white pictures taken at my sister's dinner party show him surrounded by beautiful women and looking very happy. He liked beautiful women and they liked him, so he was inevitably the star of any dinner party.

At some point that evening he mentioned, almost casually, that he was leaving in a few days for Srinagar for a rally at which his father planned to declare him his political heir. Dynastic democracy was a new idea then, but if Indira Gandhi could do it why not Sheikh Abdullah, so nobody in Kashmir seemed to mind him anointing an heir. Farooq asked if I was still doing journalism and when I said I was he suggested that I come and cover the ceremony. 'It will be a big event,' he said. 'There will be people coming from all over Kashmir for the rally in Iqbal Park, where my father will make this announcement.' I said I would ask M.J. Akbar if he was interested in the story and let him know. When I called Akbar he said not only was he interested he would use it on the cover. So off I went to Srinagar, leaving a very unhappy Aatish in the arms of my sister. He was intelligent enough even as an infant to understand whether I was just going shopping in Khan Market or going away for a longer time.

Srinagar that August was full of summer flowers and chinar trees in their full glory. I stayed at Nedou's Hotel in a room that looked on to a garden full of sunlit trees in which tourists ate spicy Kashmiri kaanthi kebabs with fat white rolls of bread. Farooq designated his sister's son, Muzaffar, to be my guide. Before the procession was due to begin he took me to meet various political people he knew, and to Hazratbal, the shrine that is believed to contain a relic in the form of a hair of the Prophet Mohammed. It teemed with pilgrims, and this gave me a chance to find out through an impromptu vox populi if the move to make Farooq the Sheikh's heir was popular. After paying obeisance at the shrine pilgrims sat in a garden on the edge of the Nagin Lake and chatted amongst themselves over cups of salty Kashmiri tea. I joined a group of elderly men who looked as if they had come from a long way away. They said they had come for the rally from a village in Uri and that they had come in the hope that they would be able to catch a glimpse of Sheikh Sahib. When I asked if they were happy that he was making Farooq his heir they said they had no problem with this at all. They believed they owed this to the man who had fought so long for Kashmir.

Just before the procession was about to begin Muzaffar took me to the Lallarukh Hotel in Lal Chowk. Gathered there on a high balcony that offered a panoramic view of the square were many members of the Abdullah family. The Sheikh sat at the centre with his wife by his side. He looked darker and taller in real life than he did in pictures, and the karakuli cap he wore made him look taller still. His face was long and thin and his most distinctive feature was his smile, which revealed pink gums and a fine collection of strong white teeth. He smiled a lot that day as he gazed down fondly at the swirling crowds around the open truck on whose roof Farooq stood waving at his supporters. When he saw his father he lifted his arms in a greeting, and the crowds, spotting the old Sheikh, went into a frenzied bout of slogan-shouting. The slogan I remember most distinctly went 'Baba pehney Khan dress, kya kar leygi Kangress.' When I asked Muzaffar what this meant he laughed and said Khan dress meant salwar-kurta, and since this was what Sheikh Abdullah wore it became a symbol of defiance against the Congress.

The noise from the square below made conversation difficult and I was too intimidated by the old Sheikh to do a proper interview, but we talked a bit and I found him as unlike a man who should have spent eighteen years in jail as anyone I ever met. Why had Nehru not been able to talk him into seeing reason? Was it not an even bigger mistake to keep Sheikh Abdullah in jail than it was to take the Kashmir issue to the UN? What had the old Sheikh done that deserved a life sentence? Some years later I tried to find answers to these questions while researching a book on Kashmir and had long conversations with bureaucrats from Nehru's time and never found satisfactory answers.

All that they came up with was that the Sheikh had been plotting with the Americans to break Kashmir away from India. When I asked for evidence of this they said he had met the American ambassador on more than one occasion and that the Americans were very keen to destabilize India by giving Kashmir to Pakistan. In retrospect these seem like absurd arguments, but in the fragile new nation state that Nehru ruled over they may have sounded credible. Pakistan and China were words that resounded in all conversations that I remember from the army stations in which I spent my childhood.

As a child I cannot remember knowing the difference between Muslims, Hindus and Sikhs, but to say that someone was Pakistani amounted to saying he was an enemy. I vividly remember an incident when a stranger got into the swimming pool at the Ambala club and panic spread among us children because one of the ayahs said suspiciously, 'That man looks like a Pakistani.' All of us jumped out of the pool and started a whisper campaign against the unfortunate stranger, who could not understand why we buzzed around him, giggling and giving him strange looks. It turned out that he was not Pakistani or Muslim.

The paranoia of the time found its way into children's nursery rhymes. China was the other bogeyman, and a nursery rhyme that we loved dancing to was 'Ching-chong Chinaman born in a jar, pickled in a teapot, ha, ha, ha.' After the war with China the paranoia about foreign powers plotting to divide India into small countries intensified, and a word that was used loosely without anyone fully understanding what it meant was 'balkanization'. All in all Nehru's India was a pretty dismal place because instead of a sense of renewal and resurgence there was a sense of decay everywhere. In the army stations where I grew up, everything seemed to be falling apart.

There were grand old clubs in fine colonial buildings that showed clear signs of having seen better days. Ballrooms with sprung wooden floors and high ceilings were turned into storerooms and offices, and elegant billiard rooms usually smelled musty and unused. Fine wicker chairs on wide verandas had about them a look of neglect. And whenever I went with my father to the mess for some event or other there would be talk of how grand everything had been in British times and how badly standards had fallen.

There was disappointment in Nehru's leadership, but it never took away from the deep regard in which he was held for decades after he died. He was credited with bequeathing to India democracy and pluralism, and if anyone challenged the achievements of Nehruvian socialism, as V.S. Naipaul did in *An Area of Darkness*, he was reviled. I was doing a course in journalism at the very new New Delhi Polytechnic in an equally new South Extension when the book came out, and when I read it and told people that I thought it was an accurate description of modern India people were appalled. Indians did 'defecate everywhere', I argued, and India did seem like a pretty hopeless place filled as it was with millions of people living in extreme poverty and extreme illiteracy, so why should we be upset if a writer coming from abroad pointed these things out? There was no point. Nobody agreed with me, and Naipaul was reviled as much as Nehru was revered.

15

ALI, ALI

One morning all the pavement shops disappeared from Marine Drive. Ali was standing on the street near where his shop should have been, looking confused and angry. When I asked what had happened, he said the 'mooncipality' people came and moved everyone away.

'There is going to be a navy parade, they told us, so we cannot be here.'

'For how long?'

'They say we will be able to come back in two days.'

'So how will you feed the children?'

'I took the food to the car park where they live…'

'So you can continue to do that,' I said, 'until they let you come back.'

I did not know then that they would never let Ali or any of the other pavement entrepreneurs come back to Marine Drive. When they tried to set up their little shops a few days after the navy parade, they were chased away by officials who came in big, empty vans into which they flung the goods they confiscated from those who dared to defy the municipality. It was a huge loss to walkers on Marine Drive because the pavement shops sold cold drinks, water, herbal juices, Indian-style breakfast and roasted corn. These were things that came in handy at the end of long walks or jogs.

When I tried to intervene on Ali's behalf, the officials told me that there was a new rule that banned hawkers on Marine Drive. 'Big people object to them,' the officials said.

'But where are they to go? They have a right to livelihood.'

'Where they go is not our problem,' the officials said with that special callousness that makes Indian officials more cruel than officials I have met anywhere else in the world.

Having seen my friend, Madhu Kishwar, fight and win a long legal battle for hawkers to be allowed to set up shop on the grounds of the fundamental right to livelihood, I tried to argue. Vajpayee as prime minister had personally intervened on behalf of street hawkers in Delhi and ordered the city to permit them to exercise their right to livelihood without being troubled. But for these officers of the Government of Maharashtra this meant nothing because they had 'orders from above' and that was it. Marine Drive was going to be free of hawkers on the grounds that 'better people' who lived in the vicinity wanted it beautified.

Most people who used this promenade were either rich or very rich. Anil Ambani had taken to jogging along this route escorted by bodyguards, and from my own building many flabby, middle-aged men walked here in expensive sneakers and fashionable running gear. Their wives usually did not accompany them, but if they did you could tell from the diamonds on their fingers that they were definitely rich. The last thing they wanted to see when they took their morning constitutional or strolled on the promenade as dusk fell over the dark grey sea were poor people. So the poor people had to go.

Ali tried to set up his little shop near Churchgate station but was chased away by other hawkers for territorial reasons.

They themselves survived by bribing the police to be allowed to occupy tiny pieces of public land. But mostly they chased Ali away because they did not want competition. If Nashta did not guarantee him between thirty-five and forty hungry customers every morning, he would have had no income left. But even with Nashta he did not make enough money to make his little business profitable. The loss of his pavement shop on Marine Drive destroyed him, and a young man who was earning more than Rs 15,000 a month was reduced to penury. I tried to help him. I discovered that in the grounds of the massive Bal Bhavan (children's home) on Marine Drive the Salaam Baalak Trust had been permitted to set up a small contact point for homeless children and got Ali a job there. This did not work well because although Ali did not mind feeding uncouth, desperately poor, runaway children, he did not care much for them. He thought that they were dirty and ill mannered and having grown up in poverty himself had little sympathy for them.

The children he was asked to take care of in the little shed where Salaam Baalak looked after lost, homeless children rescued from the railway platform of Charni Road station were dirtier and more desperate than Surekha and her friends. Without the help that they got from the Salaam Baalak shelter they were doomed to fall into the clutches of street mafias that dealt in drugs, sex and violence. Children were their easiest prey.

The Salaam Baalak Trust was set up by Mira Nair in 1989. Her first film was called *Salaam Bombay* and one of the leading characters in it was a street child. In Delhi the trust went from strength to strength and expanded its activities to include residential schools and skill training programmes for older children, but in Mumbai they operated at that time out of a small shed in the back garden of Bal

Bhavan. It was a shed that was filled all day with the smell of railway dust and the sound of trains, but it was a useful place for rescuing lost children because it offered a full view of the Charni Road railway platform. Social workers could try and rescue runaway children before they fell into the hands of drug dealers and criminal gangs.

One day, soon after I got Ali his temporary job, I went to Salaam Baalak's shed to find a very gloomy group of social workers. When I asked what had happened they said they had been served an eviction notice by Bal Bhavan. They had been ordered to move immediately, and they had nowhere to go. It seemed so wrong for a government welfare centre called Bal Bhavan to be evicting people who were helping the neediest, most vulnerable children that I offered to help. I told them that I would try and use my press card to meet the head of Bal Bhavan and plead their case.

They said that the head of Bal Bhavan was a lady and that her office was inside the main building. So it was that I found myself inside the enormous, yellow-washed pile that sits on Marine Drive with a panoramic view of the Arabian Sea. It is an old-fashioned building with the rounded curves of the art deco style that defines the other buildings on Marine Drive and looks as if it may have been built at the same time as the other buildings when the British still ruled India and this road was called the Queen's Necklace.

Once inside I found myself in a large, cool, high-ceilinged reception area and used my press card to get an audience with the IAS officer who had charge of Bal Bhavan. This lady sat in an office that was five times the size of the shed from which Salaam Baalak ran its services. Bal Bhavan contained other offices and halls that could have housed a hundred sheds that size, and I think I may have pointed this out to the neat little lady who sat behind a very big desk. She had short hair and

wore a crisp, starched cotton sari and did not seem pleased to
see me. As I remember it, this is how the conversation went:

'Yes? What can I do for you?'

'I wanted to talk to you about the eviction of the Salaam
Baalak Trust...'

'It's a government decision. I can do nothing about it.'

'They do very good work...they are helping children who
may otherwise fall into the hands of street gangs.'

'What can I do about this? They can do their work from
somewhere else. This is a government building.'

'But if it is called Bal Bhavan, should it not be helping
children?'

'We are helping children. We need that garden area for
ballet classes.'

'Ballet classes? What sense does it make for a Bal Bhavan
to be helping middle class children instead of very poor, lost
children?'

'That is not your business.'

'It is my business. I am a journalist.'

'So write about it if you want.'

She stood up, indicating that I was dismissed. I did write
a story in a column I used to write then for syndication. It
went out to many newspapers including to the *Afternoon
Despatch & Courier* that came out in Mumbai, but it made
no difference. Salaam Baalak went to court against the
eviction, and I went with them to hearings.

The government was prepared to spend money on a long
court case but not on helping very poor, completely helpless
children. The irony that escaped those who tried to displace
Salaam Baalak was that the work it was doing was the
work that Bal Bhavan itself should have been doing. Had
government welfare services worked as they should have,
it would have gone a long way towards serving India's lost

children. But like most other services of the Indian socialist
welfare state, children's homes had become just another
vehicle for providing government jobs. And for reasons I
have never understood, the officials who work in government
welfare institutions are the most insensitive and uncaring you
will have ever met.

Ali tried for many months to find some way of earning
what he could in Mumbai's mean streets but failed. So one
day he disappeared altogether from my life along with the
cell phone I gave him to help run Nashta. I next heard from
him on my birthday. He called from Chennai. 'We had to give
up the room in Dharavi,' he said, 'because I couldn't make
enough money. So we are now living with my uncle who has
a chicken farm near Chennai.'

'So are you doing well? Are you managing to make some
money?'

'Not as much as I was making in Mumbai in the old days,'
he said, 'but my expenses are much less here. And my uncle
is trying to send me to Kuwait. I have applied for a passport.'

Having seen at close quarters the plight of Indian workers
in the Gulf countries, I tried to warn him about how lonely it
would be and how difficult. But Kuwait acquired the quality
of a dream for Ali. Every time he called, and he called on
birthdays, Diwali, Eid, Christmas and New Year, all he could
talk about was Kuwait. In between he rang to ask for some
money for his mother, who needed to have an operation, and
asked if I would come to his wedding. I told him that I could
not make it to the wedding but would come whenever I was
next in Chennai to see his bride. But before this could happen
he rang one day to tell me that he was leaving immediately
for Kuwait and asked if I could help him with some contacts
there. I gave him the number of a friend but he never got
in touch with her. He still calls from Kuwait to wish me on

happy occasions and festivals, and he seems lonely and a little sad.

If he had been given half a chance in his own country, he may have become a very successful businessman. As in the case of millions of other young Indians, it was because India could not provide him with just basic things like a good school and a chance at making a living, he was forced to try his luck in a foreign country. The children Ali fed every morning were suddenly grown-ups. Surekha got married to a cousin of her mother. And this at a time when Sonia Gandhi unofficially took full charge of the government that she put in place and put on it the label of being 'pro-poor'.

16

THE DICTATOR

In a box of old photos I found a black and white photograph of Indira Gandhi addressing a press conference. It is an ordinary sort of photograph and was probably taken by a photographer from the Press Information Bureau who sent it to me because among the reporters present is me. It is not much of a picture but I kept it because it is a memento from the first time I saw Indira Gandhi in real life and at such close quarters. I remember that my first reaction was shock at how small and frail she was compared to how she looked on television and in pictures. Small, frail and very white in that way that only Kashmiris ever are.

I cannot remember what the press conference was about because I spent the whole time staring at this woman who in all my adult years had so dominated Indian politics. I remember listening more to the thinness of her voice than to her words and I remember being riveted by the way one side of her face twitched when she spoke and how carefully dyed her short, frizzy hair was so that a white streak remained on top like a crest. Was it a fashion statement? Vanity? What I remember most vividly from my first real-life encounter with the woman who was by then already a legend was that she had that quality that everyone loosely defines as charisma. It was not just I who stared at her that morning. Everyone did. Including supposedly hardboiled hacks in the press enclosure.

My first conscious political memories of Indira Gandhi are of slogans. 'Voh kehtey hain Indira hatao. Main kehti hoon gareebi hatao.' Then another slogan comes to mind as if linked to the other. 'Is deepak mein tel nahin hai, Indira hataana khel nahin hai.' The first slogan is too famous to need translation. The second needs explanation. The Bharatiya Jana Sangh's election symbol in those days was a clay lamp of the kind that lights up homes on Diwali, and the sneering reference in the second slogan is to this little diya not having enough oil in it 'to remove Indira'.

In the early 1970s when these slogans resounded at election time in the narrow alleys of Delhi's slums and in the city's elegant, high-ceilinged drawing rooms, the idea that India could be ruled by anyone other than Indira Gandhi was preposterous. A sycophantic Congress president was to say one day that 'India is Indira and Indira is India', and because he coined this slogan in the days when she temporarily became a Dictator it was seen as snivelling sycophancy of the worst kind. The truth is that it was an astute bit of political analysis. Indira Gandhi defined India and India's political aspirations in a deeper way than even her father had. Jawaharlal Nehru lived in a time in which men usually described in political conversations as 'stalwarts of the freedom movement' were still alive. They were educated, sophisticated men and women who came into politics with the idea of freeing India from colonialism, with an idyllic vision of what India could be if she governed herself and with an almost poetic idea of nationalism.

By the time Indira Gandhi became prime minister the political landscape was a place in which much smaller men loomed much too large. There were exceptions, but mostly the 'leaders' I met when I began to cover politics were either semi-literate peasants or Marxist ideologues whose commitment to their ideology limited their ability to grow. So it was no surprise that Mrs Gandhi seemed so much taller than her colleagues and opponents.

For me at a personal level it was when Indira Gandhi decided to abolish the princes that I first became aware of her immense political power. This was because I had come to know well the man who fought her on behalf of the princes: the Maharaja of Dhrangadhra. His oldest son, Bapa, was a close friend of mine from my louche teenage years when in the absence of HHD, as we called Bapa's father, we used his large government house on Thyagaraja Marg for parties and other amusements like long evenings of dumb charades. He was often in his constituency in Gujarat but would occasionally appear without warning and was so formidable a presence that our festivities would abruptly end as his three sons gathered around him respectfully saying 'Hukum' to everything he said. He was a small man but gave the impression of being taller than he was because he had a natural grandeur about him and a very strong sense of who he was. He was in the middle of his fight for princely rights when we first met. It took me a while to stop being awestruck enough to start asking him what the fight with Mrs Gandhi was about and why it was so important to him. He seemed to spend much of his time writing letters to lawyers and to 'my dear brother rulers'.

It made no sense in Indira Gandhi's increasingly socialist India to fight for privy purses to continue to be paid to some of the richest men in India or for them to retain their titles and the dubious privilege of having special red number plates on their cars with the name of their state written on them. When I summoned up the courage to ask HHD these questions he said simply, 'We were ruling princes and when we merged our states into the Union of India it was under a treaty that guaranteed us certain privileges. If the Government of India can break one treaty how can it be trusted not to break others?' HHD and his 'brother rulers' won their battle in court but Mrs Gandhi abolished what was left of princely India anyway by using Parliament to override the Supreme Court's decision.

After losing an election HHD left the house on Thyagaraja Marg and moved permanently to Dhrangadhra, where he lived out the rest of his life in a decaying palace. He would come now and then to Mumbai and stay for weeks in a large suite in the Cricket Club of India (CCI), where he lived in princely style with a small army of uniformed staff to tend to his every need. Whenever I dropped by for a chat and a glass of wine he would talk to me about India and the dreams he had once had for her future. He told me how when Jawaharlal Nehru first came to Bombay after the British left he had stood by the side of the road and shared the hopes of the ordinary people who lined the streets to welcome him. He told me that he had himself been a socialist in those times and had dreamed of bringing change and prosperity to Dhrangadhra. He said that his idealism had died after Indira Gandhi became prime minister because he saw how cynical she was about her reasons for being in politics.

It was Mrs Gandhi's cynicism that worried me personally, and at no time was this trait more visible than during the Emergency when she used the suspension of democracy to ensure that Sanjay became her heir. Even as a very junior reporter I can remember being shocked by the cynicism of her twenty-point programme. The points in it were things that as prime minister she should already have done if she had seriously tried to remove poverty, so by turning them into goals that the Emergency would be used to achieve she was mocking the intelligence of the average Indian. This was easy to do since most Indians in 1975 were poor, illiterate and politically naïve. After that first meeting where the black and white photograph was taken I made it a point to go to every meeting where Mrs Gandhi was present.

These were mostly in Vigyan Bhavan, and although I continued to be fascinated by her charisma I never heard her make a single speech that did not disappoint me. She seemed always to talk about high ideals and the 'greatness' of India and how she would die serving India, but since she had suspended fundamental rights and become a Dictator her speeches sounded merely like mocking attempts to continue fooling the people.

After every speech I would come back to the *Statesman* reporters' room and talk to older journalists about what made her who she was. There were almost no biographies of her then, and in those days before Google the only way to do any research was by actually talking to people. So it was from older political correspondents and yellowing scraps of paper in the newspaper's archives that I learned how she began her political career as a compromise candidate chosen by party bosses who thought they could manipulate her. Older journalists told me over endless cups of tea in smoke-filled rooms how it did not take her long to show the old men of the Congress party what she was really made of.

They spoke of her with awe and admiration.

'These party bosses forgot that she was Nehru's daughter and that she had been groomed for politics,' said Mr Kumar, his eyes shining behind his thick glasses. He was a small, round man with a large, round face and was always happy to talk to me about politics.

'Did Nehru want her to take over from him?'

'No. Not the way she wants Sanjay to be her heir. But she became general secretary of the Congress party when he was still prime minister.'

'Did he object? Did he try to stop her?'

'No. And she was his official hostess in the years that he was prime minister, so she saw what politics was about and must have learned about governance from him.'

'Do you think she is intelligent?'

'Well, she is a very clever politician. She broke the Congress party when its senior leaders tried to boss over her and proved by winning 352 seats for her Congress (R) in the 1971 general election that she was a real leader.'

What I discovered when I began to travel as a reporter to remote villages was that in the vast hinterland of rural India the millions of desperately poor Indians who barely made enough to eat two meals a day loved her. They believed in her 'gareebi hatao' slogan and were convinced that she would do her best to end the horrible poverty in which they lived. And it was her aggressive attempts to destroy the princes, nationalize banks and demonize businessmen that had created the image of her being the patron saint of the poor.

If she convinced the very poor that she was their saviour, she also convinced educated, middle class Indians that she was a great leader by winning the Bangladesh war. And even though her licence raj almost killed India's tiny private sector, rich Indians worshipped her. Many, many years after her death I ran into rich and powerful Indians who said that they would always support the Congress because of what Indira Gandhi had done for India. In the words of the industrialist Rama Prasad Goenka, 'I think of Indira Gandhi as India's greatest leader because she was the first Indian leader to win a war in more than a thousand years.' I remember being quite taken aback by this comment.

It was more than twenty years after Mrs Gandhi's death and I was interviewing Mr Goenka in his luxurious drawing room for the TV show I did then called India Inc. I remember that he stood against a glass cupboard filled with European bric-a-brac and that his eyes shone and his voice shook as he said this. I knew that he was one of the most loyal financiers of the Congress but not till then did I understand why.

So powerful was the impact of her victory in the Bangladesh war that even her political opponents kowtowed before her. Most memorably Atal Behari Vajpayee, who is supposed to have described her as an incarnation of Durga, India's goddess of war. Vajpayee has gone blue in the face denying that he ever said this but at the time it was widely believed, and in politics it is always perception that trumps reality. As for socialists and communists, of whom in the 1970s there were more in Parliament than MPs from what was then the Bharatiya Jana Sangh, they shared her economic ideas totally. They believed as she did in five-year plans, in the licence raj, in statist power and in the idea that India must always be a socialist country.

So in the first half of the 1970s she was invincible. My own memories of those years are spotty. In the summer of 1971 I left for England to train as a reporter with a small local newspaper in a small, ugly English town called Slough. It was the first time I had ever been outside India and the first time I travelled in an aeroplane. Foreign exchange was in such short supply with the Government of India that travelling abroad was almost impossible except for very rich Indians. In my immediate family the only people I knew who could afford an air ticket to a foreign land was one of my mother's brothers who owned a travel agency that gave him and his family access to cheaper tickets. It was he who made my travel arrangements. My one-way ticket to London cost

Rs 3,000, and the Reserve Bank of India permitted me to buy 35 English pounds.

Foreign travel was such a rare thing in those times that many of my friends became airhostesses just to be able to see another country. So on Air India and British Airways flights it was quite normal to be served your meals by Indian princesses and the daughters of generals and admirals. Somehow even then bureaucrats and political leaders lived in another sphere and mysteriously always managed to pay for their children to study in foreign universities and even take them on foreign holidays.

What is often forgotten when Indira Gandhi's life and times are analysed is that it was a time when India was among the most isolated countries in the world. Technically there was democracy, a free press and an absence of the sort of iron curtain that screened off totalitarian countries, but information about what the rest of the world was doing came to us only from a handful of foreign magazines that were censored before we got to see them. When I got to Heathrow airport I remember feeling as if I had arrived on another planet. Indian airports at the time were usually small, low-roofed barracks in which a single carousel creaked noisily around in a hall that always smelt of dirty toilets. My experience of Indian airports was limited to having gone to receive a relative or friend, so Heathrow with its vast halls and multiple luggage carousels was so confusing that I had to ask friendly strangers where I should go to find my luggage. Then there was the confusion of trying to find which exit I needed to take. I am not sure how I made it out of Heathrow airport that day. If an Indian friend had not come to receive me I am not sure that I would have been able to negotiate transport to London either.

Once I got used to being in a foreign country I found myself fascinated by everything. Escalators, the underground,

ATMs, motorways, Harrods, Selfridges, food vending machines and telephones that actually worked were for me a source of endless wonder. As indeed were London's clean, orderly streets and its magnificent theatres and museums. These were all things that we lacked in Indira's India. Slough was about the only thing I did not like. I had managed to get on the training programme that the *Evening Mail* offered only because Slough was bursting with Indian and Pakistani immigrants who worked in factories in and around this bleak town. Many spoke very little English and lived in poor working class areas that had become ghettos. I was probably taken on as a trainee in the hope that I would do immigrant stories. But in the end I did what every other trainee reporter did: police, fire, magistrate's court and local government.

India and Indira Gandhi faded away as I settled into my new role as a small town reporter, even acquiring a Slough accent to be better understood by copy takers when I phoned stories from court. This was until the Bangladesh war happened in December that year. In the six months that I had spent in England before the war began, I had managed to move to London and fallen in with a large group of Indian friends, some new and some from school, and had become a Londoner. I commuted to Slough every day and returned every evening to go to parties where Indians and Pakistanis mixed happily together until the war began. Once Indira Gandhi won the war for India she became a heroine even in the eyes of Indians like us who lived so far away. But we immediately lost all our Pakistani friends.

When I returned to India in 1974 she was still a heroine in the eyes of most Indians, even if there were burgeoning signs of big trouble. In the year I spent trying to find a job after coming back to Delhi, I followed politics in relatively desultory fashion and got only small whiffs of what

Jayaprakash Narayan was doing in Bihar, what was making students angry in Gujarat and the small corruption scandals that were finding their way into drawing room conversations.

In the tiny circle of privilege in which I moved, nobody blamed Mrs Gandhi for anything. Into this charmed circle of princes, scions of rich business houses, advertising types and old school friends would for an evening drift a bureaucrat or two. From them we learned that Mrs Gandhi was no longer as popular as she once had been because the poor had remained poor and the educated middle classes (a tiny, tiny group) were beginning to question the awfulness of public services. None of these things affected us in our cocoon of privilege. Indian realities intruded only in the form of daily power cuts, limited supplies of water in our taps and endless shortages of everything. We did not believe that this had anything to do with Indira Gandhi's economic policies.

Besides she was one of us. She spoke English and French and unlike us even spoke Hindi well enough to become popular with the masses. As the first generation of Indians who weren't fully colonized, we were different from my parents and grandparents. They spoke English but also spoke Punjabi, Urdu and Hindi. We spoke only English, except to servants, listened to American music and read books by foreign writers. I knew almost nobody who could recite a poem in Hindi, Urdu or Punjabi and nobody who could speak an Indian language well. Our Indianness came from watching Hindi films and smoking marijuana that came from the Himalayas. We were not rich but we were privileged. Everyone I knew lived within the boundaries of Lutyens' Delhi in big, old-fashioned houses with high ceilings and wide verandas. Life was comfortable. And if I, newly returned from London, complained about something, my friends and family would usually tell me to stop behaving in such a 'foreign-returned' way.

It was the Emergency that changed everything. By 26 June 1975 I had managed to get a job as a reporter in the *Statesman* newspaper. This had happened exactly a month before the Emergency came and brought with it press censorship. But in that month I had become more aware of political realities than I had ever been. I became aware that Mrs Gandhi's opponents had coalesced around Jayaprakash Narayan and that there were opposition rallies in Delhi to which huge, eager crowds were flocking. As far as I remember nobody expected that one of these rallies would inspire Mrs Gandhi to declare an Emergency. Not even after the Allahabad court judgement on 12 June that disqualified Mrs Gandhi from contesting elections. Once I became a reporter with the *Statesman* I took to wandering past her house on Safdarjung Road as often as I could. It was walking distance from where I lived, and there always seemed to be some kind of political activity on the roundabout outside her house.

As Mrs Gandhi's unpopularity grew so did the size of the rallies on this roundabout of trampled flowerbeds and dying brown grass. No matter how hot the day, no matter how many hours of waiting, the villagers who came seemed ever willing to be transported here to show their support for the prime minister who had promised to remove their poverty. Mrs Gandhi's flunkeys would appear from time to time and assure them that she would soon be there and they would continue to wait without water, food or shelter from the sun.

As a very young 'foreign-returned' reporter, their docility amazed me, as did their devotion to a leader who had done nothing to improve their lives despite a full mandate to remove poverty. Their poverty was painful and ugly to my foreign-returned eyes. I was horrified by their scrawny bodies, their torn, dirty clothes, and the visible signs of malnourishment in their bleached hair and yellow teeth. But most of all I was horrified by their passive acceptance of their lot. They seemed not to have the energy to demand more. Were they kept poor and illiterate because the fundamental rule of democratic feudalism is to keep 'the people' mired in perpetual poverty? I did not think of these things then, and as far as I remember nobody else did either, because the political crisis that came with the Emergency was too compelling to worry about anything else.

After the Emergency was declared on the hot, sultry night of 25 June 1975, conversations in newspaper offices were not about Mrs Gandhi's failure to remove poverty but about the suspension of fundamental rights. In the very British atmosphere of the *Statesman* newsroom, every journalist was upper caste, English speaking and leftist. This made everyone a natural ally of the Nehru-Gandhi family until Mrs Gandhi used the Emergency to bring in dynastic succession. Then things changed. Suddenly the suspension of democracy came to mean something new and sinister.

Petty officials took to appearing from the Press Information Bureau with pictures of Sanjay Gandhi that they insisted 'must be prominently displayed'. They were little men but when they made this demand there was a menace in their voices. Soon stories started to filter down from the highest echelons of government about how Sanjay was making policies and sacking ministers. Our informants spoke in whispers. 'The Cub ordered Inder Gujral to be sacked today.'

'And what did the prime minister say?' I whispered back to the small-time political worker who brought me this news.

'She said nothing. You will see that Gujral will go tomorrow…the new minister is a personal choice of the Cub.'

'Do ministers take orders from him?'

'I don't know…everything is being handled from the prime minister's house by the Cub.'

While I continued to run into Rajiv and Sonia Gandhi in the safe apolitical environs of Delhi's drawing rooms, Mrs Gandhi's younger son spent his time trying to rule India. And his adoring Mummy let him. The foundation stone of democratic feudalism was being laid and nobody could object because there was an Emergency that had suspended the fundamental right to free speech. Those who dared to defy Mrs Gandhi went straight to jail.

It soon became clear that India's real prime minister was Sanjay Gandhi and that his approach to politics was not just different but fundamentally undemocratic. He gave orders and dealt harshly with those who disobeyed them. He believed that India's real problems were to do with lax population control, too many visibly poor people living in too many slums and environmental damage caused by these things. To implement his new 'vision' for India he sought the services of servile officials who turned their servility into brutality when it came to dealing with ordinary people. Meanwhile, in Delhi's genteel political circles appeared a new kind of politician – the thug – whose loyalties were entirely to Sanjay.

In newsrooms we took to calling them 'Sanjay's storm troopers' and soon they were everywhere. My first encounter with Sanjay's new followers was on a hot morning when I was shopping for slippers on Janpath. I was busy trying on a pair of Kolhapuri slippers when I heard a ruckus outside and noticed that the owner of the shop started looking very nervous. 'It's them,' he whispered.

'Who?'

'Sanjay Gandhi's men…Youth Congress.'

'So?'

'If they come into a shop they take what they want and they never pay for anything.'

As he spoke a large group of noisy young men in white khadi kurta-pyjamas walked by laughing and talking in raucous tones. A look of relief spread across the shopkeeper's face when they ignored his shop and went into another further up this street of shops built by Punjabi refugees when they had come to Delhi from Pakistan. Once it became clear that Sanjay was India's real prime minister it did not take long for Delhi's drawing rooms to discover how powerful his cronies were. The denizens of these drawing rooms are easily impressed by raw power, and even if Sanjay's cronies were a rough breed they were suddenly seen being entertained by big businessmen and glamorous socialites.

In the drawing rooms the ones made most welcome were his friends from the Doon School because, as a socialite friend confided, 'at least they speak English'. Sanjay himself was too busy running the country to come to dinner parties but his friends and cronies enjoyed a glass of good Scotch whisky in the evening and the company of people like them. No sooner did they leave than stories about Sanjay would start to be told by those who knew him from his years in the Doon School.

'He was a horrible brat in school. And really cruel…'

'Tell me about it…he used to catch birds and lock them up in cages and leave them unfed and uncared for, so I released them one day and he took revenge on me by cutting up a brand new tennis racquet that my mother had bought me.'

'I remember, and Mrs Gandhi had to be called and she bought you a new tennis racquet but you said no I want my racquet back.'

'And then?'

'Then nothing. There were other incidents of this kind. He was very unpopular.'

'Do you know that if anyone got into an argument with him he would threaten the person with dire consequences?'

'Do you know he had to leave Doon because he got on the wrong side of so many people?'

Nobody could tell for sure if these stories of school days were accurate or exaggerated, but what everyone including Mrs Gandhi's ministers soon found out was that Sanjay was capable of the worst kind of bad behaviour. And that he had hatchet men in high places who did not hesitate to take violent action against those they thought had offended their leader in any way.

Sanjay's most prominent characteristic was his disdain for rules and regulations. He did not ever express an economic idea that could be considered a serious economic idea, but for his friends he was prepared to break the strict socialist regulations that his mother imposed on free enterprise. One of his close friends was the socialite Rukhsana Sultana, or 'Meenu' as I knew her from the days when she was married to Shivi, the brother of a childhood friend. I first met her in Simla when she was a young bride and her sister-in-law, Rayman, and I were boarders at St Bede's College. I remember that she was very pretty and had skin like translucent glass.

Her marriage to Shivi ended soon after their daughter Amrita was born, and she moved to a small house in Narendra Place near Jantar Mantar. Shivi was a grandson of one of the builders of New Delhi, Sir Sobha Singh, and I think the house belonged to him. Meenu took to being a gay divorcee in grand style and soon became a celebrated society hostess. I was once taken by a political friend to a 'mujra' she organized and was astonished to find that the men who came to watch the dancing girls from Old Delhi were senior politicians and rich businessmen. I have no idea how she met Sanjay Gandhi, but when I next met her she made no effort to hide her closeness to India's de facto prime minister.

'He wants me to do social work with Muslim women,' she said proudly, 'so I go every day to Old Delhi and try and make them understand how important family planning is.'

From having nearly been beaten up in Old Delhi for being mistaken for Rukhsana I knew that her visits were causing great tension in Muslim areas, but she had not noticed. 'When I first went,' she continued, peering out of the blue-tinted sunglasses she wore all the time, 'people said I should go wearing clothes like them but I chose not to. I wear chiffon and pearls because I want them to aspire to improving their lives.' Meenu was always in chiffon and pearls, always perfectly groomed and not nearly as empty-headed as she gave the impression of being. Underneath the socialite exterior dwelled a hardnosed businesswoman who knew how to mix politics and business.

Soon after Sanjay's rise to power rumours started to spread in newsrooms and drawing rooms that he was not a socialist like his mother. In newsrooms these rumours caused leftist journalists to expound upon the dangers of moving away from socialism.

'India is a very poor country, so socialism is the only way,' my political guru Mr Kumar said when he heard that Sanjay was encouraging free enterprise albeit surreptitiously.

'But he has never said that he wasn't socialist and we know that his mother has amended the Constitution to make India socialist and secular forever more.'

'That may be, but I have been meeting businessmen from Bombay who tell me that he is very sympathetic to their problems. They think that if he becomes prime minister he will do away with socialism.'

Mrs Gandhi's insertion of the words 'socialist and secular' before 'republic' in the preamble to the Constitution was unnecessary. No political leader or public intellectual in those times was anything but socialist. If a journalist began to show signs of questioning socialist economic ideas he was instantly labelled as a CIA agent. This label could ruin careers and invite the attention of Mrs Gandhi's socialist officials who knew that she was obsessed with the 'foreign hand' and convinced that the CIA was trying to get rid of her. Decades later a KGB spymaster called Vasili Mitrokhin defected to the West and revealed that many journalists in India at this time and many politicians were actually KGB agents. But it was all right to be a KGB agent because the Soviet Union was on our side.

If newsrooms were worried about Sanjay Gandhi's 'disdain for socialism', the drawing rooms were excited by what they saw as new opportunities for crony capitalism through Sanjay's cronies like Rukhsana. She quickly became both 'social worker' and commission agent. It was never established whether she really saw 'Sanjayji' every day as she boasted, but what quickly became clear was that she had the power to help entrepreneurs bypass Indira Gandhi's licence raj. Private enterprise was brutally restricted in Mrs Gandhi's 'secular, socialist republic', and those who dared to try and become entrepreneurs nearly always needed political support from Delhi. Mrs Gandhi favoured a particularly Indian form of crony capitalism that allowed only a small handful of businessmen to build big businesses.

The unwritten condition for this was that at election time they would help Congress with funds. For those who were not so pliant, doing business in India was like what doing business may have been in countries ruled by Marxist committees. Once the help of a major political leader was obtained there were the bureaucrats to contend with. Licence raj bureaucrats loved using their position to make industrialists crawl before them. As one senior bureaucrat who went on to become election commissioner said proudly to me once, 'One of the things that gave me the greatest pleasure was to see the richest men in India come to me on their knees to beg for licences.'

Their powers were reduced during Sanjay's brief rule. His natural disposition was authoritarian, and in the two years of the Emergency when he was India's de facto prime minister he made no effort to hide this. Supplicants for licences that only the Government of India could provide moved from Mrs Gandhi to her son with their petitions. And cronies like Rukhsana suddenly acquired powers beyond the power of ministers. So it was to her that the Taj Group went when they wanted to build their first hotel in Delhi. They needed special assistance because they wanted permission to build in Lutyens' Delhi, which had been declared a residential zone by Mrs Gandhi, and they got it. The Taj Mansingh came up the year after Mrs Gandhi lost power and in it Rukhsana was given a permanent suite.

To celebrate the opening of the new hotel there was a fashion show by Yves St Laurent. It was a huge event for so famous a designer to be having a show in India at a time when it was such a fashion backwater that the only other designer who had ever come to Delhi was Pierre Cardin. Tickets were hard to get for the show because every glamorous Indian woman seemed to have been invited by the Taj Group, so when Sonia Gandhi wanted to be there she called me to see if I could help. She knew that I had a friend who was a St Laurent model and believed that it would be easy for her to get a ticket.

When I asked my friend if she could find a ticket for Mrs Gandhi's daughter-in-law she said that she had given her two tickets to her parents, so the only way was to ask Camelia

Panjabi, who was at the time a powerful executive of the Taj Group and the guiding force behind the fashion show. Ms Panjabi invited me to coffee in the newly opened Machan coffee shop. It was decorated in the self-consciously ethnic style of those times. The hotel industry seemed to have made a collective decision to be deliberately Indian to an almost ludicrous degree. So to create the atmosphere of a tiger hunt there were paintings of tigers and jungles on the walls. Ms Panjabi was proud of the new hotel and told me that the hotel's interiors had been designed by the Swiss wife of the hotel's general manager, Ajit Kerkar. She told me that this Swiss lady had made every suite reflect different Indian styles from different states. When our coffee arrived my friend broached the subject of the ticket for Sonia and Ms Panjabi's manner turned from friendly to frosty.

'If Mrs Sonia Gandhi wants to come to the show,' she said to me coldly, 'then she should get someone in her office to call my office.'

'She asked me as a friend,' I protested.

'Well, that is not the way to go about it. She should approach us directly.'

In the end Sonia did come to the show but I have never understood why Ms Panjabi reacted the way she did, unless it was because the Taj Group wanted to distance itself from Mrs Gandhi's family since it was no longer in power. Everyone else seemed to want to do the same. Mrs Gandhi and her family moved out of the prime minister's house into a much smaller one on Willingdon Crescent, and for a while it seemed as if Mrs Gandhi's political career was so totally at an end that talk of her retiring to a house in the hills began to spread. She herself cut a pathetic sort of figure by showing up at the most ordinary events where everyone was usually too intimidated to make polite conversation with her.

She took to calling up foreign correspondents to complain about how badly she was being treated by the new government. Had Morarji Desai been a better prime minister it is possible that Mrs Gandhi would have been relegated forever to history's dustbin. But he was not an impressive prime minister and his deputy, Chaudhary Charan Singh, was unwise enough to try and punish Mrs Gandhi for what came to be known as the 'excesses' of the Emergency, and so it did not take long for her to return to power.

The election that made her prime minister again in 1980 was won by Sanjay Gandhi. It was he who reinvented the Congress as a new kind of party. He filled it with a rough new breed of politicians who were abrasive and totally uninterested in India. Their reason for being in politics was quite simply to enjoy power and make easy money. They made no effort to hide this either. Political conversations with his lieutenants usually went like this.

'Why do you want to be in politics?'

'Obvious, yaar, for money and power.'

'To what end?'

'What do you mean to what end, yaar? Obviously because money and power are what the game is all about.'

'Do you have any political ideology?'

'Whatever is Sanjay's political ideology is mine too.'

'Does he have a political ideology?'

'You tell me...what do you think?'

'And an economic ideology?'

'Sure...'

Sanjay's friends benefited by using his name. Money was made in different ways. Some made it through commissions on international deals and some through connections with big business. One of his poorer friends became rich overnight because a prominent businessman told him to buy real estate in a particular part of Delhi where he knew the prices were soon going to rise. Sanjay's 'poor' friend followed the tip and quickly made a lot of money. So did many others. Men who barely had enough money to get by before coming into politics quickly rose to dizzying new heights. From eking out an existence in the squalid back lanes of Old Delhi, some of Sanjay's stormtroopers became rich and respectable and moved into large houses that they could not have dreamed of owning.

In the newsrooms we who remembered Sanjay's thuggish proclivities from Emergency times spent long hours discussing what was likely to happen to India now that this new kind of politician had taken over the country. We knew it was a defining moment in Indian history and that what defined it was that an older generation of political leaders who came into public life with the desire to do something for their country was gone for good. In the Congress those with memories of the freedom movement were replaced by Sanjay's cronies, men like Jagdish Tytler and H.K.L. Bhagat, who had risen to power from Delhi's rougher localities. Men capable of murder, mayhem and just about anything in the name of their political masters, as we were to find out after Mrs Gandhi was killed and Congress workers were incited to go out and butcher Sikhs.

Mrs Gandhi's time as prime minister has been described by her critics as two wasted decades and by her acolytes as a time when, in the words of her close friend Pupul Jayakar, 'India held her head high in the comity of nations.' Many Indians continue to believe that she was India's best prime minister, and many of them live in villages to which the benefits of her largesse never reached. I remember vividly a conversation I had with farmers in a Rajasthani village more than ten years after Mrs Gandhi was killed. We were in a roadside teashop drinking very sweet, very milky rural tea, and in the gathering were old men with withered faces and white turbans and young men who wore jeans and T-shirts. There was an election on, and after I asked them the usual questions about who was likely to win I asked who they thought was the best prime minister India had ever had.

'Indira Gandhi,' one of the older men said without hesitation. When I asked him why, he looked around at the other men, then down at his worn, dusty leather shoes before saying, 'She was a real ruler.'

'Did the village benefit when she was prime minister?'

'No.' This came in a chorus from the gathering.

'Do you have electricity, water?'

'No.'

'A good school? Is there a hospital nearby?'

'No. The children have to walk ten kilometres to go to school and many women lose their babies because by the time we get them to the hospital in Alwar it takes too long.'

'So what is it you liked so much about Indira Gandhi?'

Once more it was the old man who answered, 'She loved poor people. And she knew how to rule.'

Mrs Gandhi's great skill as a politician was that she succeeded in winning the support of high-born Indians and those not so high-born. If India's poorest citizens saw her as their champion, so did rich English-speaking Indians and high officials in Lutyens' Delhi. In all my years of political reporting I have never seen bureaucrats kowtow to a prime minister the way they did to her. Bureaucrats in her time were usually upper caste and upper class and often the children of men who had served the British Raj in the Indian Civil Service, and Mrs Gandhi was exactly their kind of leader. She spoke English, presented herself elegantly and intelligibly in the forums of the world, and unlike most other Indian leaders of that time was well educated and well versed in European ways. She read books by foreign writers, spoke French and seemed always ready to defend India's interests.

So how did it matter that in her time most Indians remained as poor and illiterate as they were when she became prime minister? How did it matter that it was in her time that China under Deng Xiao Ping became a capitalist country and soon overtook India in almost every way? How did it matter that small Southeast Asian countries that had begun their journey towards becoming modern nations at the same time as India had gone ahead in winning the war against poverty? None of these things seemed to matter to Indians who worshipped Mrs Gandhi, and they were many more than those who saw her legacy as one that had kept a country with the potential to count among the richest in the world very, very poor.

Indira's legacy was dynastic democracy, serious political problems in Kashmir and Punjab and an economy run by officials who were mostly incompetent except when it came to creating reams and reams of red tape. India was almost an economic basket case when Indira's rule ended horribly with her assassination in October 1984. The wave of sympathy, as it was called by most political commentators, swept her son to power in the election that came in December that year with the largest majority in Indian parliamentary history.

17

LAVASA

For me the farce of Dr Manmohan Singh being India's prime minister and his total powerlessness became tragically obvious when Ajit went to see him to seek his intervention after Lavasa was closed down. 'He apologized to me,' Ajit said when he came home. 'He said it should never have happened and that he was sorry. Then he called Jairam Ramesh and told him that he should allow construction to continue. He did that in front of me.' When months went by and nothing happened Ajit went back to see the prime minister and told him that Jairam Ramesh had been telling people that he could do nothing because 'he had orders from above'. Dr Manmohan Singh tried once more to rectify the wrong that had been done but failed. Personally, I did not need proof that he was prime minister in name only but it came anyway in what happened to Lavasa.

The story of Lavasa began, at least for me, when we were in Italy in the summer of 2003. We were there for a wedding in Turin when Ajit asked me if I had ever been to Portofino. I said I had not but had heard that Positano, where I had not been either, was more beautiful. 'Well, we are going to Portofino,' he said firmly, 'because I am planning to build a city in the hills near Pune and it will be built around a lake, so I want to see what we can learn from Portofino, which is built around a water body.'

So we went to Portofino. It was more beautiful than its pictures. I remember that we drove on a highway through flat countryside and that I fell asleep and when I woke found myself in a landscape of soft hills. There were whitewashed villas on the hills, and I was still staring at them when the car turned downwards on to a sloping road and before us lay the emerald and turquoise waters of the Mediterranean. The road led to a picture postcard harbour that had restaurants, cafes, fancy shops and buildings painted in rust, yellow ochre, brown and terracotta. We were only there for a few hours but there was time to eat a lunch of freshly caught fish in a sunlit restaurant on the edge of the sea. Afterwards we walked along cobbled streets in the harbour and bought souvenirs in small, brightly lit shops.

When we came back to India I forgot about Ajit's plans to build a city until he first took me to Lavasa. It was then no more than a lodge on a high cliff that offered from its small garden and glass-walled dining room a spectacular view of a valley at the bottom of which glistened a large lake. In one room of the lodge, surrounded by computers and maps, stood the model of the city that Ajit planned to build. I am not good at reading models or maps and glanced at the model only briefly as Ajit told me that the city would be built in phases. It was only when he said that by the time Lavasa was finished it would be a city with a footprint the size of Paris that I was startled into paying close attention. 'It will not just be a place where people buy holiday homes but a proper city that I hope will one day become a great centre of education.'

He told me that Lausanne's famous hotel management school had already agreed to open a branch here and that he was talking to Oxford to see if they might open a business school here. He talked to Sri Sri Ravi Shankar and Sadguru Jaggi Vausdev to see if they could set up ashrams in Lavasa and talked of setting up a Centre for Indian Classical Studies. And there were talks with Bollywood people for setting up new studios and a film school.

Ajit said Lavasa would be the first new city to be built in India after Chandigarh and that he intended it to be a model for sustainable urban development. In the next five or six years I saw it grow. Hotels came up and villas and apartments in buildings that had been copied from pictures of Portofino. They were even called Portofino apartments. I saw restaurants and shops being built below the apartments, and increasingly the waterfront looked more and more like Portofino. There were critics who said that Ajit should have copied an Indian waterfront city, like Benares, and not a European one, but his market researchers found that aspirational middle class Indians were more enamoured by foreign cities than our own ancient ones.

Every time I went to Lavasa it seemed to grow and expand. A town hall came up in a fine yellow-washed building that overlooked the lake and near it a school for the children of workers building the city. It was the second Christel House School to be set up in India by an American woman called Christel DeHaan, who had made it her mission to try and give underprivileged children the best possible education. Christel DeHaan opened her first school in Bangalore, and at about the time she opened her second one in Lavasa the Bangalore school had its first high school graduates. Four of them got into Stanford University on full scholarships.

Ajit was very taken by the idea of turning Lavasa into an educational centre not just for privileged children but for the children of the construction workers who were building the city. And it was with this idea that he invited Christel DeHaan to open her second school in Lavasa. From the time I first met Ajit I had noticed his obsession with urban planning, so Lavasa was not just another project for his construction company – it was the ultimate project. The dream.

An American city manager was appointed to take care of municipal needs because Ajit believed it was possible for Indian cities to be run professionally in the manner of American cities. Buyers from Mumbai and Pune lined up to buy apartments and villas, and Ajit was more excited by this project than I had seen him in all the years we had been together. Personally, I thought he was mad to take on a project of this size but sustainable urbanization was a passion with him, and he was convinced that unless India started building new cities we would end up as a country of slums. 'By 2050, 400 million Indians are expected to move from villages to towns...unless cities get built in a planned manner, urban India will look like one big slum,' he would tell me.

Judging by what Sonia Gandhi did to Lavasa and judging by her ten-year rule, her vision for India was the opposite. It was a vision in which cities would look like slums and villages remain mired in desperate, degrading poverty so that she could bestow upon them largesse in the name of one or other member of her family. If she had a political ideology it was democratic feudalism that was in truth feudalism disguised as democracy. This peculiarly Indian political system can survive only if India's voters remain eternally poor, illiterate and ready to vote forever in feudal fashion. It is not an accident that nearly every former princely family has found its way into electoral politics.

Lavasa represents the opposite of feudal India. It represents an India in which voters are middle class enough to want to buy a small apartment in the hills as a second home. Was it because Lavasa was such an eyesore in Sonia's vision of

India that she did her best to close it down? If it had been this grand political reason it may even have been easier to forgive the damage that she did to the thousands of villagers who were part of the Lavasa project. It would not have been possible to begin building the city unless eighteen villages in the Lavasa area had not willingly participated in Ajit's dream project. But Sonia appears to have not thought of them but only of how she could put her old bête noir Sharad Pawar in his place and in the process me. If Ajit had to be destroyed too, well, so be it. She appears never to have forgiven Pawar for raising the issue of her Italian birth. And I was one of a small handful of journalists who had consistently opposed the idea of India having an Italian prime minister. We had to be punished.

Sonia must have looked really hard for reasons to destroy Lavasa and come up with none because there was environmental enhancement rather than damage and the land was not a gift from the Government of Maharashtra, as Medha Patkar and her gang of activists alleged. The land was not acquired. It was bought slowly over a period of time, with villagers cooperating in the process because of the prosperity that Lavasa brought to their lives. Before Ajit's company built the road that led to the city, the people who lived in the remote hill villages that circled the lake subsisted on a primitive economy. They burned the scrub that grew on hilltops that were already severely denuded. When the fires made terrified animals flee downwards to their villages, they killed them and then walked miles to sell their hides and meat. Lavasa transformed their lives, but as always happens, there were a few disgruntled local people who believed that they had not got enough money for their land. It was to these that Medha Patkar turned in her efforts to prove that Lavasa was depriving 'the poor' of their rights.

Having watched Ms Patkar's activities carefully from the time I first saw her standing knee deep in the Narmada river to protest against the dam that made her famous, I had felt that her activism was spurious and self-serving. Even in those early days when the Narmada movement made her an international celebrity, I found her hysterics worrying. That day on the banks of the Narmada when I first saw her, I remember thinking that there was something contrived about her straggly hair, her crumpled blouse with its sweat stains under the armpits and her cheap cotton sari.

She stood among a group of truly poor villagers who were dressed this way out of necessity, not radical chic, and I found it offensive that she tried to seem as poor and underprivileged as them. Later when I discovered that she worked strenuously to persuade a small handful of people ousted by the dam to refuse the compensation they were being given, I knew that she was a professional agitator.

Once the dam was built and the Narmada movement faded from public memory, so did Ms Patkar. To me it seemed as if to remain in the public eye she became a rebel for any old cause. One moment she could be seen protesting against slum clearance in a Mumbai suburb, and the very next she would appear in a village in Orissa, inciting Adivasi villagers to protest against a project that may have lifted them out of grinding poverty. Somehow there were always reporters and cameramen following in Ms Patkar's unkempt wake, and somehow they never asked her embarrassing questions.

Whenever I tried, and try I did, to question her methods, causes or financing in my columns, the response was usually a tirade of abuse and accusation. Over the years I discovered that I would always find myself on the other side of the causes that Ms Patkar supported because I noticed that in her efforts to speak for 'the poor' she ended up harming their interests.

This is what she did in Lavasa. Out of thousands of villagers whose lives were transformed for the better by Ajit's efforts to build a city that created thousands of jobs where there were none, Ms Patkar sought out a handful of disgruntled farmers and helped them make a case in court. It was by using this case that Jairam Ramesh, more Sonia Gandhi's hatchet man than environment minister, ordered construction in Lavasa to stop in November 2010. He had no environmental reason to stop it since Ajit had reforested denuded hills by planting more than 600,000 trees and built a city where it was possible to walk everywhere and in which all the water was reused, so he used a jurisdictional excuse to close it down.

The Maharashtra government had jurisdiction to grant Ajit's company permission to build a city in the Sahyadri hills on the condition that no structure be built at a height of more than 800 metres from sea level. This rule was assiduously followed, except in the case of one structure. This was the main symbolic gate that led to Lavasa – a stone arch on the main road that Ajit had built to the city. This gave Sonia's hatchet man an excuse to stop construction in Lavasa on jurisdictional grounds.

News of the notice came to me in an odd way. I was about to leave for Jodhpur in November 2010 for the wedding of Yuvraj Shivraj Singh. His parents are old friends of mine, and I had watched Shivraj grow from a plump little boy in the 1970s to the handsomest of all Indian princes. And then the gods got jealous. In 2005 he had a polo accident that caused severe head injuries and put him in a coma for several weeks in Bombay Hospital. It was a miracle that he survived at all and an even greater one that he was now well enough to get married.

Before leaving for Jodhpur I dropped by Vasundhara Raje's house in Delhi and ran into her son, Dushyant, who had just returned from Parliament with a piece of gossip he picked up in Central Hall. He said, 'I heard from some Congress people that there is a plan to target Ajit Uncle.'

'Target him? How?'

'I am not sure but you need to tell him to be careful and don't tell him anything on the telephone.'

I took the information seriously and imagined that there would be a tax raid or something like it. I did not tell Ajit anything on the phone because I knew from past experience that my phone had sometimes been tapped. So I resolved to tell him nothing until I saw him in Jodhpur. He was meant to arrive from Bombay on the evening that Shivraj's baraat was going to leave for Jaipur. But there was no sign of him as the baraat left. We watched from a high, trellised balcony as Shivraj in an ajkan of gold brocade and a turban of gold tissue stepped into Bapji and Hemlata's private courtyard in Umaid Bhavan and left in a vintage Jaguar of deep blue that had a red licence plate with Jodhpur 1 written on it. His clansmen walked beside the car as it moved slowly out of the courtyard into the gardens of the palace. And we ladies on our balcony rushed to the other side to watch the procession of magnificently attired princes who accompanied the car to the gates of Umaid Bhavan. It was a ceremony of such timeless grandeur that it made me very irritated that Ajit should have missed it.

After the baraat left I went with the ladies of the house to the entrance of the palace, where we waited for the procession of princes to return for the evening's feasting and festivity. To my surprise it was in this procession of bejewelled and turbaned maharajas that I found Ajit walking alongside Bapji Jodhpur, looking very pleased with himself. I asked how he had been included in this parade of maharajas, and he laughed and said that Bapji had spotted him when he arrived and brought him along.

The wedding was among the grandest I have ever attended. As someone who had memories of Umaid Bhavan from the 1970s when it was a place of empty rooms, dark corridors and decaying elegance, it was wonderful to see it luminous with so much happiness and hope. There was a sadness that tinged the festivities because almost nobody except his closest family members got to see the groom. The accident had left him with disabilities that made him embarrassed to be seen too much in public. He had speech problems and problems walking, and so it was without him that we watched concerts in the high courtyards of the Mehrangarh Fort and without him that we partied till dawn in the gardens of Umaid Bhavan. But having seen Bapji and Hemlata through those grim weeks in Bombay Hospital when nobody was sure if Shivraj would survive his injuries, I shared deeply in their happiness. It was in a mood of great good cheer that Ajit and I returned to our home by the sea in Kihim village.

Then came the news about Lavasa. It was from Aatish that I first heard it. He called to ask if I was watching the news on TV, and when I said that I was not he said, 'They are saying that construction in Lavasa has been stopped by the environment ministry.' When I turned on the television I saw that the news was much worse than even that. Every news channel was reporting that Jairam Ramesh had ordered the Lavasa Corporation to show cause why the city should not be demolished for violating environmental permissions.

Bahar Dutt (Barkha's less famous sister) stood beside Jairam Ramesh with a copy of the show-cause notice in her hands. Of course she did not ask the minister why he had taken such a drastic decision. Or why it had taken the environment ministry nearly a decade to discover that Lavasa was being built in violation of jurisdictional rules. Bahar was not alone in her lack of fundamental curiosity.

No environmental journalist asked this most vital question even once in the days that followed. They were such devotees of Jairam Ramesh's activism that they acted as cheerleaders every time he closed down some project. They never even asked why his supposed concern for the environment was confined to closing down big projects instead of trying to clean India's rivers or the air of her cities.

When I called Ajit to tell him what I was seeing on television, he said he had not heard the news and then followed a moment of stunned silence before he put the phone down. When he and his team saw that the notice ordered demolition of Lavasa and not just a halting of construction activity, they were forced to go to court against the environment ministry. Jairam Ramesh's officials immediately backtracked and said that the demolition order was a 'clerical error' but this did not change anything. Construction remained halted even after an environmental assessment committee visited Lavasa and declared publicly that the only environmental damage was that some generators were wrongly placed. Medha Patkar and her ilk kept up their campaign of vilification and were given lots of airtime in which Ms Patkar lied about farmers' land being forcibly taken from them at the behest of Sharad Pawar. Ms Patkar's lies found their way into a story in the *Sunday Times*, London. Ajit sued them and won. The *Sunday Times* apologized publicly and paid damages that were donated to the Christel House school.

Since these so-called environmentalists had the media on their side, what he said made no difference. Lavasa Corporation told its side of the story in detailed full-page advertisements in newspapers, in which they refuted every false charge, including one that claimed Lavasa was 'stealing' Pune's water. Ajit pointed out more than once that Pune had the highest consumption of water per capita of any city in the world and that Lavasa had the least, but it made no difference.

In the days, months and years that followed, I kept waiting for at least one environmental journalist to actually visit Lavasa to see who was telling the truth, but this never happened. The exception was Madhu Kishwar, who went to Lavasa and wrote in *India Today* and *Manushi* that the government's action was mala fide. In Davos some months after construction in Lavasa was stopped, Prannoy and Radhika Roy, Shekhar Gupta, Ajit and I happened to have breakfast together in the sunlit dining room of the Central Sport Hotel. Ajit explained to Prannoy in detail what had happened and I remember Shekhar backing him up and saying that Jairam's actions were as bad as anything 'Beria had done'. Prannoy listened and took notes, but NDTV never did a story and nor did the *Express*.

Arun Shourie was the city's first permanent citizen. He bought two villas and linked them together and moved his family there even before the city was fully ready for permanent residents. His wife Anita had severe Parkinson's disease that worsened in cold weather, so he needed a place to take her when Delhi's winter months began. Since Ajit and he had known each other even before I met Ajit, he decided that Lavasa was where he was going to build his second home.

Some months after he moved in and started writing a new book, Anita's sister Manju and her husband Suman Dubey came to stay with them. Arun told us how much they loved the place and how Sumi had spent his entire time taking pictures. But when weeks after they returned to Delhi came the notice from the environment ministry, it seemed as if they were on a mission from Sonia. Sumi and Manju have been close friends of Rajiv and Sonia Gandhi since long before either of them began political careers. Did Sonia look at Sumi's pictures and decide that she had found her weapon? I do not know.

But because I sensed that something like this may have come to pass and because nobody else took up the cause of Lavasa, I wrote in my column about what had happened. And this caused a minor furore in Delhi's drawing rooms. Sumi took to maligning me in every drawing room he went to, and he went to many. He did more. He rang Shekhar Gupta and told him that he should shut my column down. I heard this not from Shekhar, who kept completely silent about this until he left the *Express*. I heard from friends whom Sumi talked to. He liked to boast about his power and told them in so many words that he had warned Shekhar that he should close my column down or else, and that Shekhar had said that the column was too popular for him to close down.

It was only much later, after Sonia Gandhi's Congress was reduced to forty-four seats in the Lok Sabha, that some of her ministers told me what really happened. They requested anonymity, so I am not going to identify them, but the conversations they had with their leader went something like this:

'Have you seen what that woman writes about me? Why can't we do something about her?'

'Yes, madam. But what?'

'Well, she is living in sin with Ajit Gulabchand and he is building an illegal city in the Western Ghats. Surely we can stop that?'

'Yes, madam.'

It is never possible to verify the truth of these things. But whatever her reasons may have been to target Lavasa and try to destroy it, what is true is that in doing what she did she ignored India's interests. India needs at least 500 new cities to accommodate the 400 million people who are expected to move out of their villages in the next thirty years. When under sustained pressure from the prime minister she was forced to agree to move Jairam Ramesh out of the environment ministry, she chose once more to appoint someone she believed would be completely loyal to her. Jayanthi Natarajan. If there are still people who believe she had nothing to do with the running of the governments she appointed, then here is one more example of how powerful and controlling she was.

Jayanthi knew that she was appointed only to continue doing what Jairam had been doing but her hand was forced by the Bombay High Court to allow construction to start again in Lavasa. By then the damage done was so fundamental that Ajit was no longer able to refinance the project. So unless he somehow succeeds in rectifying the damage done, Lavasa could end up being just another suburb of Pune and Ajit's dreams of sustainable urbanization will soon be forgotten. The irony is that Lavasa won international awards for its development model and for what it did to restore and preserve the environmental sanctity of the hills in which it is built. Ajit gathered environmentalists from all over the world to discuss the kind of trees that needed to be planted and to find ways of constructing that would keep bio-mimicry in mind at all times. Had it not been for Sonia's vengeful act, India may today have had its first post-modern city.

18

SUREKHA'S BABIES

Surekha got pregnant within months of getting married. I learned that she was pregnant after finding out that she had got married. Marriages for people who live on the footpaths of Mumbai are not celebrated, just as deaths are not mourned. Grinding, relentless poverty makes such ceremonies unaffordable. So one day the child Surekha that I had known since she was a girl of ten was Surekha the married lady. She seemed to love the accoutrements of being married and took instantly to wearing earrings and necklaces and anklets on her feet. And she loved wearing shiny saris like a newly married lady.

Surekha's first son was born in a rundown government hospital. He did not live for more than a few hours. The doctors later said that the baby was born with a genetic defect. Surekha said she had seen him alive and that he seemed perfectly healthy to her. She blamed the doctors for killing him and when she got pregnant again barely nine months later asked if I could pay for her to go to a private hospital this time. She had already found a gynaecologist in Bombay Hospital but could not afford to pay for the baby to be delivered there.

When I asked her if she had told the doctor that her first baby was born with a genetic blood disease, she said that she had not because it was not true. 'It was the fault of the doctors,' she said. 'The baby was fine. I know he was fine because I saw him and even fed him. There was nothing wrong with him.'

'But the doctor should be told. If you are not going to then I will. Give me her number.'

'All right,' she said reluctantly, 'but I don't want her to think there is anything wrong with me or the baby.'

'I will make sure.'

So I called the doctor. She was a nice woman who was sympathetic when I explained in detail the conditions in which Surekha lived and how she had already lost a son just the year before. She said she had examined Surekha and was sure that there was nothing wrong with the baby but Surekha was anaemic and needed some tonics. We bought these and I tried to make sure that Surekha ate well during her pregnancy. When the time came for the baby to be born there were no beds available in the general ward of Bombay Hospital, so I paid for her to be in a private room.

The nurses on duty in the private ward gawped when they saw that one of their patients was a woman who lived 'on the footpath', and when they kept asking her about this it impressed me that Surekha handled their questions with dignity. 'So where do you live?' they asked with prurient curiosity over and over again.

'On the footpath,' she said firmly.

'But what do you mean by that...do you mean you really live on the footpath?'

'Yes. I live on the footpath.'

'And your family?'

'They live on the footpath too. I was born on the footpath.'

'But where will you take the baby when you leave?'

'He will live with me there.'

'Will he be all right?'

'Other babies live there too.'

I was present when this conversation took place and when I saw how small the baby was asked the doctor if there was some way to keep Surekha in the hospital a few days longer to give the baby a better chance to survive. She gave me a sympathetic smile but said that the shortage of beds was so severe that she could not keep Surekha in the hospital longer than three days. 'He should be fine,' she added, 'because he is a perfectly healthy child.'

'He is very small, isn't he, to be living on a footpath?'

'Yes. But I think he will be able to survive.'

So Surekha was discharged three days after the baby was born. I brought her back to her home on the pavement behind the Air India building and bought the baby all the things I thought he needed – bottles, a blanket, a mosquito net, a small mattress and some clothes. I told her she must make sure that all he was fed for the first few weeks was breast milk because this would help him grow stronger, and I checked up on him whenever I could. I told her husband how important it was for the baby to be kept in as clean an atmosphere as possible. But how clean can life be for those who live on the footpaths of Mumbai? He was born on one of those hot, steamy days that come when the rains go away.

One day when I went by I noticed that he was lying at the edge of the pavement near the Indian Express building and that there was so much traffic rattling by that he would have inhaled unhealthy petrol and diesel fumes. I told Surekha to take him into the car park away from the traffic but knew that my advice was stupid, because like the other women in the community she had to make a living by making jasmine garlands to sell in the evenings at traffic lights. She had to keep her baby with her. So inevitably early one morning, some weeks later, I was woken by the security guard in my building to be told that there were some 'poor people' waiting to see me outside the gates. When I came down I found Surekha in floods of tears, with her husband carrying the baby's tiny body wrapped in a grimy cloth. They needed money to pay for him to be cremated.

When she recovered from the loss of her second son, I told her that she must not get pregnant until she was stronger and until we could find her a room in a slum where she could take the baby for at least the first few months of his life. She and her husband did not listen to my advice and she was pregnant again within weeks. With some difficulty I found her a room in a slum in Colaba, not far from where her family lived, for Rs 2,500 a month. The slumlord was a skinny young man who insisted that he meet me personally before giving her the room because he was afraid that she would run away without paying her dues. He insisted that I pay a security deposit and a year's rent in advance.

This time I did not arrange for her to go to a private doctor because she said that she was sure that she would be better off in a government hospital. I am not sure why she chose not to go back to Bombay Hospital but think it could have been because she did not like the way she was treated as some kind of freak by the nurses. In any case I was not in Bombay when the baby came but got a call from her husband saying that she was in 'Sanjay Gandhi hospital'. When I tried to find out where this was I discovered that the hospital was an old British municipal hospital called St George's Hospital. It is a massive, rambling Victorian building set in gardens that must once have been quite beautiful but are now overgrown with weeds and wild grass. It was raining the day I went to see her, and in the high-ceilinged, cavernous reception area there were muddy stains on the floor and the smell of wet clothes.

To get to the maternity ward in which Surekha was, I walked down endless passages that reeked of toilets and antiseptic and past wards bursting with patients. The young doctors who tended the sick looked harassed and sleepless, and I found myself wondering for the nth time why the Indian state had not been able to provide such basic things as decent public healthcare. Whenever I have asked politicians this question they have given me a standard answer: we cannot afford to create facilities that are too clean for ordinary people. It has always sounded to me like a bad excuse for abdicating their responsibilities.

I found Surekha in a ward full of women with newborn babies by their side. She was sitting up in bed and eating dal-roti out of a steel bowl. 'I don't like the hospital food,' she explained with a smile, 'so I got some from home.'

'Home?'

'My mother is a very good cook.'

'But when you leave from here you are going to the room that we got for you. Right? The baby must spend his first year under a proper roof.'

'Yes. I will be very careful this time.'

So until the writing of this book Rajveer has survived. He is smaller than he should be for his age but has big eyes and a sweet face. When he was two years old he had to be hospitalized due to an illness that the doctors said was caused by malnutrition. When I asked Surekha what she fed him she said he ate what they did, which was a diet that did not include milk or vegetables.

So I started Nashta again to feed the children of the

children that the programme originally fed. Along with Surekha's little son come other children from this small street community and the children of her sister Roopa. Nashta now functions without Ali. The children are fed by street vendors who have their stalls not far from the car park in which they live.

While researching this book I spent many hours talking to Roopa, who is ten years older than Surekha. She was already married and having babies when I first started walking Julie on Marine Drive, and all her five babies were born on the pavement. 'My mother knows how these things are done,' she said. 'All the older women know how to bring a baby into the world.' Roopa has memories of her own childhood that was so difficult that whenever I have asked her to tell me what it was like she begins to cry.

'In those days we were always hungry. That is what I remember most…'

'But today the children have enough to eat, don't they?'

'Yes. Today food is not a problem because there are people who help us and children can go to the church to eat, but when I was a child we had to go to sleep hungry if we didn't earn anything during the day.'

'From begging?'

'From whatever we could do…if we brought no money then we got no food.'

'Do you blame your parents?'

'No. Their own lives are so hard, how can we blame them?'

'Do you have any happy memories of your childhood?'

'One or two…like when they took us to a fair or to see a movie.'

'In the cinema?'

'Not in the cinema but on TV in the slum in Colaba where my mother's sister has a jhuggi.'

'Is life easier for your children today?'

'Yes. My two boys are in a boarding school in Ahmednagar, and some Christian people are paying for this.'

'Do they have to go to church?'

'They do but they are Hindus. Nobody is forcing them to become Christian...'

'Did you ever go to school?'

'They put me in a school in Sholapur when I was about ten but it was a terrible place. They used to beat me up because I couldn't plait my hair properly, and then a child died and my parents brought me back to Mumbai, and after that I never went to school again.'

Roopa's husband has developed problems in his spine and can no longer work at construction sites, so Roopa is the family bread earner. She manages to get temporary jobs as a cleaning woman in offices, but these do not last more than a few months because her employers are suspicious of people who live in the streets.

People who live in Mumbai's streets spend their whole time trying to lift themselves out of poverty with an entrepreneurial spirit that never ceases to amaze me. They devise ideas for small businesses, they try to get menial jobs, they team up with scrap dealers to sell them anything worthwhile they find in garbage dumps, and if nothing else works they beg, borrow and steal. But the people I have come to know well try as much as possible to make an honest living. Surekha turned up one morning at my doorstep with that smile she always has when she thinks she has come up with a brilliant new idea.

'Can you pay for my husband to learn how to drive?' she asked.

'Yes. But for what?'

'I could try and get a job at the taxi stand,' her husband said. It was almost the first time I had heard him speak. He is a tall, thin man with a face that seems too small for his body. Like Surekha he has grown up on the streets of Mumbai, and like her he always has some new venture that he wants me to invest in.

'If he learns to drive and gets a job driving a taxi,' Surekha added, 'then we won't have to live on the footpath any more.'

'True,' I said. 'So do you know where he can learn?'

'Yes. There is a driving school in Colaba. And can my brother also learn?'

'Yes. Why not.'

By the time they took me to the Good Luck Driving School, I had agreed to pay for four young men to learn how to drive. The Good Luck Driving School operates out of a tiny room that seemed smaller that morning because of the number of tables crowded into it. Young men sat at these tables taking down details of those enlisting for driving lessons. When it was our turn it was a young man called Husain who started writing down the details of the young men who came with me.

'Name?'

'All four of these men will be taking lessons,' I replied.

'All right. So I will need all their names.'

'OK.'

'And their age.'

'OK...tell him,' I said to the young men and they did.

'Birth certificates.'

'They don't have birth certificates,' I said. 'They live on the footpath.'

'We can get them from Sholapur,' one of them said. 'Don't worry.'

'But if they live on the footpath...they will not get driving licences,' Husain said, putting his pen down and looking at the four young men with new eyes. I think it may have been the first time that people this poor had shown up for driving lessons.

'Why?' I asked.

'Because although we have no problems in giving them driving lessons, they will have a problem getting a licence from the transport department. You have to have a fixed address to get a licence.'

'We will deal with that when they have learned to drive,' I said, thinking that I could pull a string or two to help overcome this new obstacle.

So Surekha's husband and her brothers spent the next few weeks driving around in a car that had Good Luck written on it in bold letters. They smiled and waved cheerfully every time they saw me walking Julie on Marine Drive. Once they learned to drive they were very hopeful that they would be able to get proper jobs. But as Husain had predicted, the transport department refused to give them licences. I spent many days arguing with lowly clerks and high officials in foul-smelling government offices but to no avail. Finally, I tried to get through to the MP from South Mumbai, Milind Deora, for help.

Ajit had known him since he was a boy and called him to ask if he could do anything. It transpired that the transport department was more powerful than him, and in those times of jihadi terrorism no official wanted to take the risk of giving driving licences to people who lived in the streets. So another chance of them being able to lift themselves out of poverty vanished into Mumbai's diesel-scented air. The officials I talked to told me that I was wasting my time anyway, because even if they got licences which person in their right mind would hire a driver who had no fixed address. Surekha's husband and brothers have remained confined to making Rs 100 a day parking cars in the car park in which they live. There is no hope of their earning more than this and no hope of their being able to fulfil their dream of one day having a home of their own.

19

HEREDITARY DEMOCRACY

Sanjay died within months of his greatest political success. The dust of the general election that he won spectacularly for the Congress in 1980 had not yet settled and he was gone. The *Economist* said he died as he had lived: breaking the rules. And rules he must have been breaking when he took his little red flying club aeroplane into acrobatics and dives that brought him low over the trees of Delhi on that very hot June morning. When he died he seemed to take with him that force that made his mother such a formidable political leader. I met her months after his death in the palace of Sheikha Fatima in Abu Dhabi, and she seemed diminished somehow and an aura of deep sadness surrounded her. Mrs Gandhi wore a simple black sari and talked politely to everyone who talked to her, but it was as if she were merely going through the motions of being alive. When I came back to Delhi I heard on the Lutyens' grapevine that the only thing that cheered her up was Sanjay's small son, Feroze Varun, with whom she spent as much time as she could. I also heard that Rajiv was going to be brought into politics to replace his brother.

The news surprised me because from what I knew of him he was not just apolitical but not even the sort of person who had ever shown an interest in political events or political ideas. In the drawing rooms in which I met him, many times in the long months of his mother's Emergency, political conversations were forbidden because his friends thought it would upset him to know that people were saying bad things about his mother. When the Emergency ended I took my chances and catching him almost alone one evening asked what he thought of the Emergency. He said with a smile that he was relieved that someone had finally asked him this question and admitted that he had disapproved of it and told his mother this, but she had mocked him for getting his ideas from his 'elitist' friends. This conversation led inevitably to other political conversations in which I discovered that he blamed his brother for the 1977 loss and that he did not like his brother's kind of politics. I believe that was the extent of his political knowledge.

Rajiv's friends were all children of privilege and nearly all from the Doon School. The exception was Satish Sharma, who came from lower down the class order and who may never have been in a Delhi drawing room if he had not befriended Rajiv in the days when he was a pilot for Indian Airlines. He was a dull man who never had anything to say and who spent his time in Delhi's most exclusive drawing rooms drinking quietly in a corner. He usually came with Rajiv and Sonia and with his blonde Belgian wife in tow. She spent her time talking to Sonia at these gatherings. Sonia was so reserved that she talked to almost nobody and spent most evenings clutching Rajiv's hand and smiling nervously. The only time I saw her chatty and animated was if she were talking to a European friend. In those early months after Sanjay's death if someone had told me that Rajiv was going to become India's prime minister and Satish the minister for civil aviation, I would have laughed.

Not even the most astute astrologer could have read in the

stars then that Rajiv would win the biggest mandate in Indian parliamentary history and that he would usher in an era in Indian politics in which many, many children of privilege would take charge of ruling India. If Sanjay's most memorable contribution to Indian politics was the introduction of a thuggish new kind of politician, his brother's was to do the opposite. A privileged, arrogant kind of person was suddenly to be seen floating about Delhi's corridors of power to the astonishment of the elected representatives of the people of India who wore humble khadi and dirty slippers to identify with the 'common man'. Rajiv's friends gave up Western attire for khadi as well, but their kurtas were cut by the finest tailors and on their feet could be spotted Gucci loafers or, when mingling with the masses, expensive trainers. From inside the breast pockets of their khadi kurtas usually peeped a Mont Blanc pen or two, and on their wrists, in close emulation of their leader, could usually be seen a gold Rolex watch.

The other kind of person that Rajiv brought into politics was the bimbo. There was a romance attached to India having a handsome young prime minister, and this lured glamorous, empty-headed socialites into politics on a scale never seen before. They were women whose only reason for harbouring political ambitions usually was that they had a father, husband or father-in-law who had been a Congress politician. Among the ladies who abandoned drawing rooms and lives of luxurious boredom for 'public service' were actresses like Moon Moon Sen and Nafisa Ali. Politically well-connected beauties like Kiran Chaudhury and Uma Gajapati Raju and friends from Welham School who had married into princely or political families. And of not one could it be said that they had a coherent political idea in their heads. Rajiv was their inspiration was all they could say if asked their reason for wanting to suddenly mingle with the masses.

South Indian socialites who Rajiv lured into the Rajya Sabha were often better educated and more serious, but again their motive for being in public life was Rajiv. If any of these new women politicians so much as met him for five minutes, every drawing room in Delhi heard about it in seconds. 'He notices every detail,' a beauteous socialite once told me.

'Oh!'

'After I saw him in the morning I went for a manicure, and when I saw him later that day he noticed that I had changed the colour of my nail polish.'

'Wow!'

'So why do you want to be in politics?'

'Because it's such fun being in Parliament...it makes you feel so special.'

'So where would you like to contest from?'

'My father-in-law is arranging for a seat. You know he has been chief minister twice?'

'Yes.'

'And Rajivji is very keen to bring me into politics. He said that India needs younger, educated people to come into public life.'

India did. Sadly not the kind of people Rajiv brought in even if the lady I had this conversation with went on to become a minister in a state government. She had an indulgent husband who seemed not to notice her dangerous liaisons with other politicians, and like most of the other people who entered public life in Rajiv's time her main contribution was to bring her daughter into politics as soon as she was old enough. The seeds of hereditary democracy, planted by Rajiv's mother during the Emergency, began to flower in her son's time.

Since Rajiv was himself a political heir he had no problem with hereditary democracy. In fairness to him nobody else in India seemed to mind much either, because whenever the relative of a well-known political leader contested an election, he or she usually won. It did not seem to matter to the 'people' either that most of those who began political careers in Rajiv's time were motivated by self-interest and not public service or that they were nearly all children of privilege with no idea at all of the country in which they lived.

Like Rajiv their India was limited to the cocoon in which they had spent their lives. Like Rajiv they had nearly always been to the Doon School and gone on to Cambridge or Oxford, and like him they were among a tiny handful of Indians who had seen other countries and seen how good they looked compared to their own. But they had never connected this to the abysmal standards of their own country. What was extraordinary about them was their inability to ever imagine that India could and should be rich and prosperous. Among this new breed of politicians I counted many friends, and whenever I asked them what they would like to do for India the answer I usually got was 'whatever Rajiv wants'.

There were perks that came with public life and they quickly discovered them. In those deeply socialist times when the state was all-powerful, access to political power was paramount. The licence raj was in full force, so even the scions of big industrial houses were forced to crawl through the murky, smelly corridors of Delhi's 'bhavans' to beg for licences. The clever ones soon realized that it was easier to get their work done by cultivating Rajiv's friends.

Sonia had her own circle of friends who liked to boast behind her back about how they were helping her fit into her new role as India's first lady. In the years I had known her I had always seen her in Western clothes, but as the wife of the Prime Minister of India she appeared to see the importance of changing her attire. Friends advised her on the kind of saris she should wear and sometimes helped her buy them.

Friends claimed that they helped her organize intimate dinner parties in the prime minister's house. They arranged flowers and made up menus. No sooner did they leave 7 Race Course Road than they would start boasting of how intimately they knew Sonia and how great her skills as a hostess were.

'Darling, you cannot imagine how impressed Mr Cardin was by the way the table was laid...and the food. It came in courses, not the usual everything-on-the-table Indian way of serving.'

'Really?'

'And the prawns were beyond delicious...and Sonia's sari so tasteful. She gets her saris specially made by Asha Sarabhai, you know.' There was, of course, more to being a gatekeeper and this soon became obvious. In Delhi's drawing rooms businessmen from Mumbai (Bombay then) openly discussed which friend of Rajiv they should cultivate to get a licence.

In the 1980s a majority of Indians lived in villages, and these villages were places of despair and desperate poverty and not hope. Usually the village consisted of one small shop that sold boiled sweets in big glass jars, hair oil in gaudy bottles, cheap combs, Cinthol talcum powder and Lifebuoy soap. It was not till the middle of Rajiv's term as prime minister that more sophisticated consumer goods like shampoo and face cream came to rural India in small sachets that cost Rs 2.

It was a bleak socialist time. Everyone dreamed of getting a government job. Everyone. The richest Indians had a standard of living that was not much higher than that of middle class people in London and New York. Almost every young man I knew took the civil service examinations. Only if they failed to make it into some government service did they consider private sector options, and the reason for this was that a government job ensured a roof over your head and the guarantee of a permanent job. It was for exactly this reason that wherever I travelled in the wilds of rural India I met people whose only dream was to one day get a 'sarkari naukri' – a government job.

Government jobs had a special allure also because government officials lived and behaved with the grandeur of colonial rulers. While the natives lived in filth and poverty in small towns and squalid villages, there would always be one street that was spotlessly clean and lined with pretty bungalows set in neat gardens. On this street lived the police chief, the local magistrate and the district collector, and if there were houses to spare then other high officials would find accommodation on this street too.

Then along came Sam Pitroda like a magician with a big bag full of magic tricks in a children's birthday party. He seemed to have instant solutions to all of India's problems. I first met him in his large sunlit office on a high floor of the Akbar Hotel. He was a cheerful, friendly man with a head full of long silver hair that contrasted oddly with his dyed black beard and moustache. Everything about him and about his office seemed designed to show that he believed in doing things differently from the 'socialist' way. He had surrounded himself with bright, talented young people who seemed in as much of a hurry to transform India as he was.

That morning I remember being quite dazzled by Pitroda's energy and his missionary zeal. At the time his only task was to make telephones available in rural India, where telephone lines were virtually non-existent. He went about his task diligently and would have achieved a great deal had the cell phone revolution not nullified his efforts to build a network of landlines that connected villages to the world through little public telephone booths that had STD/ISD written on them. Inside the booths there was usually a single table and chair and a big, old-fashioned telephone. Owning a telephone booth became a matter of prestige in rural India, and on my travels I constantly ran into people who asked if I could help them get one. In those times before the media revolution, rural people found it hard to distinguish between journalists and government officials.

What I did not know at that first meeting with Pitroda was that he was a man with such a grandiose idea of his own abilities that he would willingly take on more 'missions' than any single person could handle. Nor did I know that he would be reckless enough to believe that he could fulfil these 'missions' by overriding the Government of India. After being given charge of a telecommunications mission, he cheerfully accepted to head a drinking water mission, a literacy mission, an immunization mission and a dairy and oil seeds mission. And I think he even accepted to lead a 'greening of India' mission. Not even the whole might of the Government of India could achieve so much in the five years Rajiv had, but he appeared not to discover this till the very end of his term as prime minister. Then he famously admitted that less than 15 paise of a rupee spent on welfare actually reached the people it was meant to.

Afterwards, when it was too late, political commentators said it was Rajiv's inexperience that caused him to not realize that to achieve anything at all he would first have to improve the shoddy standards of governance that his mother and grandfather had put in place. But as someone who knew him when he was just a pilot in Indian Airlines, my own view is that he relied for advice on friends who had no idea what it meant to run a country the size of a continent. Having known them from the days when they were just executives in multinational companies, I knew that they saw no difference between running a company and running a country. 'It's all about management,' they liked to say grandly. It was these 'management' types who formed Rajiv's closest circle of advisors. Later into this charmed circle of privilege were invited bureaucrats, often from the Foreign Service, whose main qualification seemed to be that they spoke English well. Their main disqualification often was that they knew as little about Indian realities as Rajiv's friends did.

They created around him a wonderland. They strutted about the high offices of Lutyens' Delhi announcing ambitious plans to change this and change that. At least in those first two years before Bofors when his massive public mandate seemed to gild everything he did and said. It was not just Indians who were impressed with his efforts. Foreign correspondents took to describing Rajiv and Sonia as the lead players in an 'Indian Camelot'. I wrote at the time for the *Sunday Times*, London, and quickly discovered that my editors had an insatiable appetite for news about India's handsome young prime minister and his lovely Italian wife.

Nobody noticed in those first three years that Rajiv's economic and political ideas were dangerously infantile. I personally began to notice this when I went to see one of his bureaucrats one day and he told me the plans they had prepared for 'transforming' the country's education system. The conversation, as I remember it, went something like this:

'The prime minister believes that we can solve the problem by building mini Doon Schools,' he said proudly.

'Oh?'

'Yes. Obviously we cannot improve every school in India, but what we can do is build a super structure of excellent schools where there will be the highest standards.'

'How will this make a difference...how will it make a difference in any real sense if it affects only those children who will be in these mini Doon Schools?'

'The difference will be that there will be a model for others to follow. You know that school education is a state subject, but if we can build these mini Doon Schools then state governments can copy the model.'

'Why does the prime minister not insist instead on compulsory primary education? Isn't that the real reason why China and most of Southeast Asia's countries have gone ahead of India where education is concerned?'

'Maybe. But they aren't democracies. In a democratic country like India you cannot make education compulsory. People would not accept this.'

So instead of a new education policy what Rajiv achieved was to build a handful of schools across the country that were better than your average government school. This kind of tinkering with governance was the leitmotif of Rajiv's term as prime minister. The people he surrounded himself with were to a man too clever by half. They knew nothing about the things they were dealing with but believed that they knew everything. And more frighteningly believed that Rajiv Gandhi had the power (and the mandate) to change anything he wanted to.

One afternoon I met an old friend of mine who had spent most of his life trying to revive Indian textiles and craft traditions. I knew him as a close friend of Rajiv and Sonia and was surprised when he told me that he was 'really, really upset' about Rajiv's policy on culture. 'Can you please write something about this?' he pleaded.

'You know that I don't know much about cultural policy,' I said, 'but I can find someone in *India Today* who does.' I was writing for *India Today* then on a freelance basis. My job with the *Sunday Times* paid well enough for me to have given up working full time for a newspaper. But because I wanted my byline to remain in circulation in India I had come to an arrangement with Aroon Purie to write for *India Today* part time.

'No,' my friend said. 'I want you to write it because I think you will see that it is more of a political story than a culture story.'

'OK. So tell me?'

'Do you know a man called Mani Shankar Aiyar?'

'Yes.'

'What do you think of him?'

'He is an arrogant, bumptious creature but Rajiv and Sonia love him.'

'Have you heard of his plans to set up these regional cultural zones?'

'No.'

'It is complete madness but what he has got Rajiv to agree to do is to set up these cultural centres that will club together states in certain groups. So, for instance, Rajasthan and Gujarat and Madhya Pradesh could be clubbed under one category and an IAS officer will be put in charge of the centre.'

'So?'

'Don't you see? You cannot order culture or decide cultural traditions from the prime minister's office. Culture is something that comes from the people. It cannot be imposed or clubbed in this way.'

It was this conversation that inspired me to investigate further. When I was next in Udaipur I resolved to visit the zonal cultural centre there. The west culture zone had its headquarters here and under it came a smorgasbord of disparate states and Union territories: Goa, Gujarat, Rajasthan, Maharashtra, Daman and Diu, Dadra and Nagar Haveli. The west zone had its offices in a lovely old building on the edge of the lake that is the centre of this town of palaces, temples and forts that was once the capital city of the Mewar rulers of Udaipur. In the courtyard of the west zone headquarters that afternoon were puppeteers in brightly coloured Rajasthani turbans and crafts people making bangles of papier mache. A small group of folk singers sat tuning their instruments under a large neem tree, and it was all very picturesque and charming until I met the IAS officer who had the responsibility of producing 'culture' from India's western states. She was a large, buxom lady who made it clear in the first five minutes that she had a high opinion of herself and a low opinion of those who did not share her opinions.

Our conversation began with her recounting with relish how she had prevented the Maharana of Udaipur from building a second hotel in the city. Instead of a tale of civic duty it sounded as if she had exercised her power only to show the maharana that his place was now considerably lower than hers. When we got around to speaking of the culture zone idea I asked her if she thought it was possible for officials to control culture.

'Of course it is,' she said. 'It is for us to tell people what culture is and how they must preserve it.'

'Us?'

'Government...we who represent government.'

'Isn't culture something that the people should create themselves?'

'No. It isn't like that at all. Please remember that in the old days it was the princes who kept alive the traditions of music, painting and crafts. Now it is our responsibility.'

'So you don't think there is anything wrong with the prime minister's office deciding which state should be in which cultural zone and which traditions should be preserved?'

'No. I don't at all. I think Mani Shankar Aiyar is a very clever man to have come up with this idea, and I think it will work very well.'

The lady officer was so firm in her convictions that I saw no point in trying to argue. We drank some tea, chatted of this and that, and parted on an amicable note. When I left, the musicians were still under the tree, tuning their instruments and singing snatches of folk songs. The bangle makers were making their bangles and the puppeteers were twirling their marionettes about in a crazy dance. I remember thinking as I left that nothing that they did had been taught to them by government officials. So why should you need official interference at all? The zonal culture centres did not last long. Like Rajiv's other ideas they failed to take off.

His other big 'cultural' idea was to clean the Ganga. I learned about it from my friend Mapu (Martand Singh), whose brother Arun Singh was Rajiv's closest childhood friend and who was in those first months of his prime ministership Rajiv's closest advisor. He had given up a boxwallah job in Calcutta (Kolkata now) to come and work with Rajiv when he entered politics. Unlike Arun, or Roon as he was called by his friends, Mapu's interests lay in more cultural areas. He was one of the founders of INTACH (Indian National Trust for Art, Culture and Heritage) and it was to INTACH's new office in a large bungalow in Lodhi Estate that he summoned me one day to tell me about the Ganga Action Plan. He asked if I would write a document for him about it, and I agreed without at all understanding what it meant. So I read through the collection of dull books he gave me on river cleaning and the Ganga and squeezed out of them a more readable, concise document.

It was many years later on a visit to Benares that I discovered that the Ganga Action Plan was fundamentally flawed. Its well-intentioned objective was to build thousands of sewage plants in the cities and towns along the Ganga that were pouring untreated sewage into India's most sacred river.

But it was from the mahanta of the Sankat Mochan temple on the Assi Ghat, Vir Bhadra Mishra, that I realized that it would have been wiser to divert the waste away from the river. 'You do know, don't you, that until the British came to India, sewage was never put in rivers at all?'

'No. I didn't know this,' I said, looking suitably embarrassed by my ignorance. We talked on a terrace of the temple that hung delicately over the Ganga. We sat on the stone floor, gazing out at the changing colours of the river and at the panoply of devotion that plays out daily on the steps of the ghat. There were young brides with hennaed hands and arms covered in bangles, standing in their bridal clothes at the edge of the river, seeking Ganga's blessings. Priests in saffron under little umbrellas, offering religious ceremonies to believers. And foreigners in shorts, taking pictures of everything. And, too, a very dirty old man with mad eyes sitting with a monkey in his arms. The monkey was picking lice out of his armpit. Dusk was falling and the sound of religious music came from another ghat where the evening worship of the river was about to start.

The mahanta looked sad and there was despair in his eyes. He was a fine-looking man with refined Brahmanical features and a head full of white hair. When I said I had come to talk to him about the Ganga Action Plan he said after a long silence that he had spent a lifetime trying to save the Ganga.

'Do you know how many years it has been that I have tried to get people to clean the Ganga? I have cleaned human excrement off the steps of the ghats with my own hands? I thought it would set an example to others, but it made no difference because we have degenerated so much as a people we don't know the importance of anything any more.'

'Was it a tradition all over India not to put sewage into the rivers?'

'Yes. It was. And when I saw Rajiv Gandhi's Ganga Action Plan I told them that they were making a mistake and that what would happen would be that the sewage plants would not work and so the river would remain polluted. They didn't listen, so they wasted crores on building sewage plants that are lying idle along the length of the river.'

'Mapu says it is because the Ganga Action Plan became a government plan instead of being a private effort by INTACH that it didn't work.'

'Yes. That is one reason...many people have a vested interest in its remaining a government plan because there is so much money to be made out of cleaning the Ganga. But there are other reasons and the most important of these is that it is a mistake to put sewage into the river.'

'So what do you do with it?'

'You divert it and make it into manure...I have a plan that I gave the municipality of Benares. Under the 73rd amendment the municipal corporation has the powers to make these decisions. And they accepted my plan. But then the Government of Uttar Pradesh took the matter to court and that is where it has been for ten years. The vested interests are too strong.'

It was well into Rajiv's tenure as prime minister when Romesh Thapar, a former friend of Indira Gandhi, described his government as the 'baba log government'. A government of spoilt children. But the truth is that long before Bofors it became clear to those of us who knew him and his friends well that they were no more than a bunch of amateurs playing at being political leaders. They would have been exposed much earlier if they had not been propped up by brash, young bureaucrats (many from the Doon School) who reveled in the power they exercised over a prime minister who had no idea what he was doing. Often their advice took Rajiv along dangerous paths, but he remained in their thrall because he was dealing for the first time in his life with issues he had never even considered thinking about in the years when he was just an Indian Airlines pilot.

He was more comfortable with his caboodle of brash young bureaucrats than he was with older, wiser men even in matters of foreign policy. He seemed to like their projection of him as the new regional leader of all of Asia and soon developed such an exalted opinion of his ideas on foreign policy that he thought nothing of sacking the foreign secretary at a press conference in Vigyan Bhavan. A.P. Venkateswaran was a highly intelligent, sophisticated man who did not kowtow to Rajiv. He was a small, squat gentleman with a wicked sense of humour. A story he loved to tell was about how he had been present when Rajiv used his left hand to offer a traditional-minded Brahmin some sweets. He laughed every time he described the look of horror on the Brahmin's face. Had Rajiv got wind of this story? Was this why he was sacked in so summary a fashion?

This is not how Venkat's colleagues in the ministry of external affairs saw it. In a column that I wrote for the *Indian Express* (13 December 1987) it was in these words that I described a conversation I had with a high official after the sacking. 'A look of impatience crossed the face of the former high official and he interrupted me to say, "It's only people who do not understand the prime minister who talk like this. Anyone who knows him would know that there are many things that would have irritated the prime minister about someone like Venkat. After all the prime minister is a man of some style and sophistication and Venkat had this habit of sitting with his leg crossed over his knee. This used to upset the prime minister."' The comment so perfectly described the atmosphere in the court of Rajiv and Sonia

Gandhi that I use it here even though I have used it before in my book *Durbar*.

Venkat was one of the most sophisticated men I have ever met and his understanding of international events was profound, but in the eyes of Rajiv and his cohorts he was unsophisticated because he did not speak English like they did. And did not know that crossing your leg over your knee was bad manners, at least according to the rules of etiquette that Rajiv and his friends had learned in the Doon School.

Having spent most of my growing years in the shadow of this school that some call the Eton of India, I knew it well. My father and brother went to Jaipur House, and having gone to Welham Girls' High School myself, most of the boys I grew up with came from Doon. They were a genial, good-looking bunch but very much the kind of privileged young men who had never really needed to do an honest day's work in their lives. They wore their privilege casually and spoke English well but usually spoke no Indian language at all and had a better understanding of England than India. It was not their fault. It was in their generation and mine that colonization reached its apogee.

The British Raj ended three years before I was born but it really succeeded in its colonial mission after the last British rulers left India. The most effective colonial tool was language, and its first effects began to be felt in my parents' generation. Since my father lost his father when he was a young boy and my mother lost her mother when she was a very young girl, there were only two grandparents left by the time I was born. My father's mother, whom we called Bibiji, was a tall, proud Sikh woman who turned to religion for solace after becoming a widow in her thirties. She spoke only Punjabi, so we spoke Punjabi to her, as we did to my mother's father, Bapuji, who was a tiny man with very blue eyes and very white hair. He was one of the five contractors who helped Edwin Lutyens build New Delhi, but in all his years of service to the British Raj never felt the need to learn English.

By the time my parents were growing up things had changed. My mother went to the Convent of Jesus and Mary girls school in Delhi and in the summer transferred seamlessly to Waverly Convent in Mussoorie. And with my father having gone to the Doon School my parents spoke English to each other but did not lose their own languages. We were sent to schools where we learned to speak only English. Most people I grew up with would have no hesitation in admitting that English was their first language and sometimes the only language they spoke at all. This was true of Rajiv and his friends as well, but because of the confidence that comes naturally with privilege they never saw their linguistic disability as a disability.

So they had no problem at all wielding power over men and women who were infinitely more Indian than they were. It worried me that they managed to get away with doing this despite their minuscule idea of India. Was it because they wore privilege gracefully? Was it because they seemed to clearly belong to a class that was higher than that of the politicians, bureaucrats and journalists they dealt with? I do not know. What I do know is that most of my colleagues in the newsrooms of Delhi (TV barely existed) were in such awe of Rajiv that the questions that should have been asked about his policies and actions were never asked.

Would it have helped him if they had been? I am not sure but what I am sure of is that the mandate he was given by the people of India made him so confident and cocky that he began to believe he had all the answers to everything. He stopped listening even to his friends and thought nothing of letting them down if the need arose. The closest friend he let down was Amitabh Bachchan. He did this by never correcting the impression created by some newspapers that Bachchan was one of those whom Bofors bribed to sell their guns.

The Bachchan family's friendship with India's ruling dynasty went back a long, long way. Jawaharlal Nehru was close friends with Harivanshrai Bachchan and his wife Teji in the days when he was a young political leader fighting for India's freedom and Harivanshrai Bachchan was a Hindi poet so famous that his celebrity in the 1930s was almost as great as his son's would one day be as India's most famous movie star. Both families came from Allahabad at a time when it was a small town whose main appeal was as a centre for Hindu pilgrims. The friendship between the two families continued during Indira Gandhi's time as prime minister.

In the year that she declared the Emergency, Amitabh Bachchan's star rose to such dizzying heights that people talked of him as the 'one-man film industry'. Such extraordinary celebrity rarely brings with it popularity among one's peers, so when the Emergency brought with it a minister for information and broadcasting who interfered in the work of Bollywood aggressively by promoting certain actresses and censoring films he did not like, a bizarre rumour spread that it was because of Amitabh Bachchan that Mrs Gandhi did what she did.

When Rajiv asked Amitabh to contest the Allahabad seat in the 1984 election his popularity was beginning to wane a little, but he was still India's biggest movie star. He said to me in an interview years later that he took a break from his own career to enter politics at the time because the assassination of Indira Gandhi affected him deeply. 'It was an emotional thing,' he said. 'I was never cut out to be a politician.'

But in that winter election Rajiv Gandhi was so extraordinary a symbol of change and hope that Bachchan defeated the most important leader of Uttar Pradesh at the time, Hemwati Nandan Bahuguna. He defeated him by one of the highest margins ever in a parliamentary election, winning 68.2 per cent of the vote. When he came to Parliament for the first time after the election I happened to be in Central Hall. Rajiv was there to meet his victorious MPs, and as a young prime minister who had been given the most spectacular mandate in history there was an aura of hope and faith around him that made his MPs fawn over him. Until Amitabh Bachchan arrived.

When he walked in and tried to take his seat as an ordinary MP, there was almost a riot as the elected representatives of the people of India swarmed around him like ordinary fans. Had he stayed in politics and worked for Allahabad with the sincerity that he worked for cinema, who knows how far he could have gone. This is not something he believed. He once said to me that he did not think people were stupid enough to confuse the celebrity of movie stars with the celebrity of political leaders. He told me a story he had heard about Dilip Kumar. While campaigning for Indira Gandhi he asked at a public rally the question cheerleaders always ask at public rallies, 'Desh ka neta kaisa ho?' (What should the country's leader be like?) The crowd responded with shouts of 'Saira Bano jaisa ho'. Saira Bano was his wife and a famous actress.

Was it doubts of this kind that made Bachchan resign his seat just three years after winning it? Or was it because his childhood friend let him down? So close was their friendship that when Rajiv married Sonia Maino it was in the home of Amitabh's parents that the marriage ceremony took place. Indian tradition dictates that wedding ceremonies must be performed in the bride's home. So when the Bachchan name was wrongly dragged into the Bofors scandal why did Rajiv not say anything? Why did he never say, as he did in the Lok

Sabha about his own family, that the Bachchan family had nothing to do with Bofors bribes? We did not know then that Bofors bribe money would turn up mysteriously in the Swiss accounts of Sonia's best friends, Ottavio and Maria Quattrocchi, but as prime minister Rajiv would have known. And yet all the time that journalists dragged Bachchan's name through the mire in speculative, salacious articles about the Bofors scandal Rajiv remained silent.

Was this betrayal the real reason why Bachchan so abruptly ended his political career? He has never admitted this in any interview he has given but because I believe it to be true I have tried over the years on more than one occasion to get him to say this. My first attempt was soon after the scandal broke in the summer of 1987. Bachchan was staying in a suite at the Taj and I asked if I could come and see him, and I think because he needed to tell his side of the story he readily agreed.

When we met in his suite sunlight poured in through a large window and glinted off the Gujarati-style swing on which he sat. He looked troubled and vulnerable. When I asked why, he said that what had hurt him most was when his father asked him if he had done something wrong. But when I asked if the Bofors betrayal was the reason why he had decided to resign from the Lok Sabha he said the real reason was that he did not think he was cut out for politics. I did not believe him and I made it a sort of private quest to find out what the real reason was. Whenever I met him I tried in a roundabout way to bring the conversation back to politics.

Some years after Rajiv was killed I interviewed Bachchan for Ek Din, Ek Jeevan in the gaudy, extravagant, sprawling Film City that has been built with southern Indian splendour outside Hyderabad, where he was shooting for a film called

Suryavansham. We met in a hotel inside the Film City that was so ornate and glitzy that the lobby looked like a Bollywood film set. There were mirrors everywhere and great glittering chandeliers that reflected off floors of marble and shiny granite. The furnishings were in south Indian colours so bright that when Bachchan walked into the lobby in a simple blue track suit and slippers he looked out of place. We drove together in his car to the set where he was shooting but he was his usual reticent self, and although I wanted badly to ask him my political questions I did not manage to summon up the courage. I was afraid that he would mistake my genuine desire to get an answer for familiarity and that it would ruin the rest of the day.

This was a time of a deep lull in his career, when his films were not doing well and just before the astonishing comeback he made with the Indian version of *Who Wants to Be a Millionaire*, *Kaun Banega Crorepati*. That day he appeared to be doing a lesser film out of need rather than choice. His leading lady was a small, chubby south Indian actress whose name I had never heard. His role required him to wear clothes so drab that I thought he was playing the role of a domestic servant. We drove from the opulent hotel to a set where a south Indian house had been built with a typical central courtyard that led to verandas and sparsely decorated rooms. Very different from the gaudy lobby of the hotel where we met.

In a bedroom whose only furniture was a large bed and a small cupboard, I ran into the leading lady discussing wardrobe problems with the set director. And in the very realistic courtyard I met Anupam Kher, who sat eating snacks and drinking tea. It was in different parts of this fake south Indian house that I did my interview with Bachchan. We began in his makeup van, where I told him, either out of cheek or nervousness, that he looked much younger in real life than on screen. He was having his face made up at that time and looking at it in the mirror said drily that he was happy that I thought this. Not a good beginning, I thought, silently cursing myself.

Of all the people I have interviewed in a long, long career in journalism, Mr Bachchan has without question been the most difficult. His reticence is so profound that every question seems like an intrusion into a private space, so, as always, I found myself unable to extract the sort of answers from him that I needed for this episode of my series on the lives of celebrities. When I tried to be clever and ask him what it felt like when a human being became an institution he said coldly that he did not think of himself that way. When I persisted and said that people saw him that way because his celebrity had become so huge he said that I should perhaps talk to those who said this and not him. Luckily a group of fans appeared to interrupt a line of questioning that I could see was going nowhere and getting there very badly.

Since this interview was for Ek Din, Ek Jeevan, I spent a whole day with him snatching bits of conversation between shots and snacks and lunch and finally at the very end, late in the afternoon, got a chance to do a formal interview in the glitzy hotel in which the day had begun. When I asked why he had resigned from politics he gave me the answer he has always given interviewers: he left politics because he did not think he had the makings of a politician. I asked if India's poverty and the horrible conditions in which people lived were things he thought about, and he said he thought about them all the time but he did not think that he could personally do anything politically to make things better. He knew that he did not have the skills needed to be a good politician.

When the cameras were turned off I think I tried once more to ask him about Rajiv and why he no longer saw Sonia, but I got nothing out of him. I knew from my friend Chitra Subramaniam that Bachchan was not involved in the Bofors deal. She would know better than anyone since without her excellent investigative journalism, without her dogged determination, there would perhaps never have been the discovery of those bank accounts in Switzerland in the name of Ottavio and Maria Quattrocchi. Until then the media continued to try and link Bofors to Amitabh Bachchan and not once did he say to anyone that he was disappointed that Rajiv never tried to correct the lies that were told.

So was it the Bofors scandal that caused Rajiv to lose the election in 1989? It was certainly a factor. While travelling during the campaign I met semi-literate peasants in remote villages who had heard about Bofors.

'What is Bofors?' I would ask when the crowd around me got large enough. In those times before television, any stranger arriving unexpectedly in a car would cause almost every man and child in the village to gather around. And after the first question there would be silence as sunburned, lined faces under grimy turbans looked at each other. Then someone braver than the others would summon up the courage to say, 'Which party are you from?'

'No party. I am a journalist.' Only then, after another moment of suspicion, someone or other would say, 'Bofors is a scandal in which the prime minister himself took money.'

'How do you know that the prime minister took money?'

'We read the newspapers, don't we? And everyone says that he did.'

By then Rajiv's former defence minister had spent two years travelling around the villages of Uttar Pradesh. Vishwanath Pratap Singh was telling people that he would catch the

'Bofors thieves' within sixty days of becoming prime minister. He travelled in a small Fiat car with only a driver or local journalist for company, and it impressed ordinary people that a man who had once been chief minister of the state should show such humility. When he talked about Bofors he made a convincing case. He was defence minister when Swedish radio broke the story and promised to find the bribe takers as soon as possible. Soon he was out of Rajiv's cabinet and in the wilderness, but it was the wilderness of rural Uttar Pradesh and all he talked about was Bofors.

With the perspective that hindsight gives, when I look back to that long-ago election, I believe that the main reason why Rajiv lost was that he was unable to bring real change. Had schools improved or healthcare, had it become easier for ordinary Indians to get clean water and electricity, he may have survived the taint of Bofors. In the five years that he was prime minister the only real change that became evident in rural India was Pitroda's PCO booths with STD/ISD written on them.

When I first saw one of these I puzzled endlessly over what STD meant since in Indian officialese it was usually used by doctors as an acronym for sexually transmitted diseases. PCO stood for public call office, and as long as the fat telephone with its locked dial worked after they paid, most people did not care what the other acronyms stood for. They knew that one of them stood for calls within India and the other for international calls. It was only after a little research that I discovered that ISD stood for international standard dialling and STD for subscriber trunk dialling. Pitroda was always trying to impress upon people that he was from the private sector and that what he brought to Rajiv's government was the scent of free enterprise and open markets, but he seemed to quickly get sucked into lowering his standards to those of government in India. The PCO booths were shoddy and makeshift and not long after became irrelevant because of the cell phone revolution.

By the time Rajiv was killed his credibility as a leader was so damaged that despite the horror of his assassination the Congress was able to win only 244 seats. He had by then spent two years as leader of the opposition and in this time behaved so much like a spoilt prince that it did nothing to improve his image. After the incompetent, cynical government led by Vishwanath Pratap Singh crumbled under the weight of its own mistakes Rajiv used his 197 seats in the Lok Sabha to prop up a government led by Chandrashekhar, but instead of allowing this government to govern he took to treating the prime minister like a peon. At no time was this more obvious than during the first Gulf War.

Ajit knew Chandrashekhar better than I did and admired him more than I did. My disappointment with him as a leader was from having walked with him some distance during his 'padyatra' across the length of India in 1983. It was not a long distance that I walked but it was long enough for me to discover that Chandrashekhar was doing the padyatra more to project himself as a future prime minister than to try and genuinely understand the problems of the people.

On the stretch that I walked with him I was very moved by how many ordinary, very poor peasants greeted him along the route with folded hands and tears in their eyes. And very sad that he had less time for them than for the VIPs from Delhi and Mumbai who came to join him along the way. But I totally agreed with Ajit that when Chandrashekhar allowed American fighter jets to refuel in India during the Gulf War it was the right decision.

So why did Rajiv react with petulance, rage and foolishness? Why did he think he could stop the ground war by flying off to Moscow to meet Mikhail Gorbachev? Why did he end up looking like such a clown? Again with the retrospective viewfinder that time provides, when I look back what I see is a man who had developed such an exalted sense of himself that he lost touch with reality. There was much he could have done had he been guided by wiser men. He could have ended the licence raj. He could have cut the red tape that made good governance impossible. He could have invested in the infrastructure India desperately needed. He could have brought new polices for education and healthcare. He could have ended the ban on private television channels since satellite transmission was already on the horizon. He could have strengthened the Congress by making room for able, young people.

No prime minister had a bigger mandate to bring about these changes and yet he did nothing. His admirers credit him with bringing computers to India but I know from talking to Narayana Murthy and Nandan Nilekani that such a jungle of regulations controlled the import of computers that it took them as long as a year to import a single computer. History will remember him mostly for having wasted a mandate so extraordinary that he could have changed India into a modern nation in every way.

Two years after he was killed I happened to be travelling through villages in rural Rajasthan. My task was not journalistic. I am not sure why but I accepted to investigate how projects financed by NABARD (National Bank for Agriculture and Rural Development) were working on the ground. Since I was usually short of money, it may have been because some foreign NGO offered me a substantial sum to do this research. So I drove a hundred kilometres out of Udaipur to an area in which roads had not reached. The only way to get to the villages where I was to find out about

NABARD projects was by riding pillion on a social worker's scooter. It was a hot, dusty ride that I survived by totally covering my face with my dupatta.

The villages chosen for my research were so remote that people were not sure whether the British had left. But the most memorable conversation that morning was with a group of women dressed in the style of Rajasthani rural women. They wore colourful skirts and veils and their arms were covered in bangles. We sat on the mud floor of a house that had beautiful frescoes painted on the outside but that had nothing remotely resembling furniture inside. After asking my questions about rural development I could not resist asking a few political questions.

'Who is the Prime Minister of India?' I asked and the women giggled.

'Don't know,' one of them finally said in Rajasthani.

'Do you know the name of any political leaders?'

'No.'

'Indira Gandhi?'

'No.'

'Jawaharlal Nehru?'

'No.'

'Do you know who rules India?'

'The British.'

'Have you heard of Rajiv Gandhi?'

'No,' they said in unison, giggling happily until one woman said, 'Wasn't he the one that a woman killed with a garland?'

That is all they knew about him.

20

INDIA'S CHILDREN

When the newspapers reported her death they did not give her name. They described her only as a two-year-old girl who died after being raped by her mother's lover and his friend. In the two-paragraph story that recorded this death by rape, the little dead girl's mother was described as a nurse and a single mother who had been forced to leave her child in her lover's care because she had night duty in the hospital in which she worked. When she came back the next morning she discovered the broken, naked body of her daughter lying between her lover and his friend. They were still in a drunken stupor, totally unaware that the little girl who lay between them was dead. Empty bottles of liquor lay on the floor beside them.

In the *Statesman* there was a general disdain for 'human interest stories', but my editor did not object when I said I wanted to go and find out more about what had happened because this was a Delhi story. It was a time of press censorship anyway, and this so restricted reporting that human interest stories were almost the only ones that made it into the newspaper. Sometimes even these did not make it and came back from the censors with a red line through them. A series I wrote on the state of Delhi hospitals came back with red lines through all of them, and when I tried to find out why it was a political matter to report on the appalling state of these hospitals, the men in the censor board said press censorship forbade any criticism of government services.

It was for us a very censored time. And for me, having just got my first job after a year of unemployment, it was a particularly personal blow since I had only been employed for a month when the Emergency came into force. I longed to be able to do some real reporting and went out of my way to write stories that would pass the censors but this was not easy. The *Statesman* often had to be submitted every night for 'pre-censorship', so we would find out only the next morning that our stories had been written in vain. This extra strict censorship was imposed because we tried to defy Mrs Gandhi's orders in the first days of the Emergency by printing blank spaces where stories had been removed. We had long since given up our defiance and were with perfect servility displaying all stories related to Sanjay Gandhi 'prominently' on page one. But pre-censorship continued, and if the censors saw anything remotely resembling defiance, the newspaper would be returned so late at night that it could not be brought out till well after 8 a.m. the next day, thereby becoming useless. What the censors were worried about I never fully understood because the *Statesman* was so conservative that news editors routinely refused us permission to cover stories that showed India in a bad light.

On 27 December 1975, six months after Mrs Gandhi's Emergency, 372 miners in a mine called Chasnala drowned when millions of gallons of water flooded into the mine in which they were working. No bodies were ever found and so it was hard to say whether the official figure of 372 was more accurate than the workers' union figure that put the number of dead miners at 700. Records were so poorly kept by the state-owned Indian Iron and Steel Company that the exact number of dead was never established. When the accident happened I was horrified and with my foreign training in journalism saw it as a major story. It would have been anywhere else in the world. I begged to be allowed to go and cover the accident and said I could write it up in a human interest sort of way so that it passed the censors. But the problem was not censorship, just that my news editor could not understand why dead miners made a story that anyone would want to read. 'Not worth traveling all the way to Dhanbad to cover such a story,' he said.

Since the little girl's story came from a Delhi slum it was easier to persuade him that this was a human interest story that was worth covering. And since there was no government agency that could be blamed for the little girl's rape and murder it might even escape the notice of the censors. He agreed. By the time I got to the one-room tenement in which the little girl had lived with her mother, her rapists had already been taken away by the police but the debris from the night before still lay around. There were empty bottles and glasses and an unmade bed. The girl's mother sat on the floor weeping as a woman relative or friend attempted to comfort her.

She was a small woman with a long plait and still wore her nurse's uniform – a white sari with a green border. She sat on the floor with her legs pulled up close to her chest and her back against a wall, and when she saw me she started to cry even more.

'What did I do,' she sobbed. 'How did I know that such a thing could happen...'

The woman who sat beside her tried to comfort her. 'What was meant to happen has happened,' she said. 'Who knows God's will...he takes away what he gives.'

'I should never have left her alone with him,' she wailed.

'How did you meet him?' I asked when she calmed down a little.

'He came to the hospital for treatment.'

'How long did you know him?'

'A few weeks.'

'So why did you trust him?'

'He seemed nice...he was good to me. And he was very good to my daughter. He took her out for ice cream and bought her sweets.' This made her cry even more.

'And your husband?'

'Dead. Last year. So I have to work to bring my daughter...' at this point she began to weep so much I did not have the heart to ask any more questions.' I looked around the tiny room to see if there was a photograph of the little girl. There was one of her as a baby with her parents. Her mother held her in her arms and she looked straight into the camera with eyes ringed with kajal and with a big black kajal spot on her forehead to ward off evil. Her father smiled from under a thin moustache and had the rigid stance of those unused to being photographed. The picture looked as if it had been taken on a black and white film and then painted over against a bilious green backdrop. I wanted to ask the woman how her husband had died. I wanted to ask her when the picture was taken but I didn't have the heart to. As I was leaving, the woman who was with her told me that they had cremated the little girl that morning and that the police had come and taken the men away.

What happened to this woman afterwards? What happened to the rapist lover and his rapist friend? I do not know. What I do know is that to this day every time I read in the newspapers about a little girl being raped I remember the two-year-old who died that day. I never saw the dead child or her rapists but every time I think of her I feel once more the horror of what had happened. I imagine the little girl asleep on her mother's bed, sleeping the sleep of a child, and then being violated by two drunken men until their brutality killed her. I imagine them hitting her to keep her quiet when she screamed and hope that she may have become unconscious and not felt the pain and the terror.

Children fall through the cracks in India's vaunted welfare state every day. They become victims of brutality, rape and torture. Nearly always this happens in their own homes, and nearly always it is a close relation who becomes the rapist or the tormentor. When they run away from home they end up in the streets of Mumbai and Delhi where they become victims once more. If a country is to be judged by how it treats children then India would be one of the most callous states in the world.

Every story from the streets is worse than the next. Since nearly all runaway children end up at a railway station it is close to railway stations that organizations like the Salaam Baalak Trust have their offices. Ever since I first became a reporter I went out of my way to write stories that I hoped would help India's vast and very elaborate welfare state improve the lives of children. I did not succeed but kept on trying and when I started working for television did the same. And so it was that on a hot morning in Delhi I found myself at New Delhi railway station with my comrade-in-arms Ajmal Jami doing a story on Salaam Baalak's efforts to save runaway children. From working with street children in Mumbai I knew that Salaam Baalak was doing really good work and being prevented at every step by government agencies.

Mira Nair's mother Praveen Nair, whom I met in Delhi that morning, told me that they had begged local authorities to give them a small 'contact point' on the platform and been refused. 'We have established,' she said with a wave of her hands, 'that it is in the first twenty minutes of a child arriving at the station that it falls into the hands of anti-social elements, so we really need this contact point but they won't give it to us and so we have to make do.'

At the railway station I found that they were 'making do' by setting up a makeshift contact point on an unused veranda in a building in the railway station's premises. They decorated its grubby walls with pictures painted by runaway children and on its cement floor they arranged for children to eat and play and paint and learn. It was here that I met Jitin, a tiny boy with dirty feet and hands, who came to eat and spend spare time on the veranda but refused to live in the Salaam Baalak hostel because he still hoped to go home.

'Where is your home?'

'It's in Gwalior,' he said, giving me a suspicious look and then looking down at his small dirt-encrusted feet.

'So how did you end up in the railway station?'

'I got lost,' he said. 'I was with my uncle in Vaishno Devi and then suddenly he was gone and I was alone. A baba helped me go back to Gwalior and I tried to find where I used to live but could not. I spent two or three days there looking and then came back here.' His eyes filled with tears as he spoke and his voice broke but he refused to cry.

'He is an orphan,' the lady from Salaam Baalak whispered, 'and was most likely abandoned. We have tried to find his uncle but with no luck.'

'So why don't you want to go to the Salaam Baalak hostel?' I asked Jitin as he hungrily devoured a fat bread roll.

'Because I want to make some money,' he said, 'and then I will go back to Gwalior and find my uncle.'

'How will you make money?'

'I will go to Haridwar on the train and get money from the Ganga.'

'From the Ganga?'

'Yes. People throw money into the river and then when they go away we go into the water and pick it up with our feet.'

'Have you done this before?'

'No. But I have a friend who has and he is going to take me.'

The social worker from Salaam Baalak told me that Jitin's story was typical and that there were many children at the railway station who they had been unable to rescue because they enjoyed the freedom of being unsupervised by adults. 'They move around in gangs,' she said, 'and they travel wherever they want on the trains, and many of them have become addicts of some kind and do not like living in hostels where drugs are forbidden.'

'So is there no way of making sure that they are taken off the streets?' I asked and she gave me a weary look before saying, 'Yes, there are government hostels where they can be taken. They are custodial institutions unlike ours, but the trouble is that they are even more brutal than the streets.'

Having seen the government homes for children, I knew exactly what she meant and stopped asking questions. From the office at the railway station she took me to one of their hostels where I met children who had such horrible stories to tell that by the end of the day I could listen to no more of them. I met a pretty young girl from Agra who had ended up at New Delhi railway station because after her father died her mother married a man who did not want anything to do with her three children. 'He hated us,' she said, 'and beat us every day. But when he threw me off the terrace and I broke my arm, I told my sister and brother that we had to run away, so we got on a train and came here.'

'And where are your sister and brother?'

'My brother is in the boys' hostel but it's too late to save my sister. She is a drug addict and lives on the station with boys who do very bad things to her. But she can't give up the drugs.'

When I went back to Mrs Nair's tiny office she said that the stories of the children they managed to rescue were heartbreaking but they tried not to treat them as victims. 'We try instead to appreciate their incredible spirit of survival and it is on this that we build.' Later that day I watched these rescued children rehearse for a show they were organizing as part of a charitable event to raise funds for the Salaam Baalak Trust and wondered why it was that government homes for children, with their huge resources and vast compounds, could not do such things. Why were they so hopeless by comparison? And I remembered that in all the years that I had been a journalist I had almost never met a petty official who was in government service to do something good. He was in government service to get a permanent job, a government house, a government car and a high standard of living by Indian standards. It was the socialist way and nobody wanted to change it because those who did get government jobs were the ones who could bring the change and the ones who least wanted it to happen.

Surekha called late one night and said, 'They've taken Suraj away...the police. He is in Marine Lines police station. Can you come now?'

'It's very late,' I said, looking nervously at Ajit, 'and Sahib is here and won't be pleased.' It was past 10.30 p.m. and Ajit needed an early night.

'He has a father who is handicapped and no mother. There's nobody else who can help him.'

'I'll come tomorrow,' I promised. But by the next morning it was too late. They had taken Suraj to what street people call the 'chillers home' (Children's Home) in Dongri that is more jail than home. I knew from past experience that releasing a child once he was in was in the hands of a court misleadingly called the Children's Welfare Court was a nightmare. The judges in this court seemed always to be chosen for their profound hatred of children. I remembered that when I had tried last time around to rescue two little girls, aged seven and eight, the lady judge had treated them like criminals. The worst part of this hellhole was that the smaller the child the more likely he was to be abused in every way. Suraj was only eight and home on the pavement for his 'summer holiday' from the residential school in Ahmednagar where a Christian charity had placed him.

So I understood the urgent need to get him out of the Children's Home and knew that if I went along there might be a better chance of explaining to the judge that I was prepared to guarantee that Suraj was a schoolboy and not a beggar. It was a hot, horribly humid afternoon on which I loaded Surekha into my car along with Suraj's sister Sangita, who brought along her tiny daughter. Sangita was a thin young woman with a long, sad face. On the way she said, 'I went to try and get my brother out last night but they told me in the police station that they would throw me in jail if I didn't leave and send my brother to the chillers home. I could do nothing.'

'Well, let's hope that I can do something,' I said.

This home that has been built supposedly for the welfare of children has high walls and a thick metal gate just like jails do. When we entered through the trap door in the enormous gate, the men who wrote our names down in the register gave Surekha and Sangita little scraps of paper on which they scribbled something. 'These are your entry passes,' the gatekeeper said in Marathi. 'Be sure to give them back to us when you leave.'

'And me?' I asked.

'You don't need one,' he said. I would have asked why had my eyes not fallen upon the tiniest, scrawniest little kitten who gnawed hungrily at the pink claw of a chicken. She ate as if she had never eaten anything in her life before. Nobody else noticed this tiny creature because the people who came to this grim children's prison were all parents whose children had been taken away from them for one reason or other.

From the outside the Children's Home is a fine place. It is built in a stolid, old-fashioned style, with tall steps leading to a corridor that opens onto large rooms on both sides. It may once have been a grand home because in the neglected gardens still stand ancient banyan trees whose roots hang down to the ground. And there are fruit trees and neem trees, in the shade of which hang the red T-shirts and khaki shorts that are the uniforms of inmates. Surekha and I both knew exactly where the courtroom was and I knew that it would be filled with anxious parents. On this day it was especially full of anxious relatives who clamoured for the attention of the three judges who sat at tables covered in files. In the middle sat a plump middle-aged woman who seemed to be the presiding judge. On her left was a large man and on her right sat a younger woman, with short-cropped hair, who seemed to be a trainee.

We had to wait fifteen minutes or so before the judges turned their attention to us. 'Yes,' the presiding judge said to me. My social worker friend, Anagaha, had told me that Mrs Murthy was usually kinder than the other judges. This lady was not a Tamilian.

'Are you Mrs Murthy?' I asked hopefully.

'No. She is on leave. What do you want?'

'This is Sangita,' I said, pushing her forward, 'and her brother Suraj was picked up last night from Marine Drive...'

'Full name?'

'Suraj Mahadev Chavan,' Sangita said nervously.

'Oh, yes. He has been arrested for begging. We will have to keep him here for at least a month.'

'He wasn't begging,' I said in English. 'He is in a residential school in Ahmednagar and his father is handicapped, so he helps out by selling bangles on Marine Drive.'

'Everyone who comes here says they weren't begging,' the judge said smugly. 'The police are not mad to bring us just anyone.'

'If you keep him here a month he will miss going back to school,' I pleaded, 'and I am ready to give you a personal guarantee that he will go back to school on the 25th.'

'Sorry. This is a court and we follow procedures here, and the procedure is that he cannot be released unless the school gives us a certificate stating that he is a student there.'

Sangita and Surekha both tried to convince her that since the school was closed for the vacations this would be impossible to obtain but they could get through on the telephone and speak to someone. Suraj had no proof that he was in boarding school in Ahmednagar. Meanwhile, Surekha had got through to the school and handed me her cell phone. The man at the other end confirmed that Suraj was a student there and I tried to get the lady judge to speak to him but she refused.

'Deal with this,' she said, turning to the male judge next to her.

In a clear attempt to show me my place he asked the small crowd of ladies standing behind me to move forward. They had files in their hands and looked desperate, so I did not mind waiting several minutes while he signed them, ignoring me completely. It was only when there was no excuse left to avoid speaking to me that he finally said, 'Yes.'

'Please speak to the school,' I said, handing him Surekha's cell phone. 'It is impossible for anyone to get a certificate until the school reopens after the holidays.'

'Sorry. Procedures are procedures,' he said.

'He is a little boy,' I said. 'How would you feel if it was your grandson who was locked up here?'

'Don't bring my family into this,' he said, getting angry.

'See how it feels when it's your family,' I said, getting angry as well.

'Do not speak like this...this is a courtroom and you should maintain the dignity of this courtroom.'

'Oh. And are you maintaining it?'

By now everyone else had fallen silent and the presiding judge was looking very irritated as I raised my voice and started talking about the absence of basic humanity in their attitude. I would have carried on this way but Surekha pulled me aside and told me that someone had just told her in Marathi that the judges could not care less whether she brought 'important people' with her. They would do nothing to help. Defeated, we left to try and see if Sangita could at least meet her little brother and see if he was all right. Surekha knew the procedures best, so we followed her out into the compound to an outhouse under a large banyan tree and into a room in which a man sat at a desk under a picture of Rajiv Gandhi. By now I was angry enough to give him a long lecture about the importance of basic humanity and he listened patiently to my tirade and said, 'I totally agree with you. I am new here and I feel the same way as you do but I cannot do anything.'

'Do you know that under Modi's rule these are the things that must change?' I said.

'Yes. And I am a big supporter of Modi Sahib. But it will take time for things to change.'

'So can you help us meet Suraj?'

'Let me see what I can do,' he said. 'I will find the officer who is handling his case.'

He disappeared for a longish while but since he was the only person that morning who had shown us basic kindness I was more than ready to forgive him. So we waited in his sweltering, airless office for half an hour. It was two days before the monsoon was due to come and the humidity was so high that Sangita's little baby whimpered in discomfort. Her mother tried giving her water that she carried with her in a small blue-topped feeding bottle but the child continued to whimper, so she and Surekha took her outside into a corridor in which there was more air. I went out onto a balcony that overlooked a magnificent banyan tree whose roots were nearly as tall as the building. Below it was a kitchen garden in which children worked as gardeners. Children's homes run by the state are famous for using their wards as unpaid child labour.

Finally, the official came back and told us that Kulkarni, the officer in charge of Suraj's case, was in court and would be here soon. After another long wait he arrived and took us down to a low-roofed building that was the boys' section of the children's home. It consisted of several windowless rooms built around a central courtyard. It was by now time for the evening snack, and young inmates were carrying metal tubs filled with bananas into the courtyard. When I tried to see where they were taking them the official who was with us said rudely, 'Please go out. You are not allowed in here.' I guessed that the real reason why he did not want me to go any further was that he did not want me to see the conditions in which the children were kept. Surekha and Sangita told me that the reason why children hated being in this home was that it was so crowded that at night they were forced to sleep glued to each other. 'There is not even room to move,' Surekha said, 'and then there are the beatings. Small boys are beaten by bigger boys and nobody stops them.'

Several minutes later Suraj was brought out by the official. He was so small and skinny that he looked younger than his eight years. He was barefoot and wore a red shirt and khaki shorts. When he saw his sister he burst into tears and begged her to take him away. 'They beat me all the time,' he said through his tears. 'Please take me away.' This made Sangita cry and when the official saw this he got angry. 'What is there to cry about? We are taking care of him well.'

'He was bitten by a dog yesterday,' she pleaded. 'He needs to take an injection.'

'So he should have told us this. Now it can only happen tomorrow when the nurse comes. We can't do anything tonight.'

Sangita asked if she could bring her brother something to eat, and when the official reluctantly gave permission she ran off with her baby clutched in her arms. And Surekha said, 'Suraj would not have got caught if it hadn't been for the dog having bitten him on his foot. He was with two other boys who managed to run away but he couldn't run, so they caught him.' Tears continued to pour down Suraj's small face while she talked and did not stop even when his sister returned with bottles of Limca and Fanta, biscuits and chopped fruit.

On our way home I called the only senior police officer I knew best in Mumbai at the time. Himanshu Roy had always helped me in the past. He said he was no longer in a department that could help but said, 'Call the police commissioner, Rakesh Maria. He will help you.' I thought Himanshu was just brushing me off but called the police commissioner anyway. First, his personal assistant gave me the usual 'He is busy in meetings all day' response and then to my amazement I got a call from Mr Maria himself. He assured me that he would do everything to release Suraj as soon as possible. And he did. Suraj was freed on a Saturday morning, and this meant that the police went over the heads of the judges who had behaved so heartlessly. So the story of Suraj had a happy ending. But the next day they arrested Vijay, the son of Lakshmi and Amit, and the process began all over again.

21

MISS MOOLIE'S STORY

It is Ajit's birthday and I am in Alibag on my own, unable to get thoughts of Miss Moolie out of my head. It is raining hard. The sort of monsoon day when she would have been lying languidly on the sofa, looking at me through half-closed eyes. When she used to do this it was almost as if she were trying to help me write whatever it was that I was trying to write. Instead she lies in a small grave at the end of the garden under a cluster of palm trees that I started to plant when I first brought her to this house by the sea. There was no house then and no garden, just two rows of leaning palm trees that rose out of the sand, but she seemed to decide within minutes that this would be her new home.

She raced up and down the long plot of land, digging in the sand and sniffing out sand creatures with such delight that I felt bad that we had to take her back to the confinement of the flat in Mumbai. It is exactly twenty-eight days since she died of acute renal failure. If she were alive she would have been ten years old this month.

Miss Moolie was what I used to call Julie, my present to Ajit on his birthday ten years ago. Little did I know that Julie would be so special a birthday present that she would change our lives. Ajit has always been a difficult person to find presents for and on nearly every birthday since we met I have bought him the wrong thing despite my best efforts. If I bought him clothes they were invariably the wrong kind, and if I bought him antique statues or expensive pens they disappeared to his office, never to be seen again. The plan was to find him a small dog like a Dachshund. When I called my sister, more connected with the dog world than I, to ask if she knew of any Dachshund puppies available in time for Ajit's birthday she said, 'No. But Bronwen's Beagle Ella has just had a litter. Why don't you ask her if there are any left?' So I called Bronwen Latif, an Australian friend who lived in Delhi, and she said that all the boys were taken but there were two girls left and if I wanted one of them she would be happy to give me one free. She wanted good homes for her puppies, she said, not people who could pay huge amounts of money. I thanked Bronwen and told her that I would be coming to Delhi in the next few days and would drop by and choose between the two girl puppies.

That evening after dinner I told Ajit that his birthday present was going to be a Beagle puppy. I knew that he loved dogs and had long mourned the Great Dane that he had as a boy, so I expected him to be excited by the news that he was going to finally have a dog of his own on his fifty-third birthday but I had not expected him to go mad with joy. I had not expected that he would jump out of his chair with excitement like my son did when I gave him his first puppy on his fifth birthday. He was, if anything, more excited. He leapt up and shouted, 'She is going to be Julie. I am going to call her Julie.' I told him that it sounded like the name of an extra from a Bollywood film but he was adamant. I never liked the name Julie and so always called her other names and the one that stuck was Miss Moolie. Moolie is the Hindi word for radish, and although she was elegant and beautiful and not at all like a radish the name sort of suited her.

Just before Ajit's birthday that year we went to see Julie for the first time in Bronwen's house in Nizamuddin. It was not a large house but one room had been turned into a Beagle nursery. Ella sat in a whelping box in a huddle of little black puppies whose eyes had barely begun to open. They looked like hairy black mice. Bronwen lifted one of them out for us and announced that this was Julie. When Ajit held her she was just a little bigger than his hand but even at this first meeting showed a sense of purpose. Almost the first thing she did when he lifted her up was put her right paw in the pocket of his blazer. Bronwen took a picture, which we put in a silver frame, and it still sits in a place of honour in our study in Mumbai.

The summer that Julie was born was the summer of 2001 when General Pervez Musharraf was coming to Agra for a very important summit meeting with Vajpayee. It was the first time they were to meet after Musharraf sent troops disguised as militants across the Line of Control in Kashmir three years earlier in May 1999.

The summit between Vajpayee and Musharraf was so important that the Aaj Tak channel agreed to send me to Pakistan to do a series of stories on different aspects of Pakistani life. I remember Bronwen calling me to tell me that Julie was ready to come home just as I was rushing off to Pakistan. I told her that I would not be able to pick her up until I came back to Delhi. So Julie's arrival home got postponed for a few days. Then when I came back to Delhi it had to be postponed while I went to Agra to cover what turned out to be a disastrous summit. This was three months before 9/11 changed the world, and Musharraf was still a belligerent military dictator who believed that the only thing

Pakistan needed to talk to India about was when we could hand Kashmir over on a silver plate. When the Indian side insisted that we needed to talk about other things before we got to a Kashmir solution Musharraf stormed off in a huff.

Luckily, I left before him. Not just because I knew that the summit was not going well but because I was afraid of not being able to get out of Agra once his cavalcade started to move. Half the roads in the city had been closed off for security reasons and I might not have been able to get to Delhi in time to pick up Julie that evening if my cousin had not been in charge of security in Agra that day. When I was stopped at a police barricade and ordered back into Agra city, I said if they did not let me pass I would call the inspector general of police. 'You go right ahead,' the policemen said with a sneer and nearly fainted with shock when I got Karam on the line and handed them my cell phone.

When I got back to Delhi the first thing I did was go to Nizamuddin to collect Julie. I had bought a small basket, some toys and a bowl in advance from a pet shop in Khan Market. I was supposed to leave for Mumbai in the next couple of days and wanted Julie to get used to me before taking her on the flight. She had grown since I had last seen her three weeks earlier, but although her eyes were open and she looked more like a puppy now than a large mouse she was still small enough to fit into my hands. Bronwen came to the car and bid her a tearful farewell with these words, 'You have a good life, little girl.' Then she disappeared into the house without looking back.

Julie spent the short drive back to my flat exploring the car. She climbed onto my shoulder and onto the back of the seat, and if I had not restrained her she might have climbed out of the window. For a puppy who had just said goodbye to her mother and brothers and sisters she seemed remarkably content. When we got home she wandered through the rooms sniffing at some things and nibbling at others. She was not much bigger than a large squirrel, and I dared not let her out of my sight for fear that she might disappear under some piece of furniture or fall off the terrace. What surprised me was that even on that first evening away from her mother she did not need to snuggle up and sleep in my bed as puppies like to. She slept happily in her little basket. The next day I took her with me to the pet shop in Khan Market and bought her a yellow leash and collar and a container in which to take her to Mumbai.

Ajit had pulled all sorts of strings in Indian Airlines to ensure that she did not need to travel in the hold but a prerequisite for her travelling in the cabin was that she must be in a container. The last seats in the aeroplane were reserved for us and once we were on board she was allowed out of her container and travelled on my lap, hugely enjoying the attention she got from the stewardesses and our fellow passengers. When we got out of the terminal building in Mumbai airport she insisted on walking to the car instead of being carried and she sniffed the humid monsoon air with the happy expression of someone who knows they have come home.

When we got to the flat at the end of Marine Drive that was to be her home she repeated her exploration exercise, with me following nervously in her wake. After she had satisfied her curiosity and had a bowl of milk she settled herself next to me on a sofa in the study and slept. If she had a moment of homesickness or pangs of separation from her family she hid them well. She was still curled up beside me when Ajit came home and from the moment he saw her he was in love. For her part she seemed to know right from that first day that she belonged to him. It's not that she did not love me as much, it's that she somehow managed to convey that she loved me differently, as one does a much loved nanny. It was I who looked after her basic needs but it was Ajit she thought of as the person she most wanted to be with.

Until she was three months old, Julie did not go out much except when we took her down to the garden for her morning and evening ablutions. She had many visitors, though, and she loved the toys they brought and the attention they gave her. From those very first weeks she made it clear that she liked very much her new role of being the most spoilt dog in the world. Ajit went nowhere without buying something for Julie, and so she ended up not just with special toys, treats and collars but with a Beagle-carrying bag that he picked up on a trip to Washington. When she was three months old, fully vaccinated, and ready to go out in the big bad world, she travelled in this bag when Ajit took her to the office and slept in it while he worked. From an early age she showed signs of spirit and a tendency to think of other dogs as inferior.

On one of her early excursions with Ajit when she was still small enough to fit into her bag, he took her to visit his daughter Shalaka, who had a puppy called Tango a few months older than Julie but much bigger since he was a Spaniel. Shalaka told me later that Julie's first meeting with another dog had not gone well. 'We put her on the table while Tango was on the floor and I fed her in Tango's bowl, which he did not like at all, and then when she had finished eating she looked down at him and barked, which really upset him.'

When she was old enough and we started taking her for walks on Marine Drive the only dogs she befriended were the mangy strays that lay in sad little heaps on the promenade. She seemed to sense that they were less privileged than she was and out of some Beagle sense of noblesse oblige always greeted them with a wag of her tail and a friendly sniff. But when she met dogs of higher pedigree she treated them badly. She would allow them to get close, wagging her tail when they approached, and then when they got really close she would snarl so unexpectedly that they leapt back in fright. Just as she liked stray dogs she liked stray children. In our building most of the children she met in the lift or the garden were afraid of her and tended to cower and whine when they saw her even when she was only a puppy, and this puzzled and irritated her. The only children she met who were not even slightly afraid of her were street children, and she loved them for this. It was through Julie that I was introduced to a side of the city that I knew existed but had no real knowledge of. It was through Julie that I learned to really understand poverty and how it imprisons those it has in its clutches. It was through Julie that I saw the most evil side of the Indian state.

Seven weeks after I brought Julie home the world changed in ways that nobody had imagined possible. On the evening of 11 September 2001 I was on a treadmill in my study watching the news on television. Julie was in her basket taking her evening nap with one eye half open to ensure that I did not suddenly abandon her to go off to some dinner party to which she was not invited. She was barely four months old and at that stage of a puppy's life when they do not understand or appreciate being left alone. In her case she especially resented being left alone with the cook and the bearer because although she liked them well enough she seemed to know that being left in their charge was slightly below her dignity. Julie was a snob.

I was watching the news on NDTV while working out and was only half paying attention to the seven o'clock news bulletin. So when the first visuals came of the twin towers collapsing I, like millions of other people all over the world, thought it was a shot from some Hollywood film. It took me a few moments before I noticed that the shot was being repeated over and over again. For some reason there was no commentary when I started to watch. When the commentator did finally speak he sounded puzzled and unsure. He said that it seemed as if by some accident an aeroplane had flown into one of the towers of the World Trade Centre in New York. In its usual 'liberal' way NDTV's first reaction was to describe what happened as an accident. Then, while I was watching, a second aeroplane hit the second tower and it became clear to even NDTV that this was no accident.

As I watched, mesmerized, the horror of what had happened slowly sank in. I rang Ajit, who was on his way home from work, and told him that there had been a terrorist attack on the World Trade Centre. He did not register what I was saying and seemed to take it quite calmly. I think he said 'another one' or something like that because he remembered the one before and remembered arguing with my friend Maryanne Weaver because she defended the blind Egyptian sheikh who was implicated in that one.

It was only when he started getting other telephone calls that the horror of what had just happened sank in and he called me back to ask details of what I was seeing on television. Aatish, then a sophomore at Amherst College, was spending a semester in France, and my first reaction was relief that there was no chance of his having been in New York on such a terrible day. I then rang his friend Sabrina Holkar, who was a student at Columbia University, to see if she was all right and she sounded dazed but reassuringly alive.

By the time Ajit came home an hour later I had become so hypnotized by what I was seeing that I had not even bothered to take a shower. We watched with growing horror the visuals of people jumping out of high floors to escape the furnace inside the towers.

We watched as the towers crumpled like houses made of wax. Both Ajit and I knew with certainty that the perpetrators could only have been jihadi terrorists. Until we found out the identities of the hijackers we were convinced that they were Pakistanis. Of all the fanatics I have met in my long career as a journalist the most fanatical have been those I met in Pakistan. Like every other journalist who covered Pakistan in the 1990s, I had wandered in and out of Peshawar and met leaders of the mujahideen groups fighting the Soviet army. The Afghans and Arabs I met never seemed as fanatical and insecure as the Pakistanis.

On a trip to Peshawar in 1993 I met the dreaded Gulbuddin Hekmatyar for the first and only time, and I remember thinking that even he did not seem as fanatical as some of the Pakistanis I met during the same trip. He seemed somehow more secure about his identity. When I met him I knew that he was the most dangerous of the mujahideen leaders and so it was after passing many rings of security that we entered an ordinary-looking house in which he sat in a very ordinary room. Instead of being the aggressive jihadi I was expecting to meet I was a little disappointed at how ordinary he was. I was in Peshawar with a group of Indian journalists on an exercise that has come to be called 'track two diplomacy'. We met Pakistani politicians, journalists and academics in different cities and spent long hours talking about the enmity between our two countries and ways in which it might be lessened. This particular trip was organized by Rehmat Shah Afridi, who owned the *Frontier Post* newspaper and was ostensibly a respectable businessman but who was surrounded by rumours that his real money came not from the newspaper business but from drug smuggling.

He was a small, stocky man with twinkling eyes and a way of speaking very softly. The only hint he gave of having anything to do with the drug trade was a conversation I had with him one evening after dinner in Peshawar. It was in my hotel room over a glass of excellent cognac that I had managed to bring with me across the border, and Nadira Alawi, soon to become Lady Naipaul, was with us. I think it must have been the cognac that started the conversation which ended with him saying resentfully that if opium poppies grew as easily in Western countries as grapes then they would have made drugs legal and liquor illegal. He sounded bitter when he said this and I remember wondering if there was truth in the rumours that he was a mighty drug lord.

By the time 9/11 happened he was in a jail cell in Lahore facing a double death sentence allegedly for his drug smuggling activities but more likely because of his association with Osama bin Laden. Before Osama shifted base to Afghanistan he had been a guest of Rehmat Shah in his home in the North-West Frontier Province.

That night as we watched the horror unfold in New York, Ajit and I became increasingly convinced that Pakistan must be behind it. My reason for thinking this was the way Musharraf had behaved in the two years he had ruled Pakistan. The coup that brought him to power in 1999 as Pakistan's fourth military dictator was the result of Nawaz Sharif, a democratically elected prime minister, having tried to prevent him from returning to Pakistan after a visit to Sri Lanka.

Inevitably, once Musharraf landed safely in Islamabad he made sure that Sharif was jailed and then exiled to Saudi Arabia after signing an affidavit that he would never contest elections again. Sadly for Pakistan he had run such a corrupt, authoritarian and useless government that Musharraf's coup was initially welcomed by most people in Pakistan. Musharraf brought back a semblance of order and clean government but in India he continued to be seen as a hateful military dictator who had forced upon us the Kargil war. After he became ruler of Pakistan the fragile order that he brought about domestically was matched by the chaos he created in Afghanistan and Kashmir, lending the full support of the Pakistani army to jihadi groups working towards creating violence and havoc in the rest of the world.

General Musharraf was not just one of the two rulers in the world who recognized the Taliban government in Kabul, he was the Taliban's main patron. It was under his aegis that Pakistan's leading nuclear scientist had started negotiating with Osama bin Laden to sell him a nuclear device. Had these negotiations succeeded it is possible that the 9/11 attack would have been nuclear. But we did not know this that evening as we stared in mesmerized horror at the images of devastation and death from New York.

The next morning when I took Miss Moolie for her walk on Marine Drive I found it hard to believe that the world was as it was. Ali was at his spot opposite the Oberoi Hotel doling out platefuls of steaming idlis and dosas with an expression of total concentration. Surekha and her friends were wandering about in small groups, barefoot and smiling, and there was the mysterious woman with short hair who was always there every morning carrying her daughter in her arms. She dressed like a beggar but never begged and spoke to nobody. Her daughter had the sweetest face, and one day when she smiled at me I tried to offer her mother some money but the woman refused and walked hastily on as if she was scared to talk to anyone. At the corner of Churchgate sat Devraj with his big Mongloid head and flippers for legs and his big, big smile.

The fat ladies with diamonds in their ears walked by in their expensive trainers as they usually did. The veiled Muslim ladies with their bearded men walked by as they usually did, and it was only the occasional huddle of men, talking in loud voices, that indicated that I was not the only one unable to get the horrible images from New York out of my mind.

22

EARLY SIGNS OF JIHAD

They say the world changed after 9/11. I have never been sure what this means. If it means that it was on 11 September 2001 that the world became aware that the world's new enemy was radical Islam then in India we have a story that begins much earlier. For me personally my first encounters with Islam's more radical face came in Kashmir in the 1980s, some months after Indira Gandhi toppled Farooq Abdullah's government in the summer of 1984. Farooq's government had only been in office for a year when Mrs Gandhi decided to get rid of him.

She got her minions and a compliant governor, Jagmohan of Emergency notoriety, to engineer a coup in which some legislators were 'persuaded' to withdraw support to Farooq. A puppet chief minister was installed instead at the head of a government that had Congress support. When people asked why this had happened Mrs Gandhi's henchmen spread around baseless charges that Farooq was removed because he was trying to revive secessionism in Kashmir. The truth is that it was the removal of Farooq's democratically elected government that revived memories of secession but this time with a sinister undercurrent.

It was winter and Srinagar was at its most desolate – cold,

bereft of tourists and dark most evenings because electricity
supply was so low that whole days could pass without the
lights coming on even after night fell over the city's icy lakes.
It was on one such dark evening that I went in search of
Farooq Abdullah in the house of one of his party workers
where I knew he was going to dine. I had been unable to meet
him during the three days I was in Srinagar because he had
been out touring in the villages, and as I was leaving the next
day for Delhi the next morning this private dinner party was
my only chance of meeting him.

The dinner was in one of those typical tall, narrow
houses that you find in the old part of Srinagar in which the
architecture is so linear that every room is built upon the
one below with a narrow staircase leading to all of them.
There was a power cut that night, so I remember walking
into a small candle-lit room in which Farooq and his host
were already seated on the carpeted floor, eating a Kashmiri
meal with their hands. The room smelled of roasted meat and
candlewax, and Farooq, ebullient as ever, joked about the
darkness that had descended on the Kashmir Valley after the
fall of his government.

Then as dinner ended and cups of steaming kahwa
were passed around we started talking seriously about the
political situation, and he said to me that one of the most
ominous recent developments was that the Jamaat-e-Islami
was suddenly flush with funds from Saudi Arabia and the
money was being used to promote an ugly kind of religiosity.
Kashmir's traditionally moderate Islam, which even allowed
women to pray in mosques, was being replaced by Wahabism,
he said, and told me that I should definitely try and find
out more before going back to Delhi. So I did. On my last
morning in Srinagar I went to the Jamaat-e-Islami's offices in
the old city, where a bearded, middle-aged man sat in a tiny

room filled with pamphlets in Urdu. He said that the jamaat was doing nothing that it had not done before. It was simply spreading the message of Islam.

'But you seem to be spreading this message more aggressively than you usually do. Right?'

'It is Allah's will,' he said piously.

'And where is the money coming from to implement Allah's will?'

'We have benefactors in many countries.'

'Countries like Saudi Arabia?'

'Many countries,' the old man said, giving me a suspicious look.

'But why do you need to spread Islam in a state where the majority of the population is already Muslim?' I asked with a persistence that was clearly irritating him.

'We are just doing what we have always done. We serve Islam as we have always done.'

He refused to admit that there was a new, deliberate attempt to spread a new kind of Islam in the Kashmir Valley. But it became more and more evident that something new was happening every time I went to Srinagar. I went often in those times because I was gathering material for a book on Kashmir that I had already started writing. On one visit I ran into Vijay Dhar in the lobby of his Broadway Hotel, and he told me sadly that he had just been forced to close down the Broadway cinema under pressure from 'the militants'. It was on this same visit that I found that video lending libraries had been ordered to be closed by the same shadowy militant groups.

On another visit, while I was eating a delicious lunch of haaqe spinach and Kashmiri rice in the restaurant of the Broadway Hotel, I remember noticing a bearded young man having a conversation with the barman. The bar adjoined the restaurant. After the bearded young man left I asked the barman what he had said to make him look so frightened and he whispered, 'The bar has to be closed down. He told us that if we do not close it we will be forced to because liquor is banned in Islam.'

Some days later I remember being assailed by the smell of liquor while driving through a bazaar in an older quarter of Srinagar. When I stopped to see where it was coming from I saw a group of bearded young men taking bottles out of a liquor shop and smashing them on the pavement outside. As Islamism spread came news of incidents of acid being thrown in the faces of girls who did not cover their heads. An organization called the Dukhtaran-e-Millat came into being, and its leader, Asiya Andrabi, is so heavily veiled that the only thing you can see of her face are her spectacles. Today it is hard to find a woman in Srinagar who does not wear hijab, hard to remember that Kashmiri women never had a tradition of covering their faces.

It was not just in Kashmir that radical Islam began to make its presence felt in India long, long before 9/11. Towards the end of the 1990s I remember encountering it in a slightly bizarre way on a visit to the southern commercial city of Coimbatore. Aatish studied at the time in an American boarding school in Kodaikanal, and the usual way that I got there was by taking a flight to Coimbatore and then a taxi up into the hills from the airport.

On my way back to Delhi once, I had some time to kill and decided to investigate what lay behind the Valentine's Day bombings some months earlier. They were the work of jihadi groups whose main target had been L.K. Advani, who was due to address a public rally in Coimbatore on 14 February 1998. Bombs went off across the city hours before the rally, leaving fifty-eight people dead and 200 wounded.

By the time I got to Coimbatore that day the groups behind the bombings had been identified, so I was less interested in the police investigation and more curious about the mood among local Muslims. I asked where the largest Muslim area of the city was and found myself in a locality called Ukkadam, which was a place of narrow alleys in the shadow of a large mosque.

As I write these words and memories of that day form into images in my head, what I remember being most puzzled by was that the women in the streets wore salwar-kameez with dupattas covering their heads. In southern India Muslim women usually wear saris and look no different from Hindu women, but here in Coimbatore were women who seemed to go out of their way to wear Punjabi clothes in their effort to look Islamic. When I stopped a young woman and asked if I could talk to her she said, 'No. We are not allowed to talk to anyone without permission from the imam.'

'Why not?'

'Our Prophet has said that women should stay in their homes and not talk to strangers.'

'Oh, come on. Where in the Quran has the Prophet said this?'

'I am sorry I cannot talk to you,' she said.

'All right, so introduce me to someone who can talk to me.'

She directed me to the office of a male lawyer who was as evasive about the Imam's new role as she had been. 'We are guided by the imam,' he said, 'because he knows better than we do what the rules are of the Quran.' Of course I never got to meet the imam because like most imams he remained elusive during the time I was in Ukkadam. But what I began to notice after this visit to Coimbatore was how many Muslim women in Mumbai were suddenly veiled when they walked on Marine Drive. And how in Hyderabad I had been mystified by pictures of Osama bin Laden on the cover of an Urdu magazine. He was almost unknown in India before 9/11, and if I knew about him it was mostly because of trips to Peshawar during mujahideen days when the United States backed radical Islamist groups with arms and funds in their war against the Soviet Union in Afghanistan.

Like the pieces of a puzzle, memories of half-forgotten conversations started to fit together in my head after 9/11. I remembered my trip to Pakistan just before Musharraf's visit to Agra for the summit meeting with Vajpayee. While wandering about rural villages not far from Lahore to try and talk to women about their rights under Islam, I stopped at a village bus stand where a small group of women waited to catch a bus. Among them was a young woman in a pale pink salwar-kameez who had covered her face with her pink dupatta so that only her eyes showed. When I asked her if she thought that women had equal rights in Pakistan she said, 'We have the rights given to us in the Quran by our Prophet.'

'And do you work? Do you have a job?' I remember asking innocently.

'In Islam women are not supposed to work if it means working with men who are not related to them.' She looked pointedly at my cameraman and crew, so I asked if she thought that I was breaking the rules of Islam, and she said curtly that I was free to make my own conclusions.

Later that same day in Lahore I was berated by another young Pakistani woman for not respecting the dress code of Islam in a Muslim country. I was dressed in what I thought was a perfectly appropriate salwar-kameez but my head was uncovered, and this caused offence not just to the young woman but everywhere I went. On this trip I stayed with my friend Nuscie, and that evening she organized a small dinner party at which I met some of Lahore's leading citizens. When

I told them that I had detected distinct signs of an ugly kind of religious fundamentalism wherever I went, they said that it was only because I was Indian. They were in denial, as were most other liberal Muslims in India. And this was two months before 9/11.

The world had been changing long before the attack but it was as if nobody wanted to see what was happening. Not even the mighty United States of America. Not until 9/11 did the Americans do anything to curb the activities of their close friend Saudi Arabia, or their other close friend Pakistan. This is no excuse for us in India. We should have been able to see that Muslims were moving away from the liberal traditions of Indian Islam and towards the harsh Saudi version of the religion, but for some reason nobody did until after 9/11. And then the reaction from Hindus and Hindutva groups was violence and brutality. In the reams that have been written about the Gujarat riots that have so stained Narendra Modi's name, nothing I have read has made the link between the terrible massacres of Muslims in February 2002 with the 9/11 attacks. But a link there was, even if a subtle one. I remember meeting Hindus in villages a year after the violence who said that Muslims deserved what had happened to them because they were at the root of violence all over the world. They mentioned the attacks in New York and Washington almost as often as they mentioned the burning of Hindu pilgrims in the Sabarmati Express that had been the direct cause of the violence.

Shekhar Gupta had asked me to write a piece for the *Express* on Gujarat a year after the riots, and I had readily agreed because I had not been back to Gujarat since the violence. So I had taken the night train from Mumbai to Godhra, where the burned carriages of the Sabarmati Express still stood on a siding. In the Muslim quarter of this

ugly dump of a town I spent hours talking to the families
of those who had been arrested for attacking the train and
causing the death of the fifty-nine Hindu pilgrims returning
from Ayodhya. I did not meet one person who admitted to
having been at Godhra railway station that day, leave alone
setting fire to the train carriage. The police had arrested them
wrongfully, they all said.

Afterwards I drove to Ahmedabad, stopping in villages
that were worst affected by the violence. It was a horrible
journey. I met terrified Muslim families who were still in
hiding because they were too afraid to return to their villages.
I met women who had been raped and women who had seen
their children cut to pieces in front of their eyes. And in
villages with 'Hindu Rashtra' written before the names of the
villages, I met Hindu killers who told me proudly that they
would have been in jail if it had not been for the protection
they got from Modi.

When I came to see him at the end of this awful journey I
meant to ask him about these things, but I had barely entered
when I had to leave. It was as if he had agreed to see me
only to throw me out. He was seated at a large desk with his
arms folded in front of him and staring straight ahead as if
he had not noticed my arrival. When I greeted him he turned
his face towards me and after several icy moments of silence
said, 'You knew me in the days when I was in Delhi, so how
could you have written that I engineered the violence?' Then
he looked away and I was dismissed. There was no interview.
No further conversation. It is true that I knew Modi in Delhi
when he was just a humble BJP worker, but it is also true that
I did not know him well enough to know if he was capable of
doing what his critics say he did in Gujarat in 2002.

23

CORRUPTION AND A CRUSADER

By the middle of Sonia Gandhi's second tenure as India's de facto prime minister there was deep anger against her rule. The economy had begun to collapse, and even as ordinary people were feeling the pressure of the job market drying up there came stories from a hyperactive government accountant about misuse of public money. The comptroller and auditor general (CAG) of India is usually so faceless a bureaucrat that he would go unrecognized in Delhi's corridors of political power. But this was not what Vinod Rai wanted, so he took to making public his findings through the media. No sooner did he do this than media trials began of people who had supposedly benefited wrongly from cronyism in the acquisition of cell phone spectrum and licences to mine coal in nationalized coalmines. By the time he had finished making his revelations it began to feel as if the government was steeped in corruption and 'crony capitalists' had ravaged the country's natural resources.

India was more than ready for a movement against corruption. So when Anna Hazare appeared on the corner of Jantar Mantar on a balmy April morning in 2011, a slow trickle of people began to come and lend support from the very first day. On the morning that I went to see what was happening I saw schoolgirls in blue uniforms lined up to go and salute the little man who reclined against bolsters on a white stage. Behind him was a backdrop of Bharat Mata and patriotic songs played to keep the spirits up of those who were on hunger strike with this social activist from Maharashtra who was till then almost unknown. I knew of him only because of a half-forgotten story I had read in some newspaper about how he had transformed the village of Ralegan Siddhi by introducing modern methods of water management. And by tying up and beating youths who refused to follow his strict diktats against alcohol.

That morning was the first time I saw him in real life. Beside him sat a group of people among whom I recognized only Kiran Bedi, the former police officer, and Prashant Bhushan, who I knew from TV debates as a leftist lawyer. The man who was to become the most famous of them all, Arvind Kejriwal, was someone so obscure that I did not recognize him at all.

I spent some time in Jantar Mantar that morning, and as I watched the steady stream of ordinary citizens coming to pay homage to the man who had decided to go on a hunger strike against corruption I noticed celebrated TV anchors appear one after the other. By that evening nearly every news channel had set up makeshift studios below the stage on which Anna sat and were telecasting live every move that he and his companions made. Anna's hunger strike against corruption had caught the imagination of private news channels in a way that almost no other story ever had. They virtually moved to the venue of the hunger strike for the next few days.

The inevitable result was that soon all of India had seen images of the little man 'fasting unto death' on the white stage, and soon there were huge crowds at Jantar Mantar. Young men came from distant cities and villages, and when asked why they had come they said, 'Corruption is the biggest problem in our country...and we are moved that this old man has decided to go on a hunger strike against it.' Soon protests against corruption started erupting in streets across India. The protesters were mostly educated, middle-class people who had long suffered at the hands of corrupt officials and policemen and who believed the CAG when he said that a small handful of very rich industrialists had made huge fortunes out of resources that belonged to the people of India. Anna himself could not have imagined that his hunger strike would strike such a resonant chord across India.

Personally, I was unimpressed with Anna and his movement and deeply perturbed by the extreme left opinions of his comrades. Prashant Bhushan repeated over and over on television that India had been ruined by corruption that was the direct result of economic reforms. Neither Anna nor his companions appeared to understand that it was not private enterprise that had ruined India but statism, and this worried me more about the anti-corruption movement than anything else. But what the movement accidentally achieved was to show up the complete amateurishness of the government that Sonia Gandhi ran.

When middle class urban Indians wearing Anna caps took to the streets in cities across India the first reaction of the government was panic. Every demand that Anna and his comrades made for an almighty ombudsman called a Lokpal was accepted and in haste was created a new anti-corruption law that most sensible people knew would do nothing to reduce corruption. When this law was rejected and Anna announced that he would be going on hunger strike once more, and this time not at a street corner on Jantar Mantar Road but on a huge elevated stage in Ramlila Maidan, the government foolishly arrested him, making him a bigger hero than ever. He caught the imagination of not just the Indian media but the whole world, and then there was no stopping him from becoming for a brief moment the most famous man in India.

His celebrity was ephemeral since it came not from his decades of hard work but from the media. But for a while it seemed as if Anna could become a new Gandhi. Or at the very least a new Jayaprakash Narayan. For those of us who remembered JP's movement against corruption from the 1970s, it seemed for a while like déjà vu. What we did not notice was that the big difference between JP's movement and the one that Anna led was that JP achieved national recognition from the issues he raised and not from a fawning, hysterical media. In Anna's case it was the media that made him bigger than he really was, it was the media that papered over his absence of political understanding, his emphasis on a single solution to all of India's problems: a Lokpal. Anna became such a star that even Sonia Gandhi's assiduous cultivation of editors and TV anchors did not save her government from getting some very bad publicity.

When the media realized that they had created a false god the news channels soon lost interest, and Anna disappeared into the rural landscape from whence he came. The first sign of this came at a 'mega' rally he was scheduled to have in Mumbai. A vast ground was booked for the event amid the tall, shiny office blocks of Bandra-Kurla Complex, and I made a special effort to go. I parked my car some distance from the venue, thinking that I would have to walk through milling crowds to get to the stage on which Anna sat, but I was wrong. There were no crowds and the handful of people who came showed little enthusiasm for Anna. The rally was such a dismal failure that it ended early with Anna's health being used as an excuse. The only enduring effect of the Anna movement was that Kejriwal went on to form a political party and through a metamorphosis went from activist to full-time politician. But by then what had become clear was that people were very, very angry with Sonia Gandhi's government. Nobody called it Dr Manmohan Singh's government any more because he had retired into a world of shadows and silences from which he emerged only occasionally to go off quietly on some trip abroad.

24

SONIA'S HEIR

The editor was known to be close to Sonia Gandhi. He was one of a small group of senior journalists who regularly went to tea at 10 Janpath. And one of an even tinier handful who was granted a full interview. Towards the end of 2011 we met in a Delhi coffee shop for our usual exchange of political gossip. This time he had more information than I did. No sooner did our coffee arrive and the waiter removed himself to a safe distance than he said to me in a furtive whisper that the time had come for 'the yuvraj to claim his inheritance'.

'Oh?'

'Yes. I have it from the highest level that after the UP election Dr Manmohan Singh will hand over to Rahul Gandhi.'

'Just like that?'

'Just like that. They are expecting to do very well in UP because they did so well in the Lok Sabha elections...twenty-nine seats is a lot for a party that hasn't won in UP since Rajiv Gandhi was prime minister. And Rahul will lead the campaign and then come triumphantly to take Delhi.'

Rumours of this transfer of power had wafted around Delhi's murky corridors of power ever since Dr Manmohan Singh began his second term as prime minister. They subsided after Congress faced a humiliating defeat in the Bihar election a year before this conversation. Rahul had put his heart and soul into the campaign, or so I thought, but managed only to bring the party's measly nine seats down to four. I reminded the editor of this and he said the same thing was unlikely to happen in Uttar Pradesh where the two mighty caste chieftains, Mayawati and Mulayam Singh, who had between them ruled India's largest state for more than twenty years, were now unpopular and discredited.

Mayawati was chief minister at the time and appeared to have spent most of her term in office building ostentatious sandstone memorials to Dalit pride. They were scattered all over UP, and the one I passed every time I went to a TV studio in Noida was like a Disney version of Rashtrapati Bhavan. It was made of sandstone, sprawled over many acres, and had impressive domes, but somehow the proportions were all wrong and somehow the gigantic statues of Mayawati and her mentor Kanshi Ram were grotesque rather than grand.

On travels in UP I heard from people who had voted for the Bahujan Samaj Party that the memorials had not gone down well even with her most committed supporters. Instead of infusing Dalit pride they served mostly to remind people of money that could have been better spent. So in Delhi the rumours that Congress was expecting a spectacular victory in the UP elections were easily believed. The equation was simple when seen from the tree-lined avenues of Lutyens' Delhi. Mayawati had lost popularity and this had not benefited her old rival Mulayam because people had not forgotten that in his time criminals were more powerful than officers charged with law enforcement.

Days after my conversation with the editor, I met an old friend who had been a Gandhi family loyalist since the time of Sanjay Gandhi's glory. I asked him about the possible transfer of power and he confirmed that this was the plan. 'But what if you lose in UP?'

'We won't. Because this time Rahul is going to lead the campaign.'

'He led the campaign in Bihar and that seemed to not make much difference.'

'Ah, but he didn't really campaign. He addressed a few meetings, that's all. In UP he is going to be really campaigning. He will be the face of the campaign.'

'But will it really make a difference at a time when the Anna Hazare movement has made the Congress the epitome of corruption?'

'It has sort of died out now and there won't be any impact in UP. Local issues matter there.'

'So the plan is that there will be this victory in UP and then a triumphant Rahul will come back to Delhi and Dr Manmohan Singh will graciously vacate the seat for him?'

'Yes. In any case he has acted mostly as a regent in his second term...it's no secret. And only the other day he himself said that he would hand over power to Rahul Gandhi whenever he wanted to become prime minister.'

This was the plan and in the eyes of Dynasty loyalists it may have been a good one. Rahul would have three years before the general elections to show his mettle, and this would increase Congress chances of winning a third term. Rahul Gandhi began to make his presence felt in the state for many months before the election. He took to turning up in remote villages to eat meals in Dalit homes. There were always reporters around to take pictures that showed scrawny underfed Dalits looking on with puzzled expressions as the white, handsome Yuvraj of India sat on the dirt floor of their frail huts eating their meager meal with his hands. Mayawati, as the most important Dalit leader in the land, was not amused. She declared publicly that she had heard that after spending the night in Dalit homes the 'Yuvraj of the Congress Party' washed with a special soap.

Mayawati's barbs did not deter Rahul. He continued his poverty tours and sometimes took with him foreign friends like David Miliband. Nearly always there were reporters around to record these events. So there was a small army of TV reporters in the villages of Bhatta-Parsaul on the day he went to expose the 'brutality' of Mayawati's policemen. She was building the Yamuna Expressway, India's first access-controlled highway, and needed to acquire land in these villages that came in the way of her grand highway. But the farmers of Bhatta-Parsaul resisted and two policemen were killed by protesting farmers, forcing the police to respond, as Indian policemen usually do, with violence. Three farmers were killed in police firing, and this became an incident of the kind Indian political leaders traditionally use to make political capital. It was with this idea in mind that Rahul descended on the villages with television reporters following in his wake.

When he got to the dusty, fly-blown villages that sit like khaki scars in a landscape of green fields, he planted himself on the edge of a large freshly dug pit and announced in full view of TV cameras that seventy-eight bodies were buried beneath the dirt. This was not just alarming but a really big story, so reporters from all over the country descended on the villages of Bhatta-Parsaul and made their own inquiries, only to discover that Rahul had not just exaggerated but lied. Not a single body was found and nobody managed to find the women that he said had been raped by Mayawati's policemen.

When the story became this interesting I considered it my duty to go and see for myself. So I set off from Delhi on a hot, sunny morning and drove towards UP. As soon as I crossed the border I found myself in the salubrious, modernistic urban landscape of Noida. Having travelled often on this road in earlier times I remembered that there had once been dirt-poor villages here, bad roads, squalor and poverty. Now on either side of the four-lane highway there were flowering trees, parks and modern buildings of glass and chrome, some of which contained the Film City where most national TV channels have their studios.

On my right I passed one of Mayawati's memorials filled with sandstone domes and giant statues and then I came to Pari Chowk (Fairy Crossroads), where upon a grassy roundabout stood white plaster statues of Bollywood-style goddesses. Here the highway and modernity ended and I found myself once more in the Uttar Pradesh of yore. Ugly semi-towns and semi-villages lined the bumpy road that replaced the highway. In the narrow streets of these squalid settlements stood pools of stagnant water, rotting garbage and stray cattle. The village of Bhatta had an unpaved main street lined with open drains, and it was in this street that I stopped to talk to farmers. There were Hindus and Muslims and nobody was prepared to identify themselves, but everyone was happy to tell me why the protest had started.

'We heard that the government was buying our land at Rs 7 lakh a bigha and selling it to builders for Rs 45 lakh.'

'How many bighas make an acre in UP?'

'Five.'

'So you are saying that an acre of land sells for Rs 2 crore?'

There was a moment of confused silence in the gathering before someone said that the land was not worth that much yet but it would be when it was sold to those who were building the highway. Since Mayawati had been arrogant enough not to explain to people how they would benefit from the highway there was hostility and suspicion, but I did not meet anyone who was unwilling to sell his land if the price was what they considered right. Most farmers I met that morning said they were eager to sell their land because there was so little money to be made from farming but they had no idea what the market price of their land was because there was no land market. The price farmers paid for paying no taxes on their earnings was a licence raj that controlled not just the price of their land but the price of their produce. Officials controlled the markets in which farmers sold their land. It was in every sense a licence raj that in the name of protecting farmers had served mostly to keep them in poverty.

The only real prosperity farmers saw was when urbanization crept into their villages from big cities and towns and they were able to sell their land for whatever price they asked. Those of socialist disposition did not like this, and in the conferences they held in the air-conditioned halls of five star hotels in Delhi and Mumbai spoke passionately about how farmers ended up ruining their lives after selling their land because when they got too much money suddenly they spent it on cars, liquor and high living.

From Bhatta I went to Parsaul, where I was told I would find the women who had been 'raped'. I sat in the shade of a large neem tree and women gathered round. They wore tattered saris and had rough, calloused hands and told me in detail about how the policemen had come into their homes at night in search of their men. 'This was after the firing in which policemen were killed.'

'Yes. But the men were not here. They were hiding in the fields,' said a middle-aged woman.

'And then what happened?'

'They roughed us up and demanded to know where the men were hiding...can you imagine this happening in a state ruled by a woman chief minister?'

'Was anyone raped?'

'Not in this village. But we have heard that women were raped in Bhatta.'

'In Bhatta they told me women were raped in Parsaul...'

'No. Not here...'

So I went back to Bhatta and asked the farmers who told me about rapes in Parsaul where I could find the 'raped' women. An uncomfortable silence fell over the gathering until someone said, 'You know that these are things women do not like to talk about.'

It was clear that Rahul Gandhi had been taken for a ride. There were no dead bodies in the villages of Bhatta and Parsaul and no raped women, but this did not bother him and he led a delegation of farmers to the prime minister to complain about Mayawati's government. The media carefully reported this without comment. The Bhatta-Parsaul drama was merely the start of Rahul's campaign to win Uttar Pradesh. He spent nearly all of 2011 wandering about the state telling people how the Congress was the only party that was on the side of the poor and on the side of Muslims and Dalits, but it made no difference. The Congress lost as badly as it had in Bihar. The only difference was that in the Bihar election Rahul's campaigning reduced Congress seats from nine to four and in Uttar Pradesh his strenuous campaigning brought a slight increase in the number of Congress seats from twenty-two to twenty-eight. In the two states that should have given Rahul his chance to become prime minister in the middle of Dr Manmohan Singh's second term, the Congress came last out of the national parties.

25

A CRUCIAL ELECTION

The election in Uttar Pradesh came months after Rahul Gandhi's excursion to Bhatta-Parsaul. He worked hard to win. Months before the election was announced he would appear regularly in very poor villages to be photographed helping villagers. Sometimes he could be seen carrying cement on his head in a line of workers at a construction site, sometimes he would appear to lead a farmers' agitation against land acquisition, and always there were those shots of him, behaving as if he were just on ordinary Indian, on news channels and on the front pages of newspapers.

Anybody covering politics in Lutyens' Delhi knew that the image was a complete fake and that when he returned from his travels he partied hard in a few select drawing rooms with a select group of friends. Everyone knew that he was fundamentally confused about political issues and very confused about economic ones, but the media was accustomed to being totally servile when it came to the Dynasty. So Rahul's rural forays were more often than not reported as serious political exercises. NGOs, high officials and important political leaders were equally reticent.

My friends in the Congress made it a point to avoid being seen talking to me in public. But we would meet privately and then they would open their hearts about their difficulties with Rahul's leadership. So it was that just before the Uttar Pradesh election I found myself in the drawing room of an old friend who was a cabinet minister. We sat in a musty, windowless room amid cupboards filled with European bric-a-brac, chatting about the election, and he seemed despondent.

'So what do you think is likely to happen?' I asked.

'We could do well, judging by the Lok Sabha results, but I am not sure we will,' he said shaking his head sadly.

'Why not?'

'It's Rahul. He seems to be more of a social worker than a politician.'

'Why do you say that?'

'Well, many reasons…but I will give you one example. He called me to discuss campaign strategy and I had just started to give him some ideas when he interrupted me and said we would have to postpone the meeting because he had to meet someone important. So I got up and as I was leaving saw that the important person he was meeting was one of those NGO jholawala types. He is more comfortable with them than he is with politicians and that cannot be good.'

Not only was Rahul more comfortable with NGO types but so was his mother. In Dr Manmohan Singh's second tenure as prime minister it was Sonia who ruled through the National Advisory Council filled with the sort of people who liked saying 'But what about the poor?' whenever a policy was discussed. It is possible that their desire to help the poor was genuine, but they continued to devise centralized welfare programmes that sounded good on paper but rarely worked in real life. So on the ground in India's vast rural hinterland nothing changed, and in cities and towns that voted overwhelmingly in 2009 for Sonia Gandhi and Dr Manmohan Singh, jobs began to dry up as the NGO economists in Sonia's kitchen cabinet conjured up huge welfare schemes for the poor without noticing that real jobs could only come from real investment and this could only come from rich people.

By the time of the UP elections in early 2012 there was a general sense of discontentment everywhere, but Congress strategists continued to hope for a victory. Winning was crucial because it was clear that this was a rehearsal for the general elections due in two years. The shadow of Narendra Modi had not yet begun to loom over the country, so the Congress had reason to be optimistic even if there was more than a little pessimism among the party's rank and file about Rahul's ability to lead.

When I arrived in Lucknow to find out for myself what was happening I discovered a city that had been transformed by Mayawati into a Dalit memorial park. Magnificent sixteenth century Muslim monuments that once decorated the city's skyline were now dwarfed by sandstone parks built as memorials to Dalit pride. They all seemed carefully guarded and closed to the public. And although I stopped at their gates to find out why they did not allow people to visit them, all I discovered from those who guarded the gates was that they were open on certain occasions.

Lucknow was so filled with visiting politicians and journalists that I was unable to find a room in the very nice Taj Hotel. So I found myself forced to stay in the much less attractive Clarks Hotel that I remembered from earlier visits as a grubby dosshouse. It had not improved. The lobby reeked of stale food and incense, and in the restaurant yellow turmeric stains on tablemats added to the general air of dirt and decay. When after a hasty bowl of tomato soup I went up to check the condition of my room I realized that the first thing I would need to do was buy some clean bed linen. The sheets on the bed smelled of hair oil from the head of the person who slept in them before me. Luckily in Lucknow's main bazaar, Hazratganj, there was a Bombay Dyeing shop where I bought a bedroll that contained a blue sheet, pillow and a soft blue quilt. Decades of reporting from mofussil India have taught me that a clean bed and a clean toilet are absolute necessities. Having taken care of these needs I asked my Dalit driver, Ranjit, to set off in the direction of Rae Bareli.

He was a talkative young man who told me that Mayawati had been a good chief minister from his viewpoint because she had done a lot for the Dalit community. 'Like what?' I asked as we drove out of the city onto a broken, bumpy road that took us through urban settlements that looked like villages that had spilled out of their rural boundaries without purpose or design. In crowded bazaars whose shops advertised computer classes and cell phones stood stray cows eating plastic out of open garbage dumps. Armies of pigs loitered about along with diseased street dogs and half-naked filthy children. No different a scene from how I remembered it from earlier travels in the 1970s when Indira Gandhi was the candidate from Rae Bareli.

Between the squalid little towns there appeared like a vision from another lost time mango groves full of dark shade and soft light and fields in gentle shades of green. But for the most there were few signs that Mayawati's government had brought real change or development. When I mentioned this to Ranjit he said, 'You have to go into the Ambedkar villages to see the difference.'

'Are there any on the way?'

'Yes. Yes. Many...there is one that I know well about twenty kilometres before we get to Rae Bareli. Shall we stop there?'

'Yes. Yes. We shall.'

So we drove past more settlements that were like hideous sores, neither town nor village, and without minimum civic services, until he spotted a rusting board that said 'Ambedkar Gaon'. The village was called Mastipur. We drove off the main highway onto a surprisingly good rural road, and Ranjit explained that once a village was chosen to be part of the Ambedkar scheme it was given electricity, water, a road and 'kalonis'. When I asked what a 'kaloni' was he explained that this was a single-room house that the government built free for homeless Dalit families.

The village of Mastipur had the usual open drains, flies and filth and did not seem to be 'developed' in any way, but when local residents gathered on plastic chairs outside the house of the sarpanch they said that their lives had improved a lot. The sarpanch was not as happy as them. He said that since his election two years ago the government had not given him any funds for 'kalonis' and hinted that without this he might find it hard to win the next election. He also wanted the government to pay for a water tank so that water could be made available in individual homes. The biggest problem in this village, as in villages across India, was unemployment. The young men who gathered around as I talked to the sarpanch said that there were many among them who were college graduates but had not been able to get jobs.

When we drove out of Mastipur, Ranjit was muttering to himself and changing gears with a little too much aggression. I asked him what the matter was and he said he was angry that Mastipur was chosen to be part of the Ambedkar village scheme. It was a much richer village than his own village near Sitapur that did not even have electricity yet. 'We tried to get it declared an Ambedkar village because it is really poor but someone cancelled us out of the list.'

'Who?'

'Some officials must be,' he said. 'You know how much money is involved in these schemes, so there is always corruption.'

'So how would it have made a difference in your life?'

'I would have had a kaloni,' he said. 'At the moment I have only a rented room in Lucknow where my wife and son live. We have nothing in the village.'

'Not even your parents' home?'

'Oh, they have a kaloni but it is too small for all of us to live there. This is why I am forced to live and work in Lucknow.'

'Don't you like Lucknow?'

'Yes…but my wife is unhappy because she is alone all day and has nothing to do. I want to buy a TV but I can't afford one.'

'How much would it cost?'

'The cheapest would cost Rs 3,000,' he said wistfully.

The next Ambedkar village we stopped in was called Mubarakpur. It had more charm than Mastipur because it sprawled around a large pond, on the edge of which stood magnificent banyan trees. The village headman had gone to Rae Bareli to help organize Sonia Gandhi's rally, and so it was from his daughter, a pretty young girl in jeans and a T-shirt, that I learned of changes since the village came under the Ambedkar scheme a year earlier. 'We have a pucca road,' she said in educated Hindi, 'and we get regular supplies of electricity and water, and many people have been given kalonis.'

'So you are happy with Mayawati?'

'Yes, Mayawati has done a lot for us…' Even as she said the words a bearded Muslim gentleman interrupted her to say that Mayawati had done nothing that the Congress had not done. 'What is the difference between the Mahamaya

Awas scheme and the Indira Awas scheme?' When I asked if he would tell me something about how Muslims felt about the coming election he told me curtly that he had no time because he was on his way to attend Sonia Gandhi's rally. 'There is a bus going,' he announced to the gathered villagers, 'for those who want to come.'

The rally began at almost exactly the time that I arrived in Rae Bareli. We heard the chopper flying overhead, so Ranjit suggested that we watch it on television instead of trying to get to the ground where it was being held. He knew a restaurant that had excellent food, he said, so we could eat lunch while we watched. The Suryesh shudh vegetarian restaurant was filled with other people who had the same idea.

Nearly every table was taken, but resourceful Ranjit found us one close to the large TV screen. The first images that flickered onto the screen were of the helicopter landing in a khaki cloud of dust. The next images were of Sonia Gandhi on a stage sitting next to her daughter, and holding her hands together in the awkward, jerky namaste that was typical of the way she greeted crowds. She looked uncomfortable and nervous especially in contrast to her daughter, to whom the common touch came so naturally that many of my colleagues in the media raved in gushing tones about how it was she who should be in politics and not her brother. Priyanka smiled and waved to the crowd and then playfully pinched her mother's cheek to make her smile. Sonia had suffered for more than a year from an unnamed illness and this was one of her first public appearances in months. A friend who had tea with her weeks earlier said she had appeared very frail and was being careful about her diet, but there was no sign of this in Rae Bareli that afternoon. In aggressive tones she told the good people of Rae Bareli that 'we have sent you Rs 100,000 crore from Delhi but the local government has eaten it up'. She said nothing else of consequence in her singularly dull speech.

After eating a delicious thali lunch of spicy vegetables and soft rotis we drove on to Amethi on a road that I described in my notes as such 'a bumpy ribbon of a dirt trail that I could no longer make notes in my notebook'. There were small signs of development since I was last here twenty years ago but almost too few to mention. We drove past a Ryan International School, an imposing structure called St Peter's College and village bazaars in which along with Airtel and Docomo advertisements were advertisements for 'Amul Macho underwear'. We stopped in a village of mud huts called Kumharpurva and asked people if there had been any change at all in their lives since Rahul Gandhi became their MP eight years ago, and they said in unison that there had been none. There were no women in the gathering and the half-naked men had scrawny bodies and bad teeth and that vacant look in their eyes that indicates malnourishment. They said they would be voting for Congress again because they did not know who else to vote for.

The enduring impression I came away with from Rahul Gandhi's constituency was that it seemed to have remained stuck in an earlier time. The only perceptible change since his father was MP from Amethi was the ubiquitous presence of cell phones and cable TV. Otherwise there were almost no changes at all. I stopped in a village school and found classrooms that looked more like cowsheds. Children sat on a dirt floor in a half-built, windowless room, and a sleepy teacher sat at the only table in the class, drinking tea. Everyone I talked to in the villages I stopped in admitted that they hardly saw their MP and that he had done little for them, but they voted for him anyway because it was a matter of prestige to be represented by a member of the Gandhi family.

Their candidate, aware of the importance of his family name, launched his campaign from Phulpur that was once the constituency of his great-grandfather, Jawaharlal Nehru. A portrait of Nehru, fine featured, handsome, with a cap to cover his bald head, was the backdrop for the speech he made, and it was mostly about his family that he spoke. His more personable sister was put in charge of Rae Bareli and Amethi, and she seemed as conscious as him of the importance of the family name, so she enlisted her children and husband in the campaign. And Robert Vadra, emboldened by so much family spirit, announced that he himself had a political career in mind. It is Rahul's time now, he told TV reporters, then it will be Priyanka's time and then mine. This was alarming but not nearly as much as the hopeless quality of Rahul's campaign and the very poor quality of his Hindi.

In Benares he held one of his very rare press conferences and said he had no 'obsession' with wanting to be prime minister, except that he used this word in English while speaking Hindi. This was what he said: 'Hindustan key jitney bhi political netas hain unka obsession hai prime ministership. Rahul Gandhi ka yeh obsession nahin hai.' At the same press conference in answer to another question in Hindi he talked of a 'monumental crime'. Obsession and monumental are words that even educated English speakers from this state that is the heart of the Hindi heartland would find difficult to understand.

Sadly for him it was not just his lack of Hindi that let him down, it was his inability to offer voters more than his family name and the shabby hope that if they voted Congress their schools would be as good as those in Kerala and that Uttar Pradesh would become as 'developed' as Maharashtra. He seemed to forget his own travels in rural Maharashtra, where he had comforted widows of farmers who committed suicide.

One of these widows, Kalawati, became a household name because of Rahul Gandhi speaking so eloquently about her despair in Parliament.

A week after my travels in Rae Bareli and Amethi I travelled to Moradabad to get a sense of how Muslims felt about the election. Something that is vital for anyone covering an election in UP because the Muslim vote can swing the election in a large number of seats. I took with me Zafar Moradabadi, a poet who moved to Delhi in search of fame and fortune but who never lost his links with Moradabad. We drove on a brand new four-lane highway, on either side of which were high-rise residential developments with names like Antariksh and Siddharta Vihar. I remembered from earlier journeys to Moradabad a broken strip of tarmac as the main road and desperately poor villages as the landscape.

At a toll booth on the new highway we stopped to buy local newspapers and I noticed that all of them carried full-page pictures of Rahul Gandhi urging voters to vote back the Congress because they had been let down by those who ruled the state for the past twenty-two years. In Hindi this was the message: Picchley 22 saalon mein ghair-Congress ki sarkarein aayeen aur gayeen. Par mila kya aapko? Kabhi jungle raj, kabhi kushashan. Kya ab bhi yahi sab bardaasht kareingey aap? Sochiye zara.' In the past 22 years you have seen non-Congress governments come and go and what did you get? Sometimes lawlessness, sometimes bad governance. Is this what you want to put up with again?

In Moradabad we drove through narrow streets into even narrower streets that led to a large green domed mosque. Children in green and white uniforms sat reading their lessons out aloud in the mosque school that we walked past to get to the home of a lawyer friend of Zafar. We climbed up a narrow flight of steps to arrive in a small living room, in which one by one arrived the lawyer's friends. They included a doctor, a teacher and a poet with long hair and wild eyes. We talked of the issues that would decide the way Muslims voted this time, and they said the most important issue of all was Urdu being made an official language. The reason why it was important, they explained, was that many Muslim families were too poor to send their children to schools that were not madrasas.

'In the madrasas they teach only Urdu…so Muslims arrive in the job market and cannot compete because of not knowing another language.'

'What about the Babri Masjid problem?' I asked. 'Is that still an issue?'

'No,' said the lawyer. 'Muslims no longer fear for their security the way they used to in the past because today no riot lasts more than a few hours. Not long ago they threw pig meat into the main mosque that you passed on the way here, and this was in the middle of Ramzan. There were people gathered in the mosque for namaz and there was a lot of anger. But the police arrived quickly and calmed things down.'

'So who is going to win this time?'

'This time it will be the Samajwadi Party,' they said in unison.

'Why?'

'People are tired of Mayawati and her monuments.'

'So why not Congress?'

'Congress has no strength on the ground, and the MP from here is Mohammed Azharuddin from Congress…the cricketer. He has not come to Moradabad once after getting elected.'

'What do you think of Rahul Gandhi?'

'He is all right,' someone said, 'but he has not made much of an impression on the Muslim community.'

Tea and kebabs arrived and so did the lawyer's young son, a student at Aligarh Muslim University. He complained about police harassment wherever he went. 'They stop you all the time and start asking all sorts of questions.'

'They do that because of jihadi terrorism. If there is an incident they will get blamed.'

'Yes. But they behave very badly with us.'

'They do that with everyone,' I said.

'But for us it is more difficult to accept because we cannot forget that we ruled this country once.'

'Well, you don't now,' I said firmly, 'and you haven't for a long time and will not for a long time to come. So maybe you need to change your attitude.'

Then turning to the older people in the room I said that it was this kind of attitude that caused tensions between the communities. They said that he was talking like this because he was a young man and young men tended to be reckless in their thoughts. But nobody told the young student that he was wrong to think the way he did. Later we drove through more narrow streets that led us deep into the heart of the Muslim quarter of Moradabad to talk to the imam of the main mosque. He was an old man with a white beard that he wore Muslim-style, without a moustache. We sat in a room with open doors that allowed in the usual urban smells of diesel, spicy food and open drains. He told me how the Bharatiya Janata Party would never win in UP because although the Babri Masjid question was no longer as important as it had once been Muslims had not forgotten what had happened.

In the end this election that we all thought was going to be a rehearsal for the general election two years later became a fight between Rahul Gandhi and Akhilesh Yadav. Both heirs to political legacies, both young, and Akhilesh won because he managed to connect more easily with voters than Rahul ever managed to do. There was about Rahul Gandhi's campaign an absurd, almost childish, quality, and his inability to speak or understand Hindi well enough to communicate with people who only spoke this language caused much mirth and confusion.

Talking to reporters towards the end of the campaign he was asked by someone what he had to say about his sister having admitted that she was like a 'frog that only came out in the monsoon'. When she used this common Hindi proverb what she meant was that she needed to be forgiven for not coming to Rae Bareli and Amethi except at election time. But her brother misunderstood and said with a smile, 'Well, she is my sister, so if she is a barsaat ki maindak then I must be too.' Watching this exchange on television I felt sorry for Rahul Gandhi. Politics was so clearly not for him that it amazed me that his mother continued to insist that he pursue it.

After losing this election he disappeared from public life for a few months, as he had done after losing Bihar, and all talk of him taking over as prime minister and leading his party into the general election ended. Dr Manmohan Singh continued to keep his job, but as the months went by and it became clear to everyone that the real prime minister was Sonia Gandhi he began to look increasingly more pathetic. He was hardly seen in public except when he travelled abroad on official tours and he was hardly seen to speak in public, so jokes began to be made about how his name should have been Maunmohan Singh. Maun is the Hindi word for silent.

26

PARIVARTAN

The ground had been made ready for political change but when it came it came surreptitiously. Almost nobody noticed that it was not going to be Anna or Arvind Kejriwal or Rahul Gandhi who was going to become India's next leader but the man who had been demonized for more than a decade by the Indian media as a merchant of death. It was at a Delhi conclave organized by *India Today* the year after Anna's movement rose and fizzled out that I first saw signs of this happening, but I did not fully understand the significance of what I saw till much later. In attendance at this conclave was a glittering array of retired bureaucrats, army officers, businessmen, socialites, TV stars and journalists.

They came that year, as they came every year, to attend sessions addressed by ministers, movie stars, writers and diplomats. They preferred, as they did every year, to attend the sessions where movie stars told them intimate details about their lives but made it a point to attend sessions addressed by major political leaders. This they considered important so that they could make political conversation at the next dinner party.

So that morning that Narendra Modi came to make his speech the front row was occupied by glamorous socialites, many of whom had come all the way from Mumbai. Movie stars invited to the conclave sat beside them while Delhi people from a more drab world craned their necks to watch the spectacle of air kissing and bejewelled handshakes. The vast hall with its shiny chandeliers and plastic grandeur was full. But the audience seemed to be there not so much to listen to Modi but to confirm their opinion of him as a monster. The majority of people there were deeply 'secular' denizens of Lutyens' Delhi, and although many of them had lived through the Sikh massacres of 1984 they had hardly noticed them because in that time there were no private television channels. They had heard from their servants that half burned bodies lay in the streets and that there were mobs attacking Sikh homes, but they had not seen anything because when the trouble started they stayed at home as they always did.

If they knew about what happened in distant Gujarat in 2002 it was because this was the first time that the images of horrible violence were brought into their drawing rooms via private news channels. There had been worse riots many times before in towns they had only half heard of, like Bhagalpur and Maliana, and they knew that thousands had been killed in these riots, but it was only in 2002 that they saw what happened when communal hatred spread. So for them Modi was a monster like no other political leader had ever been. 'He has blood on his hands,' they liked saying whenever his name was mentioned.

That morning I arrived late for Modi's session, so I sat in the last row where chairs were lined up against the wall for less important people. More important people sat at tables covered in white and on which stood bottles of mineral water and bowls of sweets. While waiting for Modi to arrive I looked around at the beautifully dressed, bejewelled socialites delicately sipping mineral water and at the scruffier, smug 'intellectuals' and wondered what they would make of Modi. The titter of women and snippets of social chit-chat still filled the hall when he began to speak, but what was extraordinary was how quickly they began to listen to his words in complete silence.

He began by saying that India had to make up her mind where she wanted to go and what she wanted to achieve. The twenty-first century was meant to be Asia's century, he said, and perhaps this meant China and Southeast Asia would forge ahead, but it was India that really had the potential to become Asia's superpower if she wanted. For this to happen there had to be resolve, direction and a serious attempt to make development a people's issue. A 'jan-andolan' as Mahatma Gandhi had done with the freedom movement.

He spoke in Hindi and although there was hardly anyone in this audience who could speak this language well they understood it well enough. So they listened carefully as he painted with his words a picture of India as she was, with her poverty and her shabby development, and what she could become if she made up her mind to move forward in a clear direction. None of them had heard this kind of talk before. They knew there were poor people in India but they never met them except in the servants' quarters, and they knew that compared to the countries they went to for their holidays India looked bad but they had never questioned why.

These were people whose parents had brought them up on stories of the freedom movement replete with heroic leaders like Mahatma Gandhi and Pandit Nehru. They had been nurtured on romantic tales of how when these leaders spoke the world listened and, of course, they had read *Freedom at Midnight*, so they knew of Panditji's 'Tryst with destiny' speech. So if India was shabby, dirty and poor it could not possibly be Nehru's fault. Nor the fault of his daughter or grandson who had both ruled India in their time and who came from a family that in the eyes of this audience had the aura of royalty. The kind of Indian leaders they were impressed by were those who spoke English better than Hindi and who belonged to the same privileged class they did.

There were many in this audience who did not like Sonia Gandhi and many more who liked Indira Gandhi even less. But they had nearly all loved Rajiv Gandhi. Some of the men in the audience had been to school with him and thought of him as a 'decent chap'. It was because they thought of him as such a fundamentally decent man that they never blamed him for the massacres of the Sikhs that took place under his nose in his first days as prime minister. Even when he justified the violence afterwards as just a consequence of the earth shaking when a big tree falls they did not see anything wrong with this justification.

Besides they secretly approved of the Sikh massacres because they believed that they avenged the killing of Hindus by Jarnail Singh Bhindranwale and his men in Punjab. On the worst day of the killings in Trilokpuri I happened to be invited to a dinner party in Lutyens' Delhi in the house of a celebrated Delhi hostess. When she rang to ask me to come I told her that I was really in no mood for dinner parties but she insisted that I come because 'the theme of the dinner is to remind us that we are all Indians'. This aroused my curiosity.

There were Sikhs at the dinner party but our hostess who knew I had been in Trilokpuri all day said loudly, 'Forgive me saying this but the Sikhs deserved what they got. They needed to be taught a lesson.' The wife of one of India's richest men who overheard this conversation added, 'Bloody people... they should be shipped.' The dinner was a tense, ugly affair made worse when our hostess produced a cake resembling the Indian flag and reminded us sternly that as long as we remembered that we were all Indians things would be all right. This lady was in the gathering that came to listen to Modi that morning when I first heard him speak to a Delhi audience. I had lost touch with her over the years and had no idea whether, as with the Sikhs in 1984, she blamed Muslims for what happened in Gujarat in 2002. What I did know was that most of the audience thought of Modi as a monster because the violence that began with the burning of Hindu kar sewaks in the Sabarmati Express in Godhra had come right into their drawing rooms.

So when he spoke to them that morning of development and change they were determined not to like what they heard but they listened in mesmerized silence. After he finished speaking I ran into a publisher who reflected the general mood when she said with a shudder, 'He certainly speaks very well but he makes my skin crawl. He terrifies me.' Nobody thought then that there was any chance of him becoming prime minister, so it was an opinion I heard often that day as we chatted between sessions and when we gathered in the evening for drinks and dinner. It had become a tradition at *India Today* conclaves that the star of the conclave would speak at the final session over dinner. That year the star was Salman Rushdie. Modi was a sideshow.

The next year Modi was invited once more to the annual conclave but this time as the chief guest. My book *Durbar* had just come out and when I ran into Modi as he was coming in to make his address I was surprised that he took my hand and smiled when I greeted him. I asked if he had read *Durbar* and his smile widened. 'I have read it,' he said. And then he was swept off to the stage by the battalion of minders and *India Today* TV stars who accompanied him and I was left puzzling over why he had been so nice to me. The last time we had spoken more than a few words to each other was soon after the violence in 2002 when he had almost thrown me out of his office. I had nothing more to do with Modi or Gujarat till four years later when I got a call from an official in the Gujarat government who asked if I could visit the state to see some of their development projects in 'remote, tribal areas'. I hesitated to say yes because it seemed so obviously like a propaganda exercise, but I was curious to see whether Modi had really achieved anything in the five years of his first tenure as chief minister, so I went.

On the flight from Mumbai to Ahmedabad I happened to sit next to a lady who was the wife of a high official in the Gujarat government and cannot be named for obvious reasons. She spoke English with the ease of Indians who speak it as their mother tongue and she ordered 'only dessert', which she ate slowly as if she could not bear to finish it so soon. We got talking and I asked her what she thought of Modi. She stopped eating, crinkled her nose up delicately and said, 'I think he is a monster.'

'Why?'

'Because of what he did in 2002.'

'But they say he has put that behind him now and that his emphasis is on governance.'

'I don't know much about that...but I think what he did in 2002 is something he can never be forgiven for.'

'Did you forgive Rajiv Gandhi for what happened in 1984?' I knew even as I asked the question that I would get the usual reply.

'I don't know what happened in 1984,' she said, 'but I was in Ahmedabad in 2002 and I know what happened and blame Modi for it.'

It was a response I had heard many times and yet it never failed to annoy me. The Gujarat riots were not the worst communal riots even by Gujarat's own standards. Many more people had been killed in communal violence in successive routine riots that sometimes led to more than 200 days of curfew, as happened in 1989, but because the violence in 2002 was India's first televised communal riot it had come to be known as 'the worst communal violence anywhere in India since 1947'. This lie was perpetuated not just by the Indian media but by important international newspapers. When measured just by numbers what happened to the Sikhs in 1984 was twice as bad. In three days more than 3,000 Sikhs were killed in Delhi alone and not one Hindu. It was a pogrom, not a riot, and on a scale never seen before or since 1947. The violence in Gujarat was terrible but it was a real communal riot since both Hindus and Muslims were among the dead.

On this visit to Gujarat at the behest of the government I travelled in remote villages and forests. The official who accompanied me was a small balding man called Bhagyesh Jha, who sang Modi's praises as we drove. He said Modi had transformed governance in the state by micromanaging it. He told me that the chief minister regularly invited officials from different departments to 'camps' in which over a period of two or three days they would tell him about their problems and he would try and solve them.

Mr Jha was so enamoured by his chief minister that he attributed every improvement to him. When I commented on the excellent quality of the roads in the remote, scarcely populated areas in which we travelled he said it was because the chief minister understood the importance of infrastructure. When we stopped to examine small check dams in the villages, he said this was because of Modi's emphasis on providing water and electricity in backward rural areas. And when we stopped in a small town to visit a computer centre, he pointed out that all the students in this school were from illiterate Adivasi families, for whom Modi had devised special schemes. 'First generation literates...and they are learning to use computers.'

In a deliberate effort to try and see something that was not part of the propaganda itinerary I asked him to stop at a random rural health centre. He did not object and I was impressed to find it functional, clean and manned by a young woman doctor who was an Adivasi. At the end of this tour when we got to Ahmedabad I met Modi for the first time since that fraught, brief encounter in 2003. He sat on a stage presiding over a beautiful, effortlessly Indian commencement ceremony in a large university hall. The students wore Indian clothes, not caps and gowns, and Sanskrit shlokas were chanted as they walked onto the stage to receive their degrees. After the ceremony I got no more than five minutes to speak to Modi, and when I told him about my visit to the health centre he was pleased. He told me that this year was going to be a year in which he would concentrate on the 'girl child'.

He went on to win his second election in Gujarat the next year. His victory was facilitated by Sonia Gandhi calling him a 'merchant of death'. The remark ended up harming her more than him. This was because somehow Gujarat had moved on from that terrible moment that inspired this remark. National newspapers and TV channels continued to paint Modi as a 'fascist' and a 'Muslim hater' but it no longer worked because Gujarat became increasingly associated with development and governance and less with its long, ugly history of communal violence. Modi held annual conferences in Ahmedabad to celebrate 'vibrant' Gujarat to which investors came from India and abroad. At these conferences famous industrialists publicly admitted that investing in Gujarat was a happier experience than anywhere else in India.

By coincidence my government-planned tour of development projects in rural Gujarat happened just after Sonia's National Advisory Council forced Dr Manmohan Singh's government to pass a law giving Adivasi tribes across India the right to cultivate forest lands. Mr Jha told me that the law was going to cause incalculable harm to what was left of India's forests and wanted to show me an example of what was happening. We drove into a forest of tall, beautiful teak trees in Dahod district, which, he explained as we drove along an excellent road, was a distortion of the Hindi word do-hadd meaning two borders. While we drove he pointed to a long line of combine harvesters filled with young men who he said were Adivasis. 'They know about the new law,' he said, 'and are heading towards the forest to claim agricultural land. They do this by cutting trees and claiming that the land is theirs. Nobody can stop them even when we know that they never lived in forests or cultivated forest land.'

We stopped for lunch in a forest lodge where forest officers confirmed gloomily that this was true. They said that the law may have been passed with the best intentions but it would end up doing irreparable harm. Central planning had always done more harm than good in India, and under Sonia Gandhi's guidance it became a powerful tool to undermine the powers of state governments. Poverty alleviation schemes run by local governments were forcibly replaced by expensive, unwieldy schemes designed in the rarified enclosure of Lutyens' Delhi where Sonia and her merry band of activists set about 'alleviating' the poverty of India.

The activists and leftist economists who designed schemes were all urban middle class people who saw poverty not as something real and hideous but as something abstract and eternal. Poor people were what made India different in their mind's eye. They saw them almost as images on glossy posters for Air India. Men with harsh features and colourful turbans placed against a backdrop of deserts and camels. And women in billowing skirts with half-veiled faces and happy smiles. It was for people like these that Sonia Gandhi's National Advisory Council planned its welfare schemes.

These were schemes not designed to help them escape poverty but to keep them in poverty forever. But in the fine offices in Delhi in which central planners planned for the poor they seemed not to know this. How could they know? There was not a single person among Sonia Gandhi's advisors who had experienced a single day of poverty in their own lives. But in doing what they did they accidentally paved the way for such a man to become prime minister who understood poverty because he had experienced it and who knew that it was something that needed to be ended, not 'alleviated'.

It was after Modi won in Gujarat for the third time, in 2012, that he began to make it clear that he had every intention of becoming prime minister. He did not have the support of even his own party, so he worked alone and subtly. He arrived in Delhi soon after winning his third election in Gujarat, ostensibly with the limited purpose of addressing students in Delhi University's famous Shri Ram College of Commerce. The speech was covered live by nearly every news channel, and I remember thinking as I watched it that Modi was making his first campaign speech even if the general election was more than a year away.

Modi used this speech to lay out his 'model' of development and to emphasize that he wanted to give people the tools to lift themselves out of poverty. He gave them examples from Gujarat. He told them how Adivasi people had come to see him from a remote district of Gujarat and asked for a better road. 'But you have a good road already, so why do you need another one, I said to them. And they said to me there are bumps on the road that damage the bananas they export to Mexico.'

He told them that his government had made such a concerted effort to improve agricultural methods that Gujarat's poorest farmers were now exporting their produce. He was willing to bet, he said, that the tomatoes eaten even in many foreign countries came from Gujarat. And that the milk they drank in Delhi also came from Gujarat. He painted for them a new idea of India. An India that could be prosperous and not just an India whose only dream was to 'alleviate' poverty. Nobody, not the students in his immediate audience and not those of us who watched on television, had heard Indian political leaders speak this kind of language before. No Indian political leader had dared challenge the fundamental socialist premise with which we had all grown up: that there would always be poverty in India.

After this speech he made other speeches that were similar and that always emphasized that India had every right to dream of being prosperous. The pundits of Lutyens' Delhi did not understand what Modi was talking about but simple people did. They watched his speeches on television in small villages across the country and saw that he was offering them a new vision of India. I discovered this by accident in a Rajasthani village on a hot, humid July day in 2013. My reason for being on this rural tour was to see if my friend from the days of our carefree youth, Vasundhara Raje, was really on the road to becoming chief minister of the state for a second time. She was on a 'yatra' that would take her by the time of the election in December to every district in Rajasthan, but this was early days.

The reports she gave me of the 'amazing response' she was getting everywhere inspired me to go and see for myself. She suggested that I travel with her on a day that began in Jaipur, and I said that before coming with her I would spend a day wandering about rural Rajasthan to get a general feel of what was happening. So I left Delhi at dawn on a hot and muggy morning when the sun was just beginning to light up the shiny glass buildings of Gurgaon. The light was as deceptive and seductive as the buildings because beneath the façade of malls, golf courses and five star hotels lay Haryana's squalor and its hopeless infrastructure. But the shiny buildings offered hope to young people because with them came a new variety of jobs. In malls, cinemas, restaurants, shops, hotels and gyms. In the old India of the 1970s when Indira Gandhi ruled like an empress the only jobs available for these young people would have been as peons in government offices.

I knew as I drove past Gurgaon that morning and onto the Jaipur highway that behind this glittering façade Haryana remained a squalid, backward state, but Gurgaon looked misleadingly modern in the morning light. This was something that could not be said of the highway. When it was first built it brought great joy to travellers by reducing the journey to Jaipur from six hours to four, but now it took nearly as long as it had before because of heavy traffic and the encroachment of urban squalor. Makeshift shops in makeshift bazaars selling modernity only in the advertisements for Airtel and Docomo and shabby residential clusters that seemed to sprout overnight. They crept up along the edges of the highway as if to remind travellers not to be fooled by the four lanes and the massive articulated lorries transporting goods brought in by foreign companies like MAERSK.

To step off the highway was to be confronted with rural squalor that seemed infinitely worse than before because of the contrast with the modern highway. As soon as we turned off and headed in the direction of Alwar along lesser roads I found myself in an unending landscape of ugly settlements that were no longer villages but not towns either. Prosperity manifested itself in those same advertisements for cell phones that decorated the usual array of small, windowless shops and in the signs that advertised computer training centres, but prosperity had not come with municipal services. Socialist India had always shown an unhealthy disdain for planned urbanization and modern public services, so I realized as soon as I entered Gandhiji's 'real India' that what lay before me was a long day filled with open drains and filthy villages. I knew the landscape well from having done more than my fair share of travel in rural India.

As always I missed the rural landscape of my childhood when, at least in Punjab, villages were primitive but clean and the air smelled of nice things like jaggery being cooked on log fires in open fields. The air on this July morning smelled of diesel fumes, rotting garbage and human excrement. Eternal India, I thought, the India that foreign correspondents seemed always to see in such a romantic light that they went home and wrote whole books about village life. In the first village in which we stopped I asked for the sarpanch's house and was told proudly by the villager I asked that my car would be able to drive all the way to it. I preferred to walk so I could observe more carefully signs of change and prosperity. They were evident in small cars parked in narrow courtyards, satellite dishes sprouting out of nearly every home and 'pucca' houses everywhere.

The sarpanch's house was grander than the others and what took me completely by surprise was the air-conditioned room in which he sprawled fatly on a sofa receiving rural petitioners. I had never seen an air-conditioned rural dwelling before because usually there is never enough electricity and private generators are too expensive. The sarpanch was a large man who wore a white vest and loose striped pajamas, and in the time he received petitioners his eyes barely moved from the large colour television screen on which a cricket match played. When he saw me he shifted his bulk and looked up by way of greeting. He said he was not really the headman any more because the village was reserved for women, so he had 'made' his wife the sarpanch in his place. But judging from the petitioners that had gathered in his small living room it was clear that he was the power behind his wife's village throne.

Tokenism was a vital component of the 'idea of India' that Nehruvian socialism bequeathed India, and one of the token gestures made for the 'empowerment' of women was to force them to participate in rural politics by reserving seats for them in panchayat elections. Of course they continued to be married off while they were still children, continued to be tortured if they did not bring enough dowry and continued to be treated with less respect than rural men treated their cattle, but they could become politicians.

When I asked this particular husband of the sarpanch (in some villages the official title is pradhan-pati) if he thought that Vasundhara Raje would become chief minister again he said cautiously, 'This village has always voted for the Congress party. I am from the Congress party.'

'But do you think Ashok Gehlot can win again?'

'Yes. He has done wonderful work and in the next six months there will be so many schemes...free medicines, ipads, pensions, gifts for the girl child. You will see that Congress will come back for sure.'

'Has he been a good chief minister?'

'Of course.'

'As good as Narendra Modi?' I meant the question to provoke a reaction and I got it.

'What do you mean Modi has been a good chief minister? He has done no better than Sheila Dikshit...look how much

she has done for Delhi? So should she be prime minister?'
He had sat up now and turned off the cricket match. And
he indicated with a gesture to the petitioners who squatted
before him that they would have to wait.

'I didn't say he was going to become prime minister,' I said.
'I was talking about his record as chief minister of Gujarat.
But do you think he will become prime minister?' This made
him even more cautious.

'Look here, I am from the Congress party,' he said,
glancing nervously at the squatting petitioners, 'so I could
never say such a thing. But there are people in the village who
are saying this. There are people who talk like this...every
finger on a hand is not the same size.'

'So people are talking about Modi? And saying they want
him to become prime minister?'

'Look. I cannot tell you much of these things. And
we don't know what will happen in a year's time. We are
worrying only about the Rajasthan election. This is what we
are working for.'

'And you believe that Ashok Gehlot will win another
term?'

'Yes. Definitely.'

'What has been done for the village in terms of development
in the past five years?'

'A lot. Didn't you see how good the road was when you
came in? And we have electricity and water and everything
else that we need.'

'Is unemployment a problem?'

'Not a serious one...and there is MNREGA. Poor people
get a hundred days of work a year because of MNREGA.
This is a Congress programme.'

At the end of this exchange the sarpanch's husband said
he would like to show me the new 'panchayat office'. So

he slipped on a white kurta over his vest and led the way down the narrow, uneven stairs that led to the courtyard of his house. We walked back along the road that I had taken, and I noticed that the only relatively attractive building in this village of ugly buildings was a small whitewashed temple under a tall peepul tree. The 'sarpanch' told me proudly that since his wife took over the village, she had brought in many modern things like computers. 'You will see in the panchayat house that our records are all computerized now.'

He led me to a low wooden gate that he unlocked. It opened onto a small courtyard, beyond which was a tiny veranda and office. Clearly what should have been a public building had been converted into a private office for him and his wife. In the office he pointed proudly to the computer that stood on a small table, but when he tried to turn it on to show me the 'records' he failed. There was no electricity. This annoyed him and he turned angrily to a flunkey who lurked in the shadows and demanded to know why the generator had not been turned on if there was a power cut. 'So there are power cuts?' I asked, feigning innocence.

'No. No. I don't know how this has happened.'

After this visit to the 'panchayat office' I took my leave and set off once more in the direction of Alwar. I noticed as soon as we left the village that hasty repairs were being done to a road that was in bad need of them. It is usual for chief ministers to remember how much work needs to be done when an election approaches. I had not gone far when I noticed a group of young men sitting idly under a tree. Dust and diesel fumes blew around them in visible clouds of pollution, the sun beat down mercilessly, but there they sat unbothered by these things much as if this was what they did every day.

When they saw me get out of the car they seemed happy for the distraction. I told them who I was and that I had just come from their village, where the de facto sarpanch had told me that the Congress government had done so much development work in the area that life was perfect. When I said this they laughed loudly and looked at me as if I were some kind of wandering lunatic. Then after a few moments of silence one of them said that the government had done so little in the past five years in terms of improving their lives that they were definitely voting for Modi this time.

'Narendra Modi?'

'Yes.'

'But he is the chief minister of Gujarat.'

'He is now but we want him to become prime minister.'

'Why?' Now a chorus of voices tried to answer.

'We have heard his speeches on TV and we like what he is saying,' they said in unison. 'He is talking about vikas and parivartan and this is what we need in this country.'

It was a conversation I was to have many times again during the rest of that hot, sultry, dusty day. I heard Modi's name mentioned more than I heard Vasundhara's, and if anyone mentioned the BJP it was only when it related to these two names. When people had words of praise for Vasundhara Raje it was nearly always to say that when she was chief minister they got electricity twenty-two hours a day. Since the Congress government came back to power they were lucky if they got five hours of electricity a day and even when it did come they were never sure how long it would stay or when it would go again.

I spent the day wandering into obscure villages a long way from the main road to Alwar. These villages were not very far from this important district town, but everywhere I went I saw signs of the absence of real change and evidence of what can only be described as eternal Indian poverty. Old women in rags sat by the side of village roads selling drinking water from mud flasks under burning hot sunlight. Barefoot children played on the edge of open drains, clogged solid and green with slime. And on the snot-covered faces of small babies who lay restless and hot on rough beds sat swarms of flies. Schools in these villages looked like abandoned warehouses, and weeds grew out of empty, crumbling health centres.

Closer to Alwar I stopped in a relatively prosperous village, where when I asked to meet the sarpanch I was told that he would be 'in Rajiv Gandhi'. This turned out to be the local community centre. Its full name was Rajiv Gandhi Bhavan. I discovered that these community centres had been built in villages across Rajasthan after Ashok Gehlot became chief minister, as part of his tireless efforts to please his boss. It was well known by the end of the decade that Sonia Gandhi had been India's de facto prime minister that she was susceptible to sycophancy. This 'Rajiv Gandhi' was an attractive yellow-washed structure that had stairs leading to a terrace shaded by a large and beautiful banyan tree.

It was here that the village's thinkers and intellectuals seemed to have gathered that morning. They had much to tell me about the schemes that the Gehlot government had introduced in recent months to fool them into voting for him. They spoke of the government with disdain but were particularly eager to talk about the political situation in the rest of the country. They seemed more interested in the Lok Sabha elections still several months away than they were to talk about Vasundhara Raje winning the coming election. Even when I tried to veer them in the direction of the assembly elections that were due in four months they made it clear that they were more interested in asking me what I thought about Modi.

They sent for tea and cold drinks from the village shop and spicy snacks. A hot wind blew dead leaves and dust around us, and they told me that there was real despair these days, especially among young people. 'They have no hope of improving their lives unless there is real development,' said a man who introduced himself as the village teacher. A farmer in a grimy white turban and dusty Rajasthani shoes said, 'They think that if they can give us free medicines now we will vote for Congress, but we know that if they were sincere they would have improved healthcare long ago. Everyone has to use private doctors.'

'When women get pregnant we have to take them all the way to Alwar. It is thirty kilometres away,' said a young man in jeans and a baseball cap.

An unemployed youth said, 'We want real jobs, not dole. MNREGA is dole and we know it.' The term he used in Hindi for dole was 'berozgari bhatta'.

'But why do you think Modi will be able to change these things?'

'We listen to his speeches on TV,' they said, 'and we like what he says about bringing sampannata (prosperity) to India.'

All of them said that they would be voting for the BJP this time but that their only reason for doing this was Modi. They said they listened carefully to every speech he made on television and were convinced that if there was anyone who could change India it was him. They made it clear that they had no faith in other BJP leaders. At some point late that afternoon I was forced to bring my rural tour to an abrupt end and head for Alwar because of an urgent need to use a lavatory. In the old days there was enough wilderness around for us travelling hacks to be able to do what villagers call 'jungle pani' (jungle water) in some hidden corner. Creeping urbanization now makes hidden corners hard to find. What I did not know when we drove into Alwar town was that finding a restroom in this large Rajasthani town would be just as hard. It took me nearly an hour to find a grubby restaurant that reeked of stale oil and other unpleasant things that included the smell of an unclean toilet. But by now I was no longer in any condition to be fussy, so I ordered coffee that tasted like hot sugared water and found a ladies room that smelled disgusting but was clean compared to some others I have used.

Dusk was beginning to fall when I finally found myself back on the highway to Jaipur. And the first thing I did was call my friend Rajat Sharma, with whom over dinner some weeks earlier I had discussed the possibility of a subterranean Modi wave. Rajat and I have been comrades in journalism for many years, during which he has gone from being relatively successful as a print journalist to being extremely successful as a TV anchor and owner of India TV, a very popular Hindi news channel. Rajat's political inclinations have been towards the BJP since his days as a student leader in Delhi University.

But when we met for dinner in the Italian restaurant in the Oberoi Hotel weeks before my rural expedition even he was not absolutely sure that there was a Modi wave building up quietly outside Delhi. He said that he thought something was going on that we sitting in Delhi had totally missed. He said he planned to send his reporters out into different states to detect signs of a possible Modi wave. When I rang him to tell him what I had heard and seen that day he said he was not at all surprised. There was a Modi wave, we agreed, and the only people who could not see it were the mighty political pundits of Lutyens' Delhi. This is often the case because the higher you get in journalism the less likely you are to be braving the heat, dust and filth of rural India and so Lutyens' Delhi provides a very distorted lens to high pundits.

Before leaving Delhi I had met a high pundit at a dinner party in the Pakistani high commissioner's residence. H.K. Dua had been editor of the *Indian Express*, the *Hindustan Times* and the *Tribune* before becoming a nominated member of the Rajya Sabha. Naturally that evening in that drawing room, filled like most Delhi drawing rooms with beautiful carpets, silk curtains and fine upholstery, there was not a whiff of the 'real India' but all talk was about it. When I told Dua Sahib that I thought there was a Modi wave that we had not yet noticed he said he respected my opinion but that I was quite wrong. In his usual gentle, learned way he explained why he believed it was not possible for a man like Modi to become prime minister. It was a conversation I had many times in many drawing rooms with many high pundits. Ironically, low-level Congress workers had seen a Modi wave before almost anyone else, but those who saw it did not dare say anything openly for fear of offending Sonia Gandhi, whose main political aim in these last months of the ten years she had been de facto prime minister was to ensure that her son took over the reins from her.

It was late evening when I finally got to Jaipur and an exhausted Vasundhara was just settling down to rest after a day that had been much longer and busier than mine. Her last public meeting on her 'yatra' finished well after 9.30 p.m., but she was more cheerful than I had seen her in a very long time because of the signs she had detected that she was on the road to victory. She lay happily on a sofa in her elegant study, having her feet massaged to reduce the swelling that came from being on them for long hours. After giving her the good news from my travels I asked if she thought there was a Modi factor in the support she was getting and she said without hesitation that there was. Her son Dushyant, who had travelled with her for many days of the yatra, added, 'The slogan you hear at the rallies is "Mukhyamantri Vasundhara Raje, pradhanmantri Narendra Modi".'

The next morning we left soon after breakfast to catch up with Vasundhara's rath that was parked some distance from Jaipur. It was a day of such searing heat that I thought nobody would possibly want to come out to see Vasundhara travel through their villages on her rath. The rath awaited the maharani outside the Triveni Dham temple in Shahpura, an hour's drive away. She went on ahead and I followed with Dushyant and other members of her entourage and caught up with her in the temple at the point when she was having her forehead smeared with sandalwood paste at the feet of dazzling gods who seemed made of gold and silver. Vasundhara never did anything without seeking divine blessings.

After decades of friendship I realized a long time ago that religion was one area in which our paths diverged. She was a dedicated believer and I was a dedicated unbeliever but despite this had spent many mornings sitting beside her in front of Hindu deities of all kinds while priests muttered prayers, plastered her forehead with vermilion and ash and blessed her journey. That morning while she prayed and received their blessings, drums played in the village outside and a large crowd of villagers gathered around her bus.

Having learned from many experiences of nearly being trampled to death by enthusiastic crowds, I scuttled on to the bus with Dushyant's help before she left the temple. Others ensconced in advance were her daughter-in-law Niharika and a man called Bhupendra Yadav, who Dushyant told me was someone the RSS had appointed as her aide for the yatra. He was a pleasant-faced man with a booming voice that he used effectively to urge people to clear the way once the bus began to move. Her first public meeting was in a small, unremarkable town called Ajeetgarh that took its name from a magnificent sixteenth century fortress that towered over it from a rocky outcrop. There were so many people there to listen to her on this morning of white, scathing heat that they spilled out of the shamiana onto trees and rooftops. Women in heavy Rajasthani skirts and dupattas sat closest to the stage, and I found myself wondering yet again how they managed so effortlessly to deal with the heat under so many layers of clothing.

The gist of Vasundhara's speech was the one sentence I was to hear her repeat at other meetings for the rest of the day. 'In this state if you count out my five years and the ten years you gave Bhairon Singh Shekhawat you have given Congress fifty-three years in government since 1947. And you still do not have drinking water, electricity, roads or decent schools...if you had given the BJP fifty-three years we would have turned Rajasthan into a garden.' To illustrate this point she reminded them of what Narendra Modi had done for Gujarat in fifteen years, and suddenly the crowd came alive in an uproar of frenzied slogan shouting. The one that rose above the cacophony was 'Modi, Modi, Modi'.

The rest of the day was long and relentless. Vasundhara's 'carriage' moved slowly and stopped every fifteen minutes for roadside conversations with increasingly large crowds of enthusiastic supporters. She asked the same questions: Do you have electricity? Teachers in the school? Drinking water? Doctors in the hospital? And the answer was always 'no'. By late afternoon I lost track of where we were or where the next rally was, and when it started mercifully to rain I decided to stay ensconced in the rath, eating salty tidbits and drinking sugary tea while Vasundhara and her lieutenant Bhupendra got off for rally after rally after rally. At one point she seemed to get quite tired herself and asked Bhupendra if he would address just this one meeting instead of her. His face paled in horror as he said something to the effect that the crowd would stone him to death. Vasundhara was so completely the face of the election that another leader may not have won as magnificently as she did. But over her yatra loomed very large the shadow of Modi.

By the time of the last rally in an obscure outpost called Khetri a velvety, star-spangled darkness had fallen, but the darkness did not deter thousands of supporters from coming to Vasundhara's rally from neighbouring villages. This was the biggest rally of the day, and she made sure in her speech to remind those who came that they had given the Congress fifty-three years and got nothing in return. 'If you had given us fifty-three years we would have turned India into paradise...look what Narendra Modi has done for Gujarat in fifteen years.' On cue cries of 'Modi, Modi, Modi' rose from the crowd.

Embittered BJP veterans were to whisper after Modi was officially made the party's prime ministerial candidate that these demonstrations of support were orchestrated. But on the day I spent with Vasundhara on her yatra I saw no signs of orchestration. After the rally ended I got into Vasundhara's car thinking that I could make a quick exit this way but regretted my decision in minutes. The car was immediately surrounded by wildly enthusiastic supporters who shook it as if it were a toy. For one dreadful moment I thought they were going to lift it up. Her daughter-in-law and I sat nervously in the back while she, seated in the front, smiled happily as her supporters shoved their hands in through the open window and shouted slogans as if she had already won the election.

Vasundhara's night halt was in the local circuit house, where a small army of maids had arrived earlier in the day to ensure that her room was clean and comfortable. Since no such facilities were available for the rest of us Dushyant suggested that we drive to Alsisar, where we could spend the night in a sixteenth century fortress that belonged to a friend of his. So we drove on through the dark night in the wake of his friend Gaj Singh's car, and because it was a much longer drive than he said it was going to be Niharika complained the whole way and I began to regret not having spent the night on a couch in Vasundhara's room. Then like a mirage before us appeared a golden fortress out of a dark, narrow village road. We drove into a lighted courtyard that led to a magnificent room with murals on the walls and pictures of former rulers.

Gaj Singh led us through courtyards that glowed with dull yellow lights, as if lit by lanterns as they must once have been, and entered a dining room that had wonderful blue and white Rajasthani motifs painted on the walls and chandeliers of exquisite beauty. He told us proudly that he had done most of the restoration himself. Gathered at the table were a small group of minor Rajasthani princelings and inevitably almost the only conversation was about the coming election. It was past midnight but since Gaj Singh had laid on a meal of many courses we had no choice but to eat more than we needed to before retiring to our sixteenth century bedrooms that had been improved with modern plumbing and new furnishings. A princess of Alsisar from long ago glowered down at me from a picture near my bed, so I found it hard to sleep and spent what was left of the night making notes from my travels during the day.

In my journal I wrote, 'VR's meetings all day yesterday were incredible, with the last one in Khetri on such a scale that it seemed like she had already won the election. There were fireworks and slogans and such a hysterical zeal that it was almost scary. Other meetings all day were as filled with excitement. And whole towns seemed to turn out to greet her as her rathyatra went by. But this is for her, not the BJP. And it is for Narendra Modi.'

When I got back to Delhi one of the first people I ran into was a celebrated editor and TV personality. He shall remain anonymous because our conversation was not meant to be public but I quote him here to show how oblivious most political pundits in Delhi remained about the possibility of a Modi wave. When I told him of my travels and what I had seen he said, 'It's probably because of Vasundhara Raje...reports from Rajasthan indicate that Ashok Gehlot has become very unpopular. This doesn't have anything to do with Modi... you'll see that he won't be able to win a seat outside Gujarat.'

One reason why so many wise and famous political pundits missed what was going on was because very few of them travelled outside their comfort zones in Delhi and Mumbai. They spent their time flitting between intimate dinner parties in drawing rooms and lavish events in five star hotels, and because their faces had been made famous by television they were surrounded by society ladies and powerful businessmen wherever they went. They told them that Modi had no chance of becoming prime minister and that the most likely outcome of the elections would be a government supported by the Congress from the outside. The BJP would get more seats this time than the Congress, they conceded, but with Modi leading the party there would be no allies. When the chief minister of Bihar broke his alliance with the BJP after Modi was made the prime ministerial candidate, it made these pundits even more certain of their opinions.

27

UTTAR PRADESH AGAIN

It surprised me that not even when Modi held his first rally in Uttar Pradesh in October 2013 did they think it worth going and seeing for themselves if there was a Modi wave or not. This first rally was in Kanpur, and I made it a point to go even if it meant leaving for Uttar Pradesh within hours of coming back from Tokyo. So it was that I went from one of the cleanest places in the world to one of the filthiest. Aatish wanted to come with me even after I warned him that I planned to drive and that this would mean spending the night in Agra. He said getting to Agra was now much easier than I remembered because of the Yamuna Expressway. And when we got on to the Yamuna Expressway I thought for a moment I was still in Japan. Jet lag helped induce this illusion but so did the excellent quality of the road and the speed with which it took us to Agra. But no sooner did we get off the highway and enter this historic town than the realities of Uttar Pradesh returned.

It was late evening by the time we got off the highway, and when we entered the city we found ourselves in a bazaar that seemed not to have changed since Shah Jehan built the Taj Mahal. Motorcars were a new element but they moved at the pace of unmotorized vehicles through a traffic jam of rickshaws, handcarts, cows, people and stray dogs. Little hovel-like shops clung to the edges of open drains, whose fumes suppressed those of automobile fuel. We were stuck in this bazaar for nearly forty minutes, so the time saved on the expressway was lost in this polluted, crowded bazaar. It was only when we crawled our way out of it and the walls of the fort loomed over us that it was possible to remember that we were in one of India's oldest and most historic cities. In another country Agra would have been Rome or Paris but in India our socialist rulers had reduced it to a vast shanty with the Taj Mahal shining out of it like an enormous jewel in a garbage dump.

After a night spent in comfort in the Taj Residency Hotel we left early the next morning for Kanpur. I was last in this town more than twenty years earlier to cover another election and remembered it from then as a sleepy mofussil town with wide avenues and old-fashioned houses with big gardens, so nothing prepared me for what it had become. We entered through a part of the city that seemed made entirely of garbage. Frail dwellings made of waste material stretched endlessly on both sides of a broken road. Half-naked children played in playing fields made of garbage, and even the shops seemed to sell only waste paper, waste metal and waste rubber. A pall of smelly pollution hung over this vision of hell and lifted only slightly when we got to the centre of the city and saw a brand new mall of blue glass and steel rise like a mirage from this ruined, filthy city.

For me it came as a reminder that our politicians had learned to make money, vast amounts of money, out of changing land usage in urban areas. The mall was probably owned by local political leaders or their proxies, as were malls like it across urban India. In this version of 'development' political leaders were always the real beneficiaries since the average Indian was usually too poor to be able to afford to even enter the air-conditioned comfort of a mall, leave alone buy anything at mall prices. I put these thoughts out of my head that morning in Kanpur because the mall was the only place we could find that had restaurants and toilet facilities. We had arrived many hours before Modi was due to arrive, so there was time to stop for refreshment. Aatish picked one of the array of American-style fast food restaurants and stuffed himself with greasy hamburgers while I nibbled delicately on something less fattening.

Then we went back into the noisy, poisoned streets of Kanpur to find our way to the venue of the rally. This was easily done since banners advertising it were everywhere, as were BJP workers in saffron scarves. It was still three hours before Modi was due to arrive, but since there were thousands of people walking towards the ground where the rally was to be held our car could only go up to a certain point, so Aatish and I got out and walked with them. The people who walked with us were middle class residents of Kanpur and we got talking.

'What do you like about Modi?' I asked a middle-aged man who said he worked in a government office.

'We know that he has brought vikas to Gujarat and want him to become prime minister so he can do this for India.'

Other men, similarly dressed in bush shirts and drab pants, joined the conversation. 'We have heard his speeches and we like what he has to say,' they said. When I asked if they were happy with their own state government they laughed bitterly.

'This government has done nothing,' they said. 'At least when Mayawati was chief minister the law and order situation improved. Under Akhilesh Yadav it has become goonda raj again.' It was a remark I was to hear often in the next few months. While we were talking BJP workers on motorcycles screeched by, yelling, 'Jai Shri Ram'. And the people I was talking to stopped and stared at this parade of saffron-bandanaed hoodlums and said in one voice that this kind of slogan was unlikely to win the BJP any votes.

They were tired of the politics of caste and creed that had so defined Uttar Pradesh for decades, they said, but this message had not reached the ears of BJP leaders in the state. So from the stage, decorated with gaudy Hindutva images, the most important BJP leaders of UP droned on about issues that the vast crowd was completely uninterested in. The men who spoke while we waited for Modi to arrive were former chief ministers of the state and ministers of the Government of India, but nobody wanted to hear what they had to say. The 'people' had changed and they had not noticed. When Aatish and I found standing room in the press enclosure I looked around and was struck by how much the people had changed.

My thoughts went back to earlier elections when at a rally of this kind it would have been hard to find one person who was not dressed in rags. I remembered how these poor people with skeletal bodies and yellow teeth would gaze in wonder at Indira Gandhi as if she were a being from some other planet. I remembered rallies addressed by Rajiv Gandhi and prime ministers who came after him and how it was the same poor people who came and gazed in wonder at the leaders who usually descended from the skies in helicopters.

The people who came for Modi's first rally in northern India that morning were dressed in jeans and T-shirts and everyone seemed to have a cell phone. There was an overwhelming presence of young men in their twenties who wore saffron scarves but seemed totally unlike the BJP supporters who had cheered on Advani's rathyatra in the early 1990s. The real difference was that their aspirations had changed. They had become middle class. They wanted jobs and cars and colour television. Not a temple in Ayodhya. And the men who addressed them from the stage reminded them of a time when they had been easily divided along the fault lines of caste and religion.

Among the speakers were the former chief minister of the state, Kalyan Singh, on whose watch the Babri Masjid was demolished. And Vinay Katiyar, whose poisonous speeches had in earlier times persuaded Hindus to go off and kill Muslims in the riots that followed in the wake of Advani's chariot ride to Ayodhya to build a 'grand temple to Rama' where the Babri Masjid stood. I remembered that Narendra Modi had been on that chariot with Advani and that the movement was entirely controlled by the RSS. He had moved on but the BJP and the RSS seemed not to have.

On that unusually hot October morning I remember thinking that without him the BJP would have no chance of winning despite the deep despair that had come from the economic downturn. The downturn was presided over by Sonia Gandhi and her kitchen cabinet of leftist advisors that in the past three years had brought the economy to its lowest point in twenty years. In her determination to install her son as the next prime minister she had reduced the real prime minister to a cipher. So Dr Manmohan Singh, who as finance minister in the 1990s introduced economic reforms that saved India from bankruptcy, was forced to implement policies that had failed India time and time again.

These were policies that sought not to create wealth but to redistribute it in the name of removing poverty. They had succeeded in the 1970s in portraying Indira Gandhi as a saviour in the eyes of India's poorest citizens but had not succeeded even slightly in reducing poverty. But because they had worked for her mother-in-law, Sonia Gandhi was convinced they could work again. So she forced her government to spend thousands of crores of rupees on schemes that sought to guarantee jobs in rural India, guarantee cheap food grain and give people rights to education, free medicines and forest land. Like the BJP leaders on stage that morning she had not noticed that 'the people' had changed. The only political leader who had noticed was Modi.

When he finally appeared on stage that horribly hot afternoon he was greeted like a messiah. Cries of 'Modi, Modi, Modi' rose from different sections of the endless sea of people that had waited hours for him, and he did not disappoint them when he began his speech. He used a mixture of humour and high ideals to make his point. He mocked Rahul Gandhi for having said recently that poverty was a state of mind. 'Only someone born with a golden spoon in his mouth could say this,' he said to huge applause. Then after an eloquent pause he reminded them that he himself had not been born with a golden spoon in his mouth and understood what it meant to be poor because he was born in a poor family. In a stirring, emotional speech he told them that he dreamed of an India in which everyone could aspire to prosperity and not just an India whose only dream was to 'alleviate poverty'.

Was it my imagination or did I see the 'leaders' who stood beside him squirm? To a man they had emulated the example of the Congress and spent their time in government making money and ensuring that their constituencies were passed on to their heirs. They were a despicable, ugly bunch, and in the column I wrote when I got back to Agra that night I said that I did not believe that they could help Modi win the fifty seats he needed from Uttar Pradesh if he was going to become prime minister.

Nobody knew then that he would win many more. Certainly, they did not suspect anything of the sort in Delhi's drawing rooms or political circles. In the drawing rooms there was beginning to develop a siege mentality. It was as if they sensed that if Sonia Gandhi stopped being India's most important leader they would suffer at a personal level. Many of those who inhabited Delhi's drawing rooms had known Sonia since the days when she was just a housewife even if the daughter-in-law of a prime minister. They had chatted to her about housewifely things like children's school results, holidays and high fashion. Some had wormed their way into her court after she became the prime minister's wife and become more loyal as the years went by and she became de facto prime minister of India. Whether they had regular access to her was hard to ascertain but they pretended that they did, and those that did have access carried to her gossip from the drawing rooms. So she continued to be told that there was no chance of Modi becoming prime minister.

In the drawing rooms there was not a hint of the political changes that were happening in the villages and small towns of India. I discovered this when I got back to Delhi from the Kanpur rally and attended a dinner party in the house of Salman Khurshid, who had just been promoted to minister of external affairs. The occasion was a wedding reception for his wife's niece, and Dr Manmohan Singh and many of his ministers were among the guests. It was an early winter evening when in Delhi you almost need warm clothes but not quite. Dinner was in the immense garden of his ministerial bungalow. There were lights in the trees and tables covered in white tablecloths scattered about the lawns and a shamiana under which we mingled over glasses of wine.

Since my main reason for coming was to try and speak to Salman about what I had seen in Kanpur I spent the evening trying to catch a private word with him. This was not easy. Everyone seemed to want a private moment with him. Wherever he went he took with him a small crowd of journalists, diplomats, politicians and businessmen. When I finally found my chance I told him what I had gauged of the mood in Uttar Pradesh, and he said I had misunderstood what was happening because I was not from that state. He was, he reminded me, and he knew that although there was a certain 'disappointment' with the government's performance it was not serious enough for the Congress to lose the general election. 'We may lose a few seats,' he said confidently, 'but believe me there is no chance of us not forming the next government.'

He was not alone in this view. It was wedding season and so within days of this dinner party I found myself at the wedding of the daughter of a distant cousin of mine, Raja Randhir Singh of Patiala. Randhir's masi was married to my mother's late brother, Mohkam Singh, who was very much alive at the time of this wedding. In attendance at this glamorous Sikh wedding at Randhir's farm in Chhatarpur were Jat Sikh relatives from far and near. In attendance as well were politicians from different political parties. So at some point on the evening of the pre-wedding dinner party I found myself in conversation with a motley political group. There was Akbar Ahmed from the Bahujan Samaj Party, Amar Singh, whose political allegiances were not clear on this evening, and Vijay Dhar, who had once been a close aide of Rajiv Gandhi. Inevitably, all conversation was about the general election that was drawing closer by the day. When I told Akbar about my travels in his home state he said that there was Hindu-Muslim polarization but despite this he was giving the BJP no more than 160 seats in the Lok Sabha. 'They could be the single largest party,' he said, 'but that's all.'

Amar Singh, who had once been Mulayam Singh Yadav's most important aide, said, 'Congress is the natural party of governance, so there is no chance of its losing power.' Only

Vijay Dhar said that he thought the BJP could cross the 250 mark on its own. This was all that even the BJP's allies hoped for. After the wedding ceremony the next day, at a lunch attended by royals from Rajasthan and Punjab, stars from Bollywood and the arenas of sports and politics, I ran into Naresh Gujral, a friend from the days of my youth whose father became one of India's accidental prime ministers and helped his son move from a successful career as a garments exporter to a career in politics. As a Rajya Sabha member of the Akali Dal I expected that Naresh would have noticed that there was a Modi wave, but he said he did not think there was any chance of the BJP getting a full majority. 'But I am certain that with its allies there will be enough seats...there will be an NDA government.'

Was it just 'secularism' that made so many people who lived in the political cocoon of Lutyens' Delhi believe that the Congress was always going to be in power? I believe not. As someone who has spent most of my life in this most privileged of India's enclaves I detected, more than a year before Modi began to loom over national politics, real fear that if he did become prime minister life as we knew it would change forever. Lutyens' Delhi had over decades of rule by the Nehru-Gandhi dynasty become an exclusive club in which only a certain kind of politician had privileged membership. Both Atal Behari Vajpayee and Lal Krishna Advani did because they, and their families, became bedazzled entrants into what they thought of as Delhi high society.

Modi was the first BJP leader who came from a world that was completely foreign to India's ruling class. And he resisted being co-opted as an inferior member of the club, as other outsiders like Lalu Prasad Yadav and Mulayam Singh Yadav had been. There is nothing that warms the privileged hearts of Lutyens' Delhi denizens more than the idea that democracy had thrown up leaders of this humble rural kind. These were leaders who appeared to represent the 'real India' but who slipped easily into our privileged world no sooner than they moved into their bungalows in Lutyens' Delhi.

They may not have spent much time in this city's exalted drawing rooms but they learned very quickly to relish the perks of living in bungalows bigger than small villages in the states they came from, and they learned quickly the intricacies of hereditary democracy. Their 'socialist' political parties were transformed seamlessly into private limited companies, with family members being the only shareholders.

Some months before Delhi's wedding season, when Modi took on the prime minister personally by giving a stirring Independence Day speech in Gujarat that outshone Dr Manmohan Singh's last barely audible apology of a speech from the Red Fort on 15 August 2013, he provoked fury in Lutyens' Delhi. 'How dare he insult the prime minister by choosing 15 August to give such a speech?' socialites asked this question indignantly in the drawing rooms and celebrated editors repeated it in newsrooms and television studios.

Politicians in his own party began to wander about with nervous expressions on their faces. What would happen to the rules of the game if this man made it, they whispered furtively. Were their privileged lives filled with foreign tours, golfing afternoons and leisurely working hours coming to a quick end? Their reactions amused me enough to write a piece in my *Indian Express* column hinting that the real problem with Modi becoming prime minister was not his lack of 'secular' credentials but his being an Outsider in Lutyens' Delhi.

Within a day of its being published I got a call from a woman who identified herself as Kavita Dutta and said without further introduction that the Chief Minister of

Gujarat would like to see me. I was so stunned by this unexpected call that I was not sure what she meant, but when it became clear that I was being invited for a private audience in Ahmedabad I told her that I was happy to come as soon as possible. And a day later I found myself in that city, with instructions that I should not use my own car because 'transport to Gandhinagar will be arranged'. It was.

Two officials met me at the airport and took me to an ugly new government guesthouse. It was aesthetically unattractive in a flashy way but surprisingly clean. The white floors of the suite I was installed in were spotless and more satisfying still was that the powder pink bathroom was clean. In the small living room, furnished with formica tables and faux-leather chairs, there was an excellent television set, and since it was the day of the Lok Sabha debate on the food security bill I spent my time watching.

It happened to be the first time I saw Sonia Gandhi speaking live in a parliamentary debate, so I was riveted. In a decade in Parliament she had barely ever spoken. But the food security bill was her pet project and she seemed to want to make it absolutely clear that it was because of her that nearly 80 per cent of the people of India would become entitled to specified quantities of subsidized food grain every month. This was being done, she said in her hugely improved Hindi, to eliminate malnutrition in children. It was exactly the sort of expensive tokenism that Indira Gandhi had used to promote the idea that she (and she alone) cared for the poor. Her Integrated Child Development Scheme had failed so abysmally that every other Indian child was officially malnourished when Sonia Gandhi introduced her law to end malnutrition. The ICDS failed like all centralized welfare programmes had because by the time the money meant for hungry children actually got to them it had usually been eaten up by the greedy officials who administered these programmes. If Sonia Gandhi had listened to her own chosen prime minister he would have warned her against wasting money on such schemes. Expensive, cumbersome welfare programmes for the poor became the leitmotif of her government.

When the economy was growing at nearly 9 per cent these programmes seemed affordable, if nothing else, but when GDP growth dropped below 5 per cent in the last months of Sonia's reign they began to hurt. Her programmes for the poor failed to reduce poverty and began to be seen increasingly as having benefited mostly corrupt officials. Meanwhile, since her antipathy to rich people had inspired a tax reign of terror profitable companies were no longer able to expand and provide the jobs needed. Twelve million young Indians were coming into the workforce every year, and in the decade her government was in power less than 60 million jobs were created. This had led to not just 'disappointment' with the government, as Salman Khurshid said, but a deep, dark despair. She could not have done more to prepare the ground for Modi.

Late that afternoon Bhagyesh Jha, with whom I had travelled earlier in the wilds of rural Gujarat, appeared to take me to the chief minister. On the short drive to the new secretariat he sang Modi's praises, as he had done when we last met. When we drove through the gates of the secretariat we went past the building in which I had last met Modi in 2002 and on towards a newish building that was not particularly attractive but remarkable for not being built in the Soviet-style socialist architecture of government buildings that came up in the glory days of Nehruvian socialism. Nehru admired the Soviet Union, so lesser Indian politicians did too out of reverence for a man who with all his socialist pretensions had the vanity of a prince and was in every sense more powerful than any Indian maharaja had ever been.

From the minute I set foot in Modi's new secretariat I noticed that he had indulged his weakness for technology. Monitors of different sizes dominated the low reception desk and all of them played Modi's speeches. I remember thinking that this was a worrying sign of narcissism in a man I had come to admire. But I did not have time to dwell on the thought. Within minutes we were in an anteroom to the chief minister's office, drinking sweet milky tea. Mr Jha introduced me to a couple of gentlemen whom he described as being 'close to Modi', and I discovered that there was not much conversation possible because they spoke only Gujarati.

There was not much time for talk anyway because before I had taken more than two sips of tea and started to make notes in my head about the white chairs we sat on and the generally white impression the room made, I was ushered into the chief minister's presence. It surprised me that neither Mr Jha nor the other gentlemen in the anteroom accompanied me and discovered later that when Mr Modi gave someone time he did not allow any interference. He never answered his cell phone once in the hour I spent with him.

We sat on either side of a small table on which stood a Chinese feng shui bamboo in a small pot. Modi's office was so uncluttered that it reminded me of a windowless room in the Osho ashram in which I had once spent a night. It had been built like a cocoon to keep out sound and induce meditation and higher thoughts, and although Modi's office had huge glass windows that looked onto the old secretariat it created the same impression. Tea arrived as soon as we sat down, and once the man who brought it left, a silence fell between us. He said nothing and I, made nervous by the silence, felt obliged to break it.

'Do you remember when we last met in Gandhinagar?' I asked.

'No.'

'It was in 2003 not long after the riots. I had barely entered your room in that secretariat when you stopped me and asked how I, who knew you from your days in Delhi, could have believed that you had allowed the violence to happen. And then you said nothing more...there was no interview.'

'I remember,' he said and laughed.

Then there was another moment of silence before he said, 'I saw your article about my being an outsider in Lutyens' Delhi...you wrote correctly. I lived in Delhi but never belonged to it.'

We discussed the article for a few moments, and I told him that there were many people in his own party who were terrified that if he became prime minister he would ruin the cosy arrangement they had with the Congress in Delhi. I told him that the gossip in political circles was that L.K. Advani and Sushma Swaraj would be happy to continue sitting on the opposition benches rather than have him as prime minister. He seemed to know this already and did not dispute what I said but changed the subject and began to talk about how he had never wanted to be a politician.

'My own inclinations were towards spirituality...that's why I left home at seventeen and spent the next few years wandering about the Himalayas and traveling all over the country. I don't think I spent more than a single night in the same place in those years.'

He talked of his childhood years in the village and how he had to give up school because his father needed him to help at his railway tea stall. He told me that his teachers had tried to stop his parents from taking him out of school by telling them that he was a particularly good student but their economic situation did not allow this.

'We were very, very poor,' he said, 'and so I was unable to complete my education until much later when I worked in the RSS office in Ahmedabad and a man who became my mentor persuaded me to complete my graduation from Delhi University through a correspondence course. He saw that although my job was to clean the office in the mornings and to fetch and carry for senior leaders I had written a book in my spare time, and so he said I should definitely complete my education.' Our entire conversation was in Hindi, and I remember thinking that he spoke it without a trace of a Gujarati accent.

In the course of the next hour he told me how he had only come into politics because in 1984 when the BJP's seats in the Lok Sabha came down to two, the RSS decided that it needed help and sent some of its people into the party. He was one of them, he said, but now that he was in politics he was determined to do what he could for the country.

'Will you get a full majority? Political pundits say the BJP has no chance of that,' I said.

'Whatever they say I can tell you that after the next general election there will be a BJP government in Delhi.'

I remember thinking that his confidence was surprising, and I remember thinking that there was something calm and likeable about him that I had never seen before. After an hour went by, it was I who ended the meeting by saying that I had a flight to catch. He stood up immediately and as I was leaving said, 'I liked talking to you.'

28

LAST DAYS

In the drawing rooms of Lutyens' Delhi a sense of an era coming to an end began to become slowly evident in the winter of 2013. At those interminable dinner parties where political leaders, high officials and journalists come together to gossip and drink and solve the problems of India, a new nervousness crept in. Senior ministers continued to pretend that they were certain of a UPA-3 coming to be but no more did they say this with certainty, and after Rahul Gandhi gave his first full interview to Times Now editor-in-chief Arnab Goswami real despair began to set in. The interview was at the end of January 2014 and everyone watched it, and after watching it even the most loyal supporters of the Dynasty began to whisper amongst themselves about the possibilities of defeat.

At convivial gatherings on cold winter evenings as we huddled by fires in the draughty drawing rooms of old-fashioned bungalows, conversations would go something like this: 'Why did he give this interview? Who advised him to choose Arnab?'

'The Congress media managers are furious...they say it was some friends of Sonia Gandhi who told him to do this.'

'Well, whoever it was they have almost made sure that Rahul Gandhi will never become prime minister.'

'Did you notice how every time there was a question that he found difficult he said that he was in politics because he wanted to empower women?'

'Arnab asked him about the violence in 1984 against the Sikhs and he said Rahul Gandhi was in politics because he wanted to empower women.'

'And then he asked him about something else altogether and again he said Rahul Gandhi wants to empower the people. He did not answer a single question directly.'

The interview was an unmitigated disaster. The first problem was that he chose to give his first formal interview in English and not in Hindi. This strengthened the impression that he represented the privileged denizens of Delhi more than the people of India. The second problem was that of all of Indian television's English anchors Arnab had been chosen. Arnab has made belligerence the defining characteristic of his anchoring style, and once he gets a victim into his studio rarely lets him get away with vague answers. Nobody seemed to have prepared him for the kind of questions he would be asked. So he spent most of his answers talking in abstractions. Democracy is about processes, he said, and Rahul Gandhi is sitting here because he wants to empower the people. And most puzzling of all was his repeated assertion that 'the system' had destroyed his grandmother and his father and would probably destroy him. As Arnab's questions became tougher and more direct Rahul's answers became more abstract.

When I finished watching the interview I watched it again on YouTube and found myself marvelling at how many times he repeated that 'the system' was what he was in politics to change. It was as if nobody had told him that 'the system' for ten years had been a government that was controlled by his mother with an iron hand. And that 'the system' had been created by his great-grandfather and perpetuated by his grandmother and father after that. By the time I finished watching this interview for the second time I was certain that the Congress would lose the election with or without a Modi wave. But in the make-believe world of Lutyens' Delhi I continued to meet high officials who told me that the Dynasty was too powerful to be defeated easily. They admitted that things did not look good but invariably added that there was not the smallest chance of Modi getting a full majority and so he would not be able to form a government because the BJP had no chance of winning allies with him leading the campaign.

'As long as L.K. Advani was the face of the BJP there was a chance of allies like Mayawati and Nitish Kumar helping win UP and Bihar. But now that chance is gone.'

'But with Advani leading the campaign do you really think they would have done better than they did in 2009?' I asked the senior bureaucrat I spoke to in his vast office in Shastri Bhavan. He reflected on this for a moment before saying that there would have been a better chance this time because there was definitely 'disappointment' with the Congress.

Delhi has always been distant from Gandhiji's 'real India' but no more than it was in those early months of 2014. As usually happens when the term of a government is coming to an end and an election campaign is about to begin there were farewell parties in the homes of ministers and high officials, and the consensus at these events was that the Congress would somehow manage to stay in power even if it meant supporting a friendly government from the outside. There were precedents for this arrangement. Indira Gandhi supported Charan Singh's ephemeral government for a few months, and Rajiv Gandhi supported Chandrashekhar's equally ephemeral government in similar fashion. Funnily enough the first sign I personally got of the times changing was when I saw Sonia Gandhi's courtiers suddenly trying desperately to win favour with the handful of BJP leaders who were regular fixtures in the drawing rooms.

Of these the most prominent was Arun Jaitley, and no sooner did he appear at a dinner party than Sonia's courtiers could be seen making a beeline for him. In the irreverent words of a friend who saw a famous woman courtier in action, 'If there was such a thing as a verbal blow job I saw her give Jaitley one.' By March that year I decided that it was time to go and see for myself what was happening in the real India. And since I had not been to Bihar in a longish while I decided that my first stop on the campaign trail would be Patna. Once more the Maurya Hotel was the only place to stay.

It had improved. In my notebook I wrote this description of my first impressions of the Maurya Hotel on 19/3/14. 'Maurya Hotel. View of Gandhi Maidan. Boys playing cricket at 7 a.m. and a small outcrop of new buildings in the vicinity that gives the impression of change. Some there is. In my bathroom the shower worked perfectly and there was wallpaper on the walls. The sheets and towels are that worrying shade of grey but did not smell. There was a small pile of handmade soap instead of Hamam and a disposable bag for laundry. But driving around the city yesterday was like being in the ultimate urban nightmare. KFC and Coffee Day sprout out of streets lined with rotting garbage, broken buildings and decay...'

This was the first time I returned to Patna after Nitish Kumar had become chief minister. He was in his second term in office, and in Delhi's newspaper offices and TV studios everyone spoke of him as a man who had 'transformed'

Bihar. There were even those who said he had no alternative but to break his alliance with the BJP in Bihar because he believed that instead of Narendra Modi being the National Democratic Alliance's candidate for prime minister it should have been him. While driving around Patna I could not see the smallest hint of change except in the form of the American fast food restaurants that rose like giant plastic flowers out of the squalor. The saddest sight for me personally was of the elegant, beautifully preserved Khuda Bakhsh library that despite being more than a hundred years old looked better than any other building in Patna. In a more civilized city it would have been a magnet for scholars, bibliophiles and tourists because it contains thousands of valuable manuscripts from ancient times, but in Patna nobody has bothered to even improve the condition of the street in which it stands.

It rises out of a narrow, crowded alley which that day seemed to be in use as a dump for old vehicles. Rusting cycle rickshaws stood on the edge of open drains, and there were the other usual sights of Bihar's capital city – rotting garbage, skinny, diseased dogs and cattle that seemed to have only the rotting garbage by way of nutrition. The only enclave of Patna that was relatively fit for human habitation was where political leaders and high officials lived in houses left over from the Raj. Even this enclave was aesthetically more pleasing because it was the season when red silk cotton trees shed their flowers, so the pavements were adorned with fallen flowers as if for a festival. Since I had been to Patna many times without once visiting the gurudwara that marks the birthplace of the tenth Sikh guru, Govind Singh, I decided to go this time if only to see what people felt about their MP, actor Shatrughan Sinha. He won a handsome victory from the Patna Sahib constituency in 2009, winning more than half the votes polled.

Before going to the gurudwara I stopped to talk to people in a chaotic, crowded bazaar that reeked of open drains. Here I talked to passersby and shopkeepers, and every conversation followed the exact same pattern. 'What do you think of Shatrughan Sinha's role as your MP?'

'He hasn't been here once since he got elected.'

'But has he used his MP fund to do something for the area?' This question evoked rude laughter before someone or other said, 'Look around you...what do you think?'

'So will he win this time?'

'Yes. But only because of Modi.'

'What have you heard about Modi that gives you so much faith?'

'We have seen his speeches on TV...we know people who have gone to Gujarat to work and they tell us that it is a wonderful place, so we hope that if he becomes prime minister he can turn Bihar into Gujarat.'

When I asked where the gurudwara that gave this parliamentary constituency its name was, I was directed to a very narrow alley that was so crowded and dirty that I changed my mind about going to the gurudwara. The thought of walking barefoot in such a filthy place was frightening. So I paid silent homage to Guru Govind Singh from a distance and left. I then went in search of the city's main mosque with the idea of talking to Muslims to see what they felt about Modi. Every single person I talked to said firmly and in no uncertain terms that 'not a single Muslim would be voting for Modi'.

The next day I left for Gaya having formed a poor impression of Nitish Kumar's 'achievements' as chief minister. If Patna city's centre looked bad its outskirts looked much, much worse. Urban squalor turned seamlessly into rural filth with pools of stagnant water on both sides of the road, mud and thatch shacks and charmless bazaars whose hovel-like shops seemed overwhelmed by advertisements for Lux Cozi underwear, Airtel services and Nokia mobile phones. Beyond the bazaars were small, ugly buildings that identified themselves as schools with names like Usha Martin World School and Kishor's School. There was even a sign on a fenced-off wasteland that proclaimed itself to be a Kid Zoo. Ironically, these things were symbols of change and a semblance of order. The last time I had travelled on this road to Jehanabad was more than ten years earlier to report on a massacre in which a Dalit village had been burned to the ground by upper caste killers. Militant caste militias ruled this whole area in that time. Nitish Kumar may not have succeeded in cleaning up Patna or bringing the development Bihar so badly needed, but he had improved law enforcement.

The first village I stopped in was called Jamalpur. The upper caste Bhoomihar peasants were the dominant community. They were delighted to talk to a reporter from Delhi mostly because they were very interested in what was happening in national politics. They made it clear immediately that they had every intention of voting for Modi because they believed that he was the only political leader capable of bringing real parivartan and vikas, and this they said was what Bihar needed desperately.

'Why?' I asked as they led me to what looked like the village community centre. There were benches and rough wooden tables laid out in a shed that had a sloping thatched roof but no walls.

'Why do we want change and development? Because look at this village…we have electricity that comes so irregularly that we cannot water our fields.'

'Do you have drinking water?'

'Yes. There are hand pumps that we get it from. But no water in our homes.'

'And television?'

'Everyone has a television and we get both Doordarshan and cable when there is electricity.'

'Cell phones?'

'Everyone has cell phones.'

'So what is the biggest problem that you face?'

'Unemployment. There are no jobs for our children. Even those who go to college and get BA and MA degrees find it impossible to find work. So they continue to work in the fields.'

'What about MNREGA? Has that not helped in any way?'

'Yes. There is MNREGA but most of the money is eaten up by officials who make lists of false names and say that they have given them jobs. There are even the names of dead people in those lists. So we have filed RTIs to get the information. We have a man in the village who we call Kejriwal because he has filed so many RTIs to get information.'

Snacks arrived in small china plates and tea in stout, ribbed glasses. And the conversation kept turning to national politics. They told me that they had been very impressed with Arvind Kejriwal when he first appeared on the scene but they lost faith in him when he gave up being chief minister of Delhi within days of getting the job. What did they think of their own chief minister, Nitish Kumar, I asked, as their 'Kejriwal', a man whose real name was Satish Sharma, appeared with a fat file of Right to Information applications in his hands. Nitish Kumar was better than Lalu Yadav, they said, because at least under him the law and order situation had improved but he was an ineffectual leader.

'Why?'

'He has a janata durbar (people's court) where we go regularly with our complaints. And nothing is ever done about them. He has not been able to create jobs or reduce poverty. You want to see real poverty, come and see how the musahar (mouse catchers) live.' The community gets its name from what once was their only source of employment and nutrition.

They led me to a railway track on the edge of the village which we had to walk across to get to the musahar quarter. No road led to this large, shallow pit in which tiny mud huts were built in higgledy-piggledy fashion. Severely malnourished children stood around listlessly in alleys not wide enough for two people to pass each other easily. I asked if I could go into one of the huts, and a scrawny man with a wrinkled face was summoned and ordered to show me his home. He led me wordlessly into a tiny hovel in which I could barely stand. It was completely bare. Outside in a tiny courtyard was a mud stove with a pot on it. When I asked the owner what he did for a living he said his only source of income came up during the harvest season when he made a few rupees by working in other people's fields.

'What about MNREGA? Has that not helped you?' I asked.

'No.'

'Have you heard of MNREGA?'

'No.'

'How is it that MNREGA has not reached these people who need it more than anyone in this village?' I asked my upper caste guides.

'We told you that there was big corruption in this programme,' they said without a hint of guilt. Clearly it was upper caste farmers who had benefited from it and not the landless musahar community, whose poverty was so extreme that 100 guaranteed days of work a year may have transformed their lives.

We walked back across the railway track to the upper caste quarter, and I was taken on a tour of the rest of the village. There were the usual open drains and smelly alleys, but the houses were all pucca and TV dishes rose out of the roof of every dwelling. A fine new temple stood on the edge of neat fields. Throughout the tour I heard complaints about corruption in everything. The Bihar government had announced a teacher training programme that they could get into only after bribing officials. When they tried to get loans from banks they paid Rs 80,000 as a bribe to get a Rs 5 lakh loan. Finally, when I asked them why they believed that Narendra Modi could change things they said, 'We go to Gujarat to work and we have seen that Gujarat looks much better than Bihar.'

When we got back on the highway to Gaya I asked the driver to select a Muslim village for our next stop. He chose Baarah. My first impression of it was that it seemed more prosperous, better planned and cleaner than the village I had just visited. In the centre was a large mosque with a green dome and attached to it a 'madarsa'. The village was governed by a woman sarpanch called Roshanara, who lived in a house that was large and well appointed by rural standards. There were pictures of Mecca on the walls and a small group of men sat at a table in the living room who did the talking on behalf of Roshanara. 'She is only a lady,' they explained. 'She doesn't know about politics and elections and such things.'

'But isn't she the sarpanch?'

'Yes. Because this is a village that is reserved for women only.'

When I asked what was likely to happen in the general election, a man called Guddu said, 'Every Muslim in Bihar will vote for Nitish Kumar. We owe him a special favour this time because he broke relations with the BJP to save Bihar from Hindu-Muslim riots.'

'Are you saying that if Modi wins there will be riots?'

'Yes. We know this from what happened in Gujarat.'

'Has Nitish Kumar been a good chief minister?'

'A very good chief minister,' Guddu said. 'He ended the jungle raj that existed when Lalu was chief minister and he has done a lot for us.'

'Do you have electricity in the village?'

'Yes. We have electricity for twenty-two hours a day.'

'But it isn't there now.'

'This is because it has just gone. It goes sometimes but it comes back soon.'

It did come back before I left, but in the hour I spent in Roshanara's home talking to her male relations I heard not one complaint about Nitish Kumar's government. Everything was perfect, they said; they wanted for nothing except that Modi should not ever become prime minister. When I asked if they were frightened of him they said it was not fear they felt but loathing. 'Muslims cannot vote for Modi because he hates us. And after what happened in Muzaffarnagar, Muslims in UP will never vote for Akhilesh Yadav either. You just wait and see.' There had been communal riots months earlier and the main victims were Muslim despite the 'secular' government of Mulayam Singh Yadav and son.

All the way to Jehanabad we passed private schools on either side of the highway with names like Harvard Kids School and Little Angle (sic) Public School. Again, an area that I visited when I was last in Jehanabad was so desolate that people were afraid to come out after dark. Sadly the town of Jehanabad itself had not benefited from 'development'. From being a dusty half-village it had become a town but one that had not learned to manage waste, so it was surrounded by walls of rotting garbage.

The only halfway decent urban centre that I saw on

this visit to Bihar was Gaya. And this was because foreign Buddhists from Japan, Thailand and China had built hotels that were clean and modern and Buddhist temples of grace and beauty to honour the place where the Buddha found enlightenment. It was a very different place from the Gaya I remembered from the 1980s when I had come here to cover a Kalachakra sermon given by the Dalai Lama. Then there was just the temple with its Bodhi tree and hostels for pilgrims that were neither clean nor beautiful.

By the time I left Patna for Delhi the next day I was certain that Modi would win many more seats in Bihar than the wise political pundits of Lutyens' Delhi were giving him. No state in India seemed to need parivartan and vikas more than Bihar.

29

THE CANDIDATE FROM BENARES

Benares. I returned to this oldest of Indian cities days after Modi announced that he would be contesting from here. I had not been back for fifteen years, so the first surprise was the airport. It was new, modern and efficient and very different from the ramshackle shed I remembered from when I was last here. All airports built in socialist times looked like ramshackle sheds. As happens to journalists at election time my conversation about the campaign began as soon as I got into the taxi. By a fortuitous coincidence the taxi company owner was a Muslim called Feroze and the driver a Hindu called Munna. Feroze happened to be at the airport to receive some other guests and asked if he could take a ride with us to his home in a village halfway to the city.

'Of course,' I said a little too eagerly and followed this up with, 'How do Muslims feel about Modi being the candidate from Benares? Are they frightened?'

'No. But he will not get their votes. Not just because of him but because the BJP is not popular.'

At this point Munna joined the conversation. 'You see,' he explained, 'ever since Murli Manohar Joshi won from here five years ago he has never come to the city. He has come to the airport many times, met people there and then flown straight back to Delhi.'

'So if he were the candidate this time he would lose?'

'Definitely,' they said in unison. 'He has done nothing at all for Benares. And people are no longer so easily fooled. They expect their MPs to work, not just sit in Delhi.'

Munna and I continued talking after Feroze got off at his village. I noticed that the road into the city had not changed much since I was last here. It was broken and full of ditches like many other roads in UP, but what surprised me was that it should not have been improved along with the airport since Benares was not just another UP town. I asked Munna why he thought it was in such a state of disrepair. He said that Akhilesh Yadav had been a useless chief minister and nothing had improved in the state under him.

'The airport has.'

'No. That was built before he became chief minister.'

'So what are the things that have not improved?'

'Law and order has broken down and we are back to those times when his father was chief minister and Yadavs thought they could get away with murder.'

'And what has happened in terms of development?'

'There has been no development at all. Mayawati was a much better chief minister but people voted her out because she spent so much money building statues. If she hadn't done this statue building business she would have won the election.'

We drove past villages and scruffy roadside bazaars that had not changed in the fifteen years I had been away, and when we got to Benares I noticed that nothing had changed much here either. Munna had by then taken on the role of tour guide and talked endlessly about how bad public services were in the city. Then he pointed to a drain that had barely a trickle of water in it, saying, 'That, can you believe, is the Assi river? Look what they have done to one of the rivers from which Varanasi gets her name.'

By the time I got to the Ganges View Hotel on the Assi Ghat he had filled me in on details about corrupt police officers and officials who were chosen only because they were from the Yadav caste. He told me of honest officials being victimized by Akhilesh Yadav's government when they tried to do something good for the city. And he told me that whether Muslims voted for Modi or not Hindus most certainly would. 'He will be prime minister. You'll see,' he said as I walked up the steep steps that led to a hotel that continues to have more charm than any other in Benares. It used to be the family home of a man I know only as Shashank Bhai, who continues to live here and treats guests who come to stay as if they were guests in a private home. He has left the public areas much as they would have been when it was a private home. So the atmosphere is that of an old-fashioned haveli with terraces on higher floors that look onto the ghat, the temples that line it and the Ganga.

From earlier visits I remembered that one of my favourite things about the Ganges View Hotel was to wake very early in the morning and watch the first light of dawn spread slowly over the Ganga. By the time I finished drinking my morning tea the river would become gilded with sunlight and look so beautiful that I would be reminded why Indians believe it to be more sacred than any other river and why poets have written paens to the morning light in Benares. This time Shashank Bhai had given me a room in a new wing on the highest floor. The room was cluttered with heavy furniture and badly lit but the view from the terrace was magical.

On my first afternoon in Benares I decided to go to Benares Hindu University in the hope of getting a sense of what young students thought of the election. I chose the Sanskrit department to begin my enquiries. From the outside it looked like a fine building with terracotta-coloured arches on a yellow-washed façade, but inside I found corridors filled with broken furniture, dust and decay. It was in one of these corridors that I sat and chatted with students from different parts of India. They came mostly from indigent Brahmin families and admitted that they were learning Sanskrit because they wanted to keep alive the traditions they were brought up with but they knew it would not help them find employment. Except as priests. Everyone I talked to said the biggest problem in their eyes was unemployment. The second biggest problem was corruption.

'But we believe that Modi will bring real change,' said Satyendra Kumar Sharma from Aligarh.

'What sort of change?'

'Every sort of change. Economic policies will be made that will create jobs for young people like us. And education policies will be made so that merit becomes important as the criteria for admission. In a university like this there are so many reserved seats that it is almost impossible for a student to get in on merit.'

Other students gathered round and joined the conversation, and a small group formed around the dusty table on which I sat. Each of them said that they believed that Modi would bring real change. Except for one student who said he would be voting for the Congress because his family always had. The others laughed at him and told him that he needed parivartan in his thinking as much as the country did. When I asked why as young people they did not find Rahul Gandhi more attractive since he was closer to their age than Modi, they said that they had not even considered voting for him because they found it hard to take him seriously and because he came from a family that they blamed for India being the way it was.

In my notebook this is what I wrote the next morning as I sat on the terrace of the Ganges View Hotel drinking sweet 'desi chai' and watching the pearly grey light become lighter and lighter on the Ganga at 5.45 a.m.: 'Went to BHU's Sanskrit Department yesterday where in a corridor of fine proportions but ruined by dusty piles of broken furniture I talked to a group of mostly Brahmin students about the election. 99.9% of them wanted Modi to become prime minister and for different reasons. Some said he was the only one who could rid the country of corruption. Some said he would improve the economy enough for jobs to be created – everyone said employment was the biggest problem – and some said he was the only one who would have the courage to end reservations. Only 30% of seats now come under the general category.'

The overwhelming impression I formed from talking to these young students was of deep, deep despair. After we finished our conversations one of them took me to meet the head professor of the department, who was on the verge of retirement. Perhaps because of this he talked more freely than he may otherwise have done and told me with great sadness in his voice that he felt he had wasted his life teaching young people a language that would not help them get jobs. 'What can they do with Sanskrit? They can become priests of course but should our governments not have been able to create more jobs for scholars of Sanskrit? What kind of country is this that scholars of Sanskrit have no place in it?'

That evening I went to Pappu's chai shop on the Assi Ghat with Aatish. He had been in Benares for more than a week by then and planned to stay a whole month to do some research for a book and to cover the election campaign for *Open* magazine. And Pappu's chai shop had become his evening haunt because it was here that local politicians came to discuss the events of the day and it was here that the city's politicians and thinkers gathered to gossip every evening. They sat on wooden benches on the edge of a drain and drank endless glasses of Pappu's tea, which he made perched on the edge of his stove. Pappu's chai shop is more open-air shed than shop, so anyone turning up for a glass of tea sat outside it inhaling fumes from traffic that swirls around an old banyan tree with a small temple under it.

A political conversation was already underway when we arrived. A man called Subedar Singh from the Samajwadi Party was speculating about whether it was still possible for Modi to be defeated. 'The only chance Congress has of defeating him is if they bring Priyanka Gandhi against him,' he said.

'Could she defeat Modi in Benares?' I asked.

'No. But she can reduce the margin of victory. She can bring it down to a difference of a few thousand votes like Murli Manohar Joshi won last time.'

'Do you see Priyanka Gandhi being brought in at this stage?'

'No. Because Congress will need her if Rahul Gandhi flops completely.'

'Does he seem like a flop?'

The men on the wooden benches looked at each other before one of them said quietly, 'Yes. He hasn't understood why people are disappointed and angry.'

'As Modi says, he was born with a golden spoon in his mouth, so how would he know what it is like to live an ordinary life?'

'What are people most angry about?'

'Everything. Look at the state of our schools. Look at the problems that people have just getting their children through school. Look at our hospitals...so many years after independence should this be the state of the country?'

'People have become impatient...young people don't find jobs. How will they live?'

'So why do you think Modi can solve all these problems?'

'He is talking about parivartan and vikas and that is what the country needs. '

'What does Benares need?' I directed my question to a man called R.P. Singh, who was a retired museum curator.

'We need the city to be cleaned up and we need the Ganga to be cleaned up.'

There was an older man from the BJP who said he was certain that Modi would win even though he conceded that Murli Manohar Joshi had been a very bad MP.

The next day I drove out of Benares towards Mirzapur and stopped to talk to people in villages with names like Raja Talao and Gadowli. My plan was to try and catch up with the campaign of Laliteshpati Tripathi, the great-grandson of Kamalapati Tripathi, who had in his time been the mighty Congress satrap of this part of Uttar Pradesh. I drove past private schools called Motherland Public School and National Convent School and stopped in small rustic bazaars to listen to the complaints of people who had nothing but complaints. They were complaints that were exactly the same as I had heard many times before in elections past, but the big change I noticed this time was the total absence of the traditional Indian villager. Gone were those older kind of villagers with prematurely wrinkled faces wrapped in grimy turbans and dusty sandals on their calloused feet. The villagers I met that day wore jeans and T-shirts and had cell phones in their pockets.

It was in a village on the banks of the Ganga that I found Laliteshpati. He had his American mother's light skin and his father's jowly face. His floppy light brown hair was held back by a bandana in Congress colours, and he sat in the village square surrounded by men who told him their woes. He listened attentively and spoke softly in the local dialect, explaining why the Congress had not been able to do more for them in its long years of rule. Aatish and I travelled with him in his car to the next village and I asked him why he had decided to become a politician. He said it was because he was so moved by the people's 'faith in democracy' that he had decided that he would like to try and do something for them. An accident had laid him up in bed for three months, he said, and in this time he had thought long and hard about what he wanted to do with his life and had concluded that he would like most of all to go into politics to help improve the lives of people who, despite the terrible deprivations they suffered, had never lost faith in democracy.

It was as good a reason as any, I thought, as we drove on through dusty, wretchedly poor villages to the next meeting that Laliteshpati was due to address. It was a small meeting under a large banyan tree. Village musicians sang songs in praise of Congress leaders to elevate the mood. And a fat English-speaking acolyte of the candidate tried to convince me that he would 'definitely win' and that Modi's effect was limited to Benares, but there was a tangible air of defeat at this gathering. Laliteshpati had won a seat in the UP assembly two years earlier but it seemed unlikely that he was going to win the Mirzapur Lok Sabha seat. Nobody knew then that the Modi factor would end up winning nearly every seat in the state for the BJP. What was clear on that hot, dusty journey was the despair that hung like a heavy pall over everything.

This had much to do with the disappointment caused by Akhilesh Yadav having been able to do nothing different or inspiring in the two years he had been chief minister. He was given a full majority by the people of UP in the hope that as a young man, albeit a political heir, he would understand how desperate people were for change. Not only did he fail to change anything, he did not show any sign even of being anything more than a proxy chief minister for his father. Every time there was a crisis it was Mulayam Singh or one of his cronies who seemed to take charge. And whatever little hope Muslims had that Akhilesh would at least strengthen secularism died when the Muzaffarnagar riots were handled with the usual absence of fairness in the administration. More than sixty people were killed in the riot that began on 27 August 2013. The rioting got so bad that the army was called to restore order, and despite this it was only in the middle of September that curfew was lifted in the affected villages. Of the dead nearly 70 per cent were Muslims and nearly all of the 50,000 people who were forced out of their villages into unsanitary camps were Muslims.

By now the possibility of a Modi wave had begun to be felt even in Delhi, and within days of my arrival in Benares famous TV anchors and political commentators began to descend on this ancient city in droves. They set up TV studios on the ghats where they interviewed political pundits, academics from Benares Hindu University and local intellectuals and wandered about the narrow alleys of the old city talking to random people. What did they think of Modi, they asked, and did they still hold him responsible for the violence in 2002, and other questions of this kind. And the people they talked to replied with cryptic words and smiles.

Many of the journalists who came to Benares were 'secular' in their fundamental approach to the Modi factor, so their views were similar to those of Sonia Gandhi. By late April she seemed to understand fully that there was a bigger wave for Modi than her campaign managers had told her, so she went on national television for the first time ever to urge people to not vote for him. In Hindi and in English she urged voters to remember that the very 'idea of India' (a phrase born in Delhi's drawing rooms) was in danger of being destroyed. She reminded them that her party represented the values that were at the heart of the idea of India. These values, she said, were love, harmony, respect for each other and it was these values that constituted 'Bharatiyata'. So the choice was between this idea of India that she as leader of the Congress embodied and 'them', who represented hatred, falsehood and discord. I speak to you from my heart, she said, to warn you to be careful of the choice you make because 'they' will bring 'ruination'.

The appeal fell on deaf ears and especially in Benares, where Modi's challenger was now Arvind Kejriwal and not the Congress candidate. Kejriwal gave up being chief minister of Delhi to stand against Modi in Benares. He arrived a day before Modi was to arrive and file his nomination papers as the candidate from Benares. This was seriously bad timing for Kejriwal, so bad that hardly anyone noticed his arrival. He travelled from Delhi by train to show that he was a humble man of the people and different from the man who was trying to become prime minister. He held small corner meetings in narrow alleyways and at these meetings told people that Modi represented only rich people and he represented the poor. Echoing Rahul Gandhi he said, 'You do not want to elect a man who represents "Ambani-Adani",' from small rickety stages over cheap public address systems that distorted his voice.

A small army of Aam Aadmi Party volunteers arrived from Delhi to help him, but they were such strangers to Benares that they asked journalists directions to their leader's small, poorly attended meetings. But when they saw the crowds that greeted Modi on the day that he came to file his nomination papers, they seemed to give up the fight. While half the citizens of Benares lined the route that Modi was due to take from Benares Hindu University to the collectorate, Kejriwal sat under a banyan tree on the Assi Ghat in sulky silence. When the occasional curious pilgrim asked why he was on a maun vrat (a silent protest), AAP volunteers said it was in protest against his workers being beaten up the day before. Nobody cared.

Modi arrived in Benares on a day of searing heat but this did not discourage people from coming out into the streets in their thousands and waiting for his procession to go by. I parked myself on a platform near a statue of Vivekananda that was being used by TV journalists who shaded their faces as they best could from the burning white sun. The platform was rickety to begin with but became dangerously rickety when a surge of enthusiastic supporters climbed on as Modi's procession drew closer. It was a high platform that offered a panoramic view of the route. TV journalists have to wait longer than print journalists on such occasions, so they are generally better prepared for waiting by ensuring regular supplies of cold drinking water. But even they were beginning to wilt by the time Modi's truck came into view.

When he got off and walked to the statue of the man he thinks of as his mentor the crowd went wild with shouts of 'Modi, Modi, Modi'. The crowd consisted mostly of young men, and after Modi's truck passed on and the frenzy died I asked some of them why they were so excited to see Modi. They said it was because they needed jobs and believed he could create them. 'He is a politician not a magician,' I said, and the youth to whom I spoke replied, 'When it comes to development he is a magician.'

※

In Delhi in those last days of April 2014 there was a sense of endings and a sense of disbelief. In the drawing rooms there were farewell parties at which senior bureaucrats talked of 'clearing their desks' as if it was an era that was coming to an end and not just a democratic transfer of power. Nobody admitted the possibility that Modi might actually become prime minister, but they sensed that change was coming of a kind that might be more dramatic than had happened in a very long while. Oddly this strengthened denial instead of acceptance, and when I told them what I had seen in Benares they dismissed my observations as 'biased in favour of Modi'. A woman columnist wrote a whole column of abuse against women she described as 'Modi's aunties'. I was in this short list.

The first event I attended after returning from Benares was Shekhar Gupta's book launch in a cavernous, chandeliered hall in the Leela Hotel. It was Shekhar's first book, and as editor of the *Indian Express* he drew a glittering array of political Delhi's most shining stars. High officials, ministers, editors and socialites were all in gracious attendance. The main speaker was P. Chidambaram. He was finance minister, so his honesty that evening was surprising. He admitted that the government that he had served for a decade had failed to understand how the electorate had changed. But he warned that there was going to be 'no new dawn' on 16 May when the election results were due. He conceded that India had changed from 'a petitioner society to an aspirational society' and that this had gone unnoticed.

He conceded that the Congress had misunderstood the results of the last general election and not paid attention to the reality that most of its new seats came from urban India. The Gandhis had been led to believe that the seats the Congress gained in 2009 came on account of Sonia's favourite welfare programme, MNREGA. Since many political pundits also misread the election results this encouraged Sonia's NGO advisors to concentrate on pouring more and more money into welfare programmes. Chidambaram did not go so far as to admit this at Shekhar's book launch, but it was the first and only time that I heard a Congress leader accept that they could lose the election because serious mistakes had been made. When it came to questions from the floor Salman Khurshid dismissed the possibilities of change by prefacing his question with, 'We are not going away, we are here to stay.' The audience responded with silence. Later when I asked him if he thought he was winning Farukhabad he said, 'I hope so.' But his wife Louise, who had handled his campaign, said she was certain that he would win. If I had told her that reports from UP indicated that he would lose badly she would not have believed me.

This sense of disbelief and denial was the mood in those last days before 16 May and continued through half that morning till it became clear that not only had Modi won but that he had become the first prime minister to win a full majority since Rajiv Gandhi. On 16 May I woke at dawn to get to the India Today TV studios in Noida by 7 a.m. When I arrived in the green room I found a group of other sleepy pundits drinking tea and coffee that tasted so much like sugared hot water it was hard to tell which was which. Even this was welcome so early in the morning.

Inevitably as we knocked down many cups of hot sugared water we started speculating about what the final result was going to be. Excitement, anticipation and a strange sort of tension made the atmosphere in this green room electric. My first conversation was with Shiv Visvanathan and Achyut Yagnik, both of whom I knew hated Modi, and they said that in their opinion the National Democratic Alliance would get

220 seats at the most. 'So you are saying Modi will not become prime minister?' Silence. The only people in the group who gave Modi more than 250 seats that morning were Ashok Lahiri and his assistant, who had done an exit poll for *India Today*, but even they stopped short of a full majority. So we went into the studio expecting a Congress defeat rather than a Modi victory.

By the time the first results started indicating a big jump in BJP seats my old friend and colleague Karan Thapar had joined our little band of political pundits. He said we must tell viewers that these were only postal ballots and that things could still change. Then when trends came in from all over the country indicating a spectacular BJP victory he said once more that we must tell viewers that these were trends and not results. He said this so many times that when the results were all in and he was still advising caution I had to urge him to stop. Karan had a personal grudge against Modi because he once walked out of his TV show when he pressed him too hard on the 2002 riots. But Karan was far from being the only person in the national media who dreaded the possibility of Modi becoming prime minister.

The English-language media is a powerful pillar in the structure that makes up that most privileged enclave called Lutyens' Delhi. Like the bureaucrats who constitute a much more powerful pillar, most journalists had traditionally been from English-speaking, upper class India. They saw the Nehru-Gandhi dynasty as representing their class interests as much as it represented the colonized officials who inherited India from the British. The very idea of Modi was terrifying because what language would they interview him in? Would he give them interviews at all or choose Hindi journalists instead? Would the cosy relationship they had with power remain? Would their 'idea of India' remain intact?

By late afternoon on 16 May it became absolutely clear that pillars were crumbling fast, and the atmosphere in the studio got infected with an unspoken gloom. When agreeing to be a political commentator on *India Today*, I had asked for permission to go for an hour to Rajat Sharma's India TV and so I did. You can count on the fingers of one hand journalists in Delhi who are close to Modi, and Rajat is one of them. So was it this that made the atmosphere in India TV that day so full of festivity? In the waiting room I ran into the actor Vivek Oberoi and a large group of political pundits from the Hindi media who openly celebrated Modi's victory. When I went into the studio Rajat introduced me as someone who had predicted a Modi wave before anyone in Delhi was prepared to acknowledge its existence. Even as he said this Sonia and Rahul Gandhi popped up on the studio's monitors. They stood outside Congress headquarters to concede defeat, and they did this ungraciously. They congratulated the 'new government' on its victory but made no mention of Modi.

Sonia looked sullen and hostile but Rahul smiled his usual genial smile as if the election had been won and not lost. He even tried to answer a question that some reporter asked, but his mother dragged him away with the look mothers get when they are about to spank a child. By that evening the atmosphere in Delhi was a curious mixture of gloom, hope and festivity. In the sandstone corridors of power that sit at the top of Raisina Hill there was the sense that an era had come to an end and the sense that nobody was sure if this would be a good thing or bad. But in the bazaars of Delhi there was celebration.

The next day's English newspapers gave as much space to hailing Modi's victory as to warning that his becoming prime minister could mean the end of the 'idea of India'.

Modi, unbothered by these prophets of doom, went to Benares the next day and after offering prayers (on live television) in the Vishwanath Mandir participated in the evening worship of the Ganga. It was the first time an Indian prime minister had been so open about his religion and a tremor of fear went up the 'secular' spine of Lutyens' Delhi. Friends who had never see the Ganga puja or Benares said that they loved the ceremony but they were worried about the message this would send to Muslims and Christians. So they readied their ammunition for the attack on Modi's secular credentials that began within months of his becoming prime minister.

30

PARIVARTAN FOR WHOM?

Surekha called in hysterics one morning. 'They have arrested Roopa,' she said, 'and a lot of other people. Please help.'

'Why? What happened?'

'We were trying to stop the police from breaking down our homes.'

'Your homes?'

'Yes. I didn't tell you but we found a small patch of wasteland near the sea and we have been living there for three months. We built jhuggis after clearing out masses of filth and rubble.'

'Why? You know that they will demolish them.'

'But there is a new government now and Modi has said that everyone will be given a home.' This was three months after a BJP government had taken charge of Maharashtra. And nearly a year after Modi had become prime minister. I would have liked to explain that nothing was going to change so quickly but I knew there was no point. This community of dispossessed, deeply disadvantaged people had voted for him because they heard on the radio that he would bring with him 'achchhe din.' They believed, as very poor, illiterate people do, that political change can happen in hours if a leader ordains it.

'Where have they taken Roopa?'

'They have all been taken to Cuffe Parade police station, so if we go there now you might be able to free them before they take them to jail.'

'Did Roopa throw stones at the police?'

'No. But she was in the crowd that was trying to prevent the police from breaking down our jhuggis, so she was taken away with the others.'

'Was anyone throwing stones at the police?'

'No. But they were trying to stop them from breaking down their homes.'

When I got to Cuffe Parade police station I noticed that a large crowd of Surekha's friends and family members had gathered outside and were raucously demanding justice. When they saw me they showed me papers that they said were proof of their residence on the wasteland. They gave me a large bundle of grubby documents written in Marathi that had what looked like official stamps on them. When I got my driver Jaywant to translate them for me he said that there was nothing in them that indicated ownership. Some tout had fooled them yet again into believing that for a small price they could be given ownership rights to take possession of empty public land. If they could establish that they had been living there for a period of time they would qualify to be given alternative housing when their shanty was demolished.

They were not wrong in believing this since successive rulers of Mumbai had made 'slum redevelopment' policies that promised squatters on public spaces free alternative accommodation on the basis of what they called 'cut-off dates'. It was a stupid alternative to building rental housing for Mumbai's low-income citizens because there was no limit to the number of people who would claim free homes in exchange for squatters' rights. So along with Surekha's family and friends there were millions of citizens of this city of eternal immigration who thought of free housing as a fundamental right. This was why squatting and demolitions had become a permanent cycle of life in the streets and slums of Mumbai.

When I went into the police station that morning to look for Roopa I found that she and the others had already been taken to jail. 'If you want to release them you will have to go to court when it opens on Monday. Today you can do nothing,' said a smug, obese policeman. So I went off instead in search of Surekha and got her to show me the wasteland on which the huts had stood. It was no more than a field of rubble by the time I got there, and although the police and the demolition squads had left, municipality officials were still there arranging for the wasteland to be cordoned off. The people whose fragile homes had been demolished sat with their meagre belongings on the pavement just outside the cordoned off area. When I talked to the officials supervising the demolitions they said only that they had orders from the collector to demolish the huts because they had been built on public land. My sympathies were with the newly homeless but I could see the point of the demolition. Land in this part of Nariman Point where the grey waters of the Arabian Sea are visible from almost anywhere is worth hundreds of crores of rupees an acre.

On the edge of the wasteland, next door to a building in which elected representatives of the people of Maharashtra are housed, there already existed a shantytown of large proportions. Among those who lived in one of the shanties was an aunt of Surekha, who told me that she had lived there for a very long time so would be entitled to a free apartment when the slum colony was resettled. Many more families would need to be rehoused if Surekha's family and friends from the footpath behind the Air India building had managed to continue squatting where they had.

So the only thing I could do to help was try and get Roopa released when the courts opened on Monday. Surekha and her aunt came with me when we went to the magnificent, crumbling edifice from which Mumbai's magistrate's court functions. Along with others whose relatives had been arrested I waited in a courtroom of peeling wall paint and filthy furniture. The judge sat at a desk with files piled so high he was barely visible. Pigeon droppings decorated the dirty wooden benches on which we sat.

When the judge spotted me he wanted to know what I was doing in his courtroom. 'I am here to help this man get his wife released,' I said pointing to Roopa's husband, who sat beside me with a raw gash on his forehead and his arm in a sling.

'He was beaten up by the police when he went to try and see his wife,' I added in the hope of a sympathetic hearing.

The judge consulted the clerks who hovered about him with files in their hands. They consulted a handwritten, ink-stained paper that listed the business of the day and pointed to an entry.

'This matter has not come up yet,' the judge said. 'Please wait outside.'

Outside the courtroom had now appeared lawyers who were bargaining with the gathered street people over terms for getting their relatives bail. When they saw me their eyes lit up and they competed with each other to assure me that they would be give me a better rate. I chose the one who seemed to have a less shark-like approach to the negotiation. He said something like 'All settled for Rs 15,000', and since this was considerably less than the Rs 50,000 that the others were asking I hired him. A young man who acted as a spokesman for the footpath people assured me that I had made the right choice. 'We have dealt with him before,' he said. 'He is a good man.'

By that evening everyone including Roopa had been bailed out but the lawyer's fees had gone up to Rs 35,000, and in addition he took Rs 1,000 each from everyone as surety. Once more India's most vulnerable citizens had come up against the Indian state and once more all they had seen was its ugliest face. What made this particular interface more saddening than others for me personally was that it was happening under a prime minister who had won the first full mandate in thirty years on the promise of change.

'It cannot happen overnight,' Ajit said when I told him what happened. 'You have to give him more than a year to change things that have become habits over decades.'

He was right of course, but whenever I have tried to explain this to those who have lived under the jackboot of the Indian state for so long I have failed. The oppression they have suffered would be more bearable perhaps if it came with the obvious jackboot of a totalitarian police state or a military dictatorship. In India, because it has come disguised as socialism and democracy, it has been harder to fight. Will things ever change? Is there hope? I do not know. What I do know is that the 2014 general election was the first concerted attempt by the people of India to overthrow the terrible legacies of the past and usher in a new dawn. This is why Modi's promise to bring achchhe din had such resonance. This is why his promise of parivartan sounded like music to so many. Perhaps bringing about change in structures enfeebled by years of bad governance will not be easy. Perhaps it will be many, many years before India is able to rid herself of the sickening poverty in which too many Indians live.

The only thing that can be said with certainty is that the 2014 general election proved that the Indian people have changed. They are no longer prepared to accept the democratic feudalism that has deprived them of nearly all their rights other than the right to vote every five years for a new government. And from this could one day come the deepening of democracy that India so badly needs.

EPILOGUE

If you were born, as I was, soon after India won freedom 'at midnight', the political speech you know more than any other would be the one in which Jawaharlal Nehru spoke so eloquently of India's 'tryst with destiny'. It seems as if woven into the very fabric of my childhood. My first memory of it is from an upstairs room in my grandmother's half-built house in Karnal, which with its huge influx of refugees from Pakistan was then a half-built sort of town. I must have been ten and it must have been Republic Day or 15 August when my mother first played it on an old-fashioned gramophone. I think it was the first time I saw a long-playing record. I was fascinated that sounds came from it, but as someone with a natural ear for beautiful words I soon became more interested in the rhythm of the speech without understanding it. After this I remember that my mother played it so often that I soon learned the words, as did other English-speaking Indians in that time of heightened nationalism.

This fervent national feeling did not exist in the rest of my grandmother's house in Karnal. My father's family was in India only because Pakistan, the country they had wanted to stay in, would not have them. They came to India only when it became impossible to live in the new Islamic republic if you were not Muslim. There was such pain and bitterness caused by this that nobody talked about Pakistan much in my childhood. It was after I became a journalist and was asked to write about what happened in 1947 for some commemorative issue on Partition that I asked my grandmother her story.

She told it to me reluctantly as if she could not bear to relive the memories. She said she was in Mussoorie on 14 August 1947. My father's younger brother, who was seventeen at the time, had developed a severe case of tuberculosis and was advised to spend time in the hills to recuperate. They had travelled there not through India but through Murree, a hill station that went to Pakistan. This is the story my grandmother told me:

'When we heard on the radio that Pakistan had been created we took a train to Lahore. But we never managed even to leave the railway station. We saw fires on all sides and hundreds of terrified people running around trying to get on to trains to India. Our estate manager had come to receive us and told me that we had to try and get on to a train as well. There's no room here for you now, he said, because they are killing Sikhs everywhere. So we got on to one train but there were too many people on it, so we got off. Then many hours later we got on to another train, and when we got to Amritsar people jumped out and kissed the ground. We found out afterwards that the train we had first got on to had arrived without a single living passenger…only dead bodies.'

My mother who was born and bred in Delhi grew up as a secret nationalist. Nehru was her hero. As I mentioned earlier, her father was one of the five contractors who helped Edwin Lutyens build New Delhi, and since he worked for the British forbade her from playing any part in the freedom movement, so she wore khadi under her silk kurtas. She told us this proudly because her nationalism seemed only to deepen after marrying into a family with ambiguous loyalties. We listened to her favourite speech in the privacy of our upstairs bedroom and I think she cried every time.

It was only after I became an adult that I began to ask questions about that famous 'tryst'. Why was the speech made in English? And did Nehru not know when he talked of the world being asleep at midnight that it was not midnight everywhere? Was he just a romantic or a real leader? Since my career in Indian journalism began a month before Nehru's daughter declared her Emergency, and press censorship, I found myself plunged into a very different India from the one in which I spent my childhood. Instead of nationalistic fervour there was fear, repression and political violence. It was in this time when democracy and fundamental rights were suspended by Mrs Gandhi that people talked about the irony of India's 'tryst with destiny' being broken by Nehru's own daughter.

Mrs Gandhi soon made it clear that the Emergency was a moment when this tryst would be with dynasty and not destiny. By that summer of 1975 she had gone from being the great goddess Durga of the Bangladesh war to being a hated dictator. A dictator who did not try and conceal her attempts to hand India on a silver platter to her younger son as if it were no more than a private estate. It was the beginning of democratic feudalism that has today become an epidemic.

India in 1975 was a dismal inheritance to bequeath her son. In most of her years as an independent nation India had been ruled till then by Nehru and Nehru's daughter, and it had failed to free the vast majority of Indians from the horrible scourges of poverty, deprivation and illiteracy. It was this failure and signs of corruption in the political class that threw up from the tiny educated middle class that existed then student leaders and politicians who managed to cause enough trouble across the country to give Mrs Gandhi the excuse to declare her Emergency. When elections came in 1977 the people threw her out along with her son and brought in new political leaders who they hoped would bring with them renewal and hope.

This did not happen because most of the new leaders were really just old leaders from the Congress party. Tired old men quite incapable of reading the winds of economic change that were beginning to blow across China and Southeast Asia. Had they been wiser men, had we been less isolated from the rest of the world in that time, it is possible that India would have been a very different country by now. When Indian voters saw that the men they had replaced Indira Gandhi with were not able to give India even a government that lasted a full five years they brought Mrs Gandhi and her son back with a full majority. Since then India has been ruled by the Nehru-Gandhi dynasty or by governments supported by it except for a handful of years. It is this that cemented the foundations of a democratic feudalism that is uniquely Indian.

Feudalism disguised as democracy is more dangerous than real feudalism because it comes without the obvious injustices of real feudalism. What is there to oppose when elections are held every five years? Every young MP may have inherited his constituency from his mother or father but he won an election before taking his seat in the Lok Sabha. And every political party may have become a private limited company but is this not what the people want? So why should they complain about being deprived of such basic things as clean drinking water and decent schools for their children? Why should they complain that Indian cities are so bereft of affordable housing that economic immigrants from desperately poor villages are forced to live in filthy shantytowns? Why should they complain that those millions of Indians who live in extreme poverty do not have any rights at all?

If there is a single reason why Narendra Modi became the first prime minister in more than thirty years to get a full mandate from the people of India it was because he was the only one who understood how urgently people wanted change. The word he used most in his election speeches was the word for change in Hindi. And every time he said parivartan his audience would roar its approval. During the election campaign I came to understand that it was more important than anything else he could promise on a hot, stifling evening in Pappu's chai shop in Benares.

It was at the end of a long, dusty day spent wandering about the bleak, dirt-poor villages of eastern Uttar Pradesh, and I would have preferred to spend the evening restfully in the discreet luxury of the Taj Hotel instead of chatting to local intellectuals in this teashop on the Assi Ghat. But I decided that a shower and air-conditioned rooms could wait.

Had I still been staying at the Ganges View Hotel I would have definitely been at Pappu's chai shop because it was walking distance. But the Ganges View had been forced to evict me because of the arrival of a large group of foreign travellers who had booked months in advance. The Taj was more comfortable but so far away from the everyday realities of Benares that it may as well have been in another city. So I decided that I needed my usual evening 'chai pey charcha' in Pappu's chai shop. Its two wooden benches that perched precariously on the edge of an open drain were occupied by the time I arrived but room was graciously made for me and a glass of chai ordered.

The men gathered there on that hot evening included local politicians, a historian from Benares Hindu University, students and retired government officials. Everyone was talking about politics as they drank tea out of thick ribbed glasses and ate peanuts out of rough paper bags. And at some point I found myself having a private conversation with the historian. I asked him what he thought was the secret of Narendra Modi's appeal and he said, 'Parivartan. He promises change and this is what every Indian citizen wants at many different levels. Of course everyone hopes that he will be able to make India a prosperous country, but everyone also knows that this cannot happen unless many, many things change first.'

'Like?'

'Everything. Look at those wires hanging up there over that banyan tree in the square. They are electricity and telephone wires and you will see them throughout the old city of Benares. Why? Surely if we can explore space we should be able to lay cables properly here on earth. Surely we should be able to find a way to keep this ancient city clean. Surely we should be able to provide our people with clean drinking water, housing, jobs, schools for their children... why have these things not happened sixty-seven years after India became a free country?'

'So why do you think they haven't happened?' I asked, shifting my gaze from the cables that hung like a dirt-encrusted cradle over the banyan tree in the ancient square. It was crowded, chaotic, filthy and covered in a pall of polluted air. Rickshaws jostled with auto-rickshaws, and cars blew their horns to edge their way through the maze of narrow alleys that led off into different quarters of the ancient city that stretches languidly along the banks of the Ganga. I found myself thinking that if Benares had existed in a more civilized country its older bazaars and unique residential quarters would have been pedestrian zones. The historian's answer brought me back to Pappu's chai shop.

He said, 'Of course corruption is one reason why these things have not happened, but it isn't just corruption that is the problem. The real problem is that until not long ago most Indians were too poor to know their rights and it was easy for politicians to keep them happy with bad public services. But now millions of people are middle class and they know that they have a right to demand better.'

It was this new middle class Indian that Modi had understood better than any other political leader. Not even in the Bharatiya Janata Party was there anyone else who had understood just how much the aspirations of ordinary Indians had changed. Surekha and her family and friends who have spent their entire lives eking out an existence on the footpaths of Mumbai have middle class aspirations, and they are the poorest people I know. When I asked Surekha and Roopa why they had for the first time voted against the Congress Surekha said, 'Because although we have always voted for them we are still lying here on the footpaths, so when Modi said achchhe din would come we believed him.'

Their parents considered themselves lucky to be allowed to live on the pavements of Mumbai but this is no longer enough for their children. They want proper houses to live in, proper schools for their children and proper jobs so that they can afford to buy nice clothes and jewellery. Their aspirations are no different from the aspirations of more privileged Indians. But India's biggest political leaders in their rarefied cocoon of Lutyens' Delhi had not noticed. At least not till Modi's rallies in the 2014 general election started attracting huge audiences across the country. Despite the media denying that there was a Modi wave, a whiff of what was happening began to infiltrate the corridors of power. Then senior political leaders began to whisper about how Indian voters were no longer petitioners but aspirants and that it was this chord that Modi had touched. But there continued to be denial at the highest levels of political power.

Sonia Gandhi made a special appearance on national television to announce that if voters made the wrong choice only God could save India. Dr Manmohan Singh in his last press conference said clearly that if Modi became prime minister it would be a 'disaster'. They invoked the mantra that has kept Congress in power for nearly all of India's history as a modern nation: secularism and socialism. They had the secret support of senior BJP leaders who sensed that the 'parivartan' Modi was talking about could sweep them away. So no sooner did the election campaign begin than they started speaking openly about how Modi was not Vajpayee and would only succeed if he became Vajpayee.

The truth was the opposite. Atal Behari Vajpayee was too Nehruvian in his political and economic ideas to change anything when he was prime minister. He seemed not to even notice how desperately change was needed and not just in political and economic ideas but in much deeper things like an education system that has served mostly to produce literate but uneducated and deeply colonized Indian children. For reasons that remain mysterious Nehru chose not to change the mass education system he inherited from the Raj even though it had been designed specifically to produce 'clerks' to run the British Empire.

In the very British public school that I went to in Dehra Dun we were as colonized as it was possible to be. We were so English in our sensibilities that we learned to sneer at girls who came from homes in which the language of communication was not English. We were taught Hindi but only as a second language and those who spoke it better than English were disdained.

Of India's ancient past, of Sanskrit and the staggering

wealth of its literature we learned nothing. Indian music, dance, art and philosophy took second place to Western, and although we saw the occasional Hindi film and sang the occasional Hindi song these took second place to Elvis Presley, the Beatles and the Rolling Stones. We were so colonized that we did not notice that we were. Nor did we notice that we belonged to a minuscule class of Indians who spoke English as our first language or that it was a minuscule class that had immense power because English was the language of India's ruling family and India's ruling class. It was the language you needed to know to take the civil service examinations, and it was the language you needed to know if you wanted to get a job in the tiny private sector that was dominated then by old British Raj companies. English-language newspapers have the tiniest circulation but remain more important than any published in what we sneeringly called 'vernacular' languages.

It was only when private television channels came to diminish the role of Doordarshan that Hindi became so much more important than English that English-speaking anchors are today forced to try their hand at it. There are Hindi newspapers like *Dainik Jagran* and *Dainik Bhaskar* that count among the biggest in the world in terms of circulation, and it is impossible to be in journalism without knowing at least one Indian language well but the power of the English media remains intact. This is because no Indian prime minister since India became a modern nation state has made any effort to decolonize the education system. It is one of the ironies of history that Indian culture was more vibrant under the British Raj than it has been since India's colonial masters left.

Until the middle of the last century Indian poets and writers wrote in their own languages and produced poetry and literature that holds its own to this day with the finest in the world. It was after 1947 that writers like Premchand and Saadat Hasan Manto faded away without leaving any heirs, and after India became independent that Urdu poets found that the only way they could survive was by writing songs for Hindi films. This remains true today. And the sad truth is that mediocre writers writing in bad English command India's literary heights. Big bookshops in major cities sell books only in English, with a mere handful reserving a small corner for books in Indian languages.

In the vast hinterland of rural India there are now more 'English medium' schools than there have ever been. They claim to use English as their medium of instruction but almost no child who goes to these schools comes out speaking English in a manner that it would be understood by anyone. Sadly they end up speaking their own languages badly as well, so the damage done by English continues to grow.

When Narendra Modi used 'parivartan' to win the 2014 election it is possible that he himself did not know the resonance he would evoke or how much change was needed in how many different arenas. Public health services exist across the country in the form of physical infrastructure but in that form alone. They are so bad that even very poor Indians are forced to rely on private doctors who can often in rural India be unqualified and unreliable.

India is technically a socialist welfare state but the institutions of social welfare are as broken and defective as a public distribution system that seeks under a new law to give nearly every Indian limited quantities of subsidized food grain. This was Sonia Gandhi's parting gift to India in the name of providing food security. In the ten years she was India's de facto prime minister she put her personal stamp on governance by playing a direct role in creating huge welfare programmes that provided free forest land to Adivasi communities, a hundred days of guaranteed employment annually to families living below a shamefully low poverty line and despite all this failed to make any real difference in reducing poverty. More than 70 per cent of the population of India lives on less than Rs 20 a day and most Indians live without clean water despite decades of rule by leaders who professed to being 'socialist' like Sonia and her mother-in-law.

Democratic feudalism could not have survived without the support of socialist and Marxist political leaders who have used 'secularism' as their excuse for supporting a false idea of democracy. Many of them would have known that there was something deeply flawed with a political system that has kept most Indians poor, illiterate and jobless. But they have continued to support it because of having convinced themselves that a man like Modi, who spent most of his life as a propagandist for the RSS, has a 'hidden agenda'. The main thrust of the 'secular' campaigners in the election that brought Modi to power was that the 'idea of India' would be destroyed if he became prime minister. This idea of India was created in the drawing rooms of Lutyens' Delhi.

There was a time when this kind of argument was believed, but Indians born decades after India was broken up in the name of Islam no longer see secularism as being threatened. They see that millions of Muslims live here more peacefully than they do almost anywhere else in the world, and in any case what they see as much, much more important is that their lives should improve. Urbanization has reduced the importance of old battles over mosques and temples and old divisions over caste and creed. What is more important to young Indians is the absence of public services and jobs.

What is more important to Indians today is that India not be seen as a weak, impoverished giant of a country that seems to be left behind by countries like China and seems to be under constant threat from small belligerent neighbours like Pakistan. But even national security and national pride pale when compared with economic issues. Most young Indians see unemployment as India's biggest problem and most young Indians see that the bleak, unyielding farms they leave behind to go in search of jobs in big cities can no longer produce more jobs.

Can Modi create jobs for the 12 million young Indians who join the workforce every year? Can he bring the 'parivartan' and 'vikas' that he promised? If his first year as prime minister is to be used as a measure it can be said that he has taken small steps in the right direction but moved more slowly than he should have, especially in trying to rectify the damage done by decades of defunct socialism. It is not easy to understand why he has moved slowly because before he became prime minister he seemed fully aware of the changes that needed to be made for the economy to grow. He talked of tourism as an important economic tool but nothing has been done to use it. He talked of bringing urban standards to rural India by investing in better public services but again has moved too slowly.

He has done better in drawing attention to urgent social problems like open defecation and India's monumental problems of dealing with cleanliness and waste management, but old habits die hard and unless the average Indian is convinced that epidemics like dengue and malaria are related to these things change will be a long time coming. Linked to the decrepitude and decay that scar India is unplanned urbanization. Villages grow into towns without anyone noticing until they become slums, and then because of the votes that these vast shanties provide they are left untouched by political leaders in the name of the poor. Modi has already indicated that he knows India is no longer a rural country but one that could be mostly urban by the middle of this century and has announced a 'smart cities' programme. He has also noticed the importance of giving Indians digital access so that this can bring about the changes that cell phones and satellite television brought. These are good initiatives and may well succeed if he can first provide sufficient supplies of electricity.

What he has not paid enough attention to is bringing about fundamental 'parivartan' in India's education system, and so it is in this area that has become most evident the one force that could defeat all of Modi's plans to bring about 'parivartan' and 'vikas': Hindutva. There is every reason for India's children to be taught more about India's civilization and culture in schools, but this change cannot be led by organizations who mix culture up with an ugly religiosity. These organizations nearly all come under the umbrella of the Rashtriya Swayamsewak Sangh and this is the school in which Modi himself was nurtured. The RSS has sought to play its role more aggressively from the time that Modi became prime minister and has often succeeded in changing the agenda from economic and political change to religious and cultural change that has about it a dangerous edge. There may always have been attempts to reconvert Muslims and Christians back to the Hindu fold but this Ghar Vapasi movement has grabbed more attention since Modi became prime minister. There may always have been Hindu fanatics making racist and derogatory comments about Muslims but again they have got more attention since Modi became prime minister. And not even when his own ministers have made foolish racist remarks has Modi made a serious effort to express his disapproval.

This is disappointing because if anything can distract him away from the path of change it is a return to the sort of provincial, small-minded religiosity that the RSS represents. The men who have always played leading roles in this fountainhead of Hindutva have been narrow-minded intellectuals to whom what matters are such things as the benefits of cow's urine as a detergent. And the misguided crusade to reconvert Muslims and Christians because of the flawed belief that it is only when everyone goes back to being Hindu that they will be true sons of Mother India.

It is a dangerous crusade whose worst consequence could be taking India back into a time of religious and social conflict that could tear it apart once more. This would fulfil the more dire prophecies of India's enemies, but this is something that RSS leaders appear not to be able to see. Just as they are unable to see that it was not because of Hindu nationalism that Modi became the first prime minister to be given a full mandate in thirty years. Not even in Benares, so deeply linked to Hindu civilization, was there any sense that it was Hindutva that made people vote for Modi.

If Modi allows his mandate to be stolen by his Hindutva friends and former travelling companions then India could lose its first real chance to take a new road. If democratic feudalism and decayed socialism held down the political elite that Modi has displaced then an ugly, defunct idea of revivalist Hindutva could become the millstone that prevents him from moving too far on the new road that stretches before him. It is a moment for India that is almost as significant as that moment in 1947 when it shook off colonial rule. It is perhaps more significant because it is a real chance to break the hold of a colonized elite who ruled in the name of the poor but kept most Indians in poverty while doing so. Modi has indicated that he knows what needs to be done. What he has not indicated as clearly is if he also knows that the one thing that will destroy all hope of change is if he allows his former travelling companions to steal his mandate. History will judge him very harshly if he does.

INDEX

25 ▪ HarperCollins India Ltd

Celebrating 25 Years of Great Publishing

HarperCollins India celebrates its twenty-fifth anniversary in 2017.
Twenty-five years of publishing India's finest writers and some of its most
memorable books – those you cannot put down; ones you want to finish
reading yet don't want to end; works you can read over and over again only
to fall deeper in love with.

Through the years, we have published writers from the Indian subcontinent,
and across the globe, including Aravind Adiga, Kiran Nagarkar, Amitav Ghosh,
Jhumpa Lahiri, Manu Joseph, Anuja Chauhan, Upamanyu Chatterjee,
A.P.J. Abdul Kalam, Shekhar Gupta, M.J. Akbar, Tavleen Singh, Satyajit Ray,
Gulzar, Surender Mohan Pathak and Anita Nair, amongst others, with
approximately 200 new books every year and an active print and digital
catalogue of more than 1,000 titles, across ten imprints. Publishing works of
various genres including literary fiction, poetry, mind body spirit, commercial
fiction, journalism, business, self-help, cinema, biographies – all with attention
to quality, of the manuscript and the finished product – it comes as no surprise
that we have won every major literary award including the Man Booker Prize,
the Sahitya Akademi Award, the DSC Prize, the Hindu Literary Prize, the
MAMI Award for Best Writing on Cinema, the National Award for Best Book
on Cinema, the Crossword Book Award, and the Publisher of the Year, twice, at
Publishing Next in Goa and, in 2016, at Tata Literature Live, Mumbai.

We credit our success to the people who make us who we are, and will be
celebrating this anniversary with: our authors, retailers, partners, readers and
colleagues at HarperCollins India. Over the years, a firm belief in our promise
and our passion to deliver only the very best of the printed word has helped us
become one of India's finest in publishing. Every day we endeavour to deliver
bigger and better – for you.

Thank you for your continued support and patronage.

HarperCollins*Publishers*India

🐦 @HarperCollinsIN

📷 @HarperCollinsIN

📘 @HarperCollinsIN

💼 HarperCollins Publishers India

www.harpercollins.co.in

Harper Broadcast

Showcasing celebrated authors, book reviews, plot trailers, cover reveals, launches and interviews, Harper Broadcast is live and available for free subscription on the brand's social media channels through a new newsletter. Hosted by renowned TV anchor and author Amrita Tripathi, Broadcast is a snapshot of all that is news, views, extracts, sneak peeks and opinions on books. Tune in to conversations with authors, where we get up close and personal about their books, why they write and what's coming up.

Harper Broadcast is the first of its kind in India, a publisher-hosted news channel for all things publishing within HarperCollins. Follow us on Twitter and YouTube.

Subscribe to the monthly newsletter here: https://harpercollins.co.in/newsletter/

▶️ Harper Broadcast

🐦 @harperbroadcast

www.harperbroadcast.com

Address

HarperCollins Publishers India Ltd
A-75, Sector 57, Noida, UP 201301, India

Phone
+91-120-4044800